Law and Society
Recent Scholarship

Edited by Melvin I. Urofsky

A Series from LFB Scholarly

Freedom of Environmental Information

Benjamin W. Cramer

LFB Scholarly Publishing LLC
El Paso 2011

Library of Congress Cataloging-in-Publication Data

Cramer, Benjamin W., 1971-
  Freedom of environmental information / Benjamin W. Cramer.
     p. cm. -- (Law and society)
  Includes bibliographical references and index.
  ISBN 978-1-59332-447-6 (hardcover : alk. paper)
  1. Freedom of information--United States. 2. Environmental law--
United States. 3. Government information--United States. 4. United
States. National Environmental Policy Act of 1969. I. Title.
  KF4774.C73 2010
  342.7308'53--dc22
                                              2010038568

ISBN 978-1-59332-447-6

Printed on acid-free 250-year-life paper.

Manufactured in the United States of America.

Table of Contents

Acknowledgements

I would like to thank all of the professors and instructors who contributed to this book: Ron Bettig, Clay Calvert, Darryl Farber, Rob Frieden, Rob Gatter, Martin Halstuk, Brian Holland, Matt Jackson, Krishna Jayakar, Neill Johnson, Lynette Kvasny, Dana Mitra, Patrick Parsons, Bob Richards, Amit Schejter, Geoff Scott, and Shyam Sundar. Honorable mention to professors Denise Bortree and Jamison Colburn for valuable research leads. Thanks also to Doug Anderson, Betsy Hall, Anne Hoag, and John Nichols of the Dean's Office at the Penn State College of Communications. And finally, I would like to thank the law-savvy environmental activists in the Pennsylvania Chapter of Sierra Club for their legal research tips: most notably Michele Barbin, Stan Kotala, Mike Nixon, Nancy Parks, Ed Perry, and Dave Sublette.

CHAPTER 1

Introduction

This book explores the intersection between government transparency and environmental law, and seeks to add to the knowledge of both fields by focusing on rarely discussed phenomena surrounding the management of environmental information by government. The American government, thanks to a variety of environmental statutes covered herein, holds vast amounts of environmentally relevant information that could be of great use to citizens concerned about the health of their communities and of the natural world. This information can be made available to the public under the specific disclosure provisions of various environmental statutes, and under the Freedom of Information Act.[1] That statute is not the ultimate arbiter of government transparency in America but has inspired more specific regulations for particular subjects, one of which is the environment.

Ultimately, this book will offer a new focus on rather obscure environmental information regulations that are much less well-known than the Freedom of Information Act, and which can be used by citizens to fight for greater transparency of government-held environmental information, and in turn, greater environmental protection. This book will analyze whether or not those laws have been truly successful in promoting the transparency of environmental information in America.

In response to growing citizen sentiment, by the early 1970s the American government enacted a variety of federal statutes meant to protect the natural environment. The first noteworthy such statute was the National Environmental Policy Act (NEPA) of 1969.[2] The National Environmental Policy Act is best known for its requirement of an environmental impact statement (EIS) for any government agency action that will have an impact on the natural environment. The requirement also applies to private parties regulated by federal government agencies. Buried within a section of NEPA that otherwise regulates the EIS process is a transparency clause pertaining to the information accumulated during that process.[3] This book will examine these two NEPA provisions – one conspicuous, one obscure – in great detail in an analysis of access to environmental information in America.

While the layperson tends to view the Freedom of Information Act and other government transparency statutes as tools for obtaining records from high-profile entities like the White House or the Pentagon, vast quantities of records are actually held by administrative agencies. Due to the nature of environmental protection and regulation, these agencies hold the most relevant documentation, and not just the Environmental Protection Agency or similarly-themed entities. Furthermore, all federal agencies are governed by the National Environmental Policy Act. Like many comprehensive administrative statutes, NEPA contains a provision requiring all agencies to review and update their internal processes in order to comply with the statute.[4] This in turn applies the NEPA transparency provision to those agencies, leading to unique disclosure requirements for agencies that one may not suspect of having an appreciable impact on the environment.

Due to its comprehensive and administrative nature, at a more general level the National Environmental Policy Act has become the primary environmental statute in America, regulating the relevant activities of all agencies in the federal government (including the Environmental Protection Agency). The statute is also the basis for several subsequent environmental laws in America, with many of those laws referencing NEPA's administrative requirements.[5] There are dozens of environmental statutes in America, and these laws fall under the regulatory umbrella of NEPA, including its transparency provision.

Environmental activists might be aware of the National Environmental Policy Act but tend to see it as a bureaucratic enigma of more use to regulators, and even among experts the statute is not very well understood, perhaps because of its mostly administrative nature.[6] Esoteric matters of reporting and investigation for an environmental impact statement are often important to local activists resisting particular development projects, but the overall benefits of environmental transparency across the entire federal government remain obscure. The general environmental community in the United States tends to be much more familiar with "action-oriented" damage prevention and amelioration laws like the Clean Water Act[7] or the Endangered Species Act.[8] The fact that the transparency of government-held environmental information is statutorily protected is not widely known even among activists and experts, and this lack of public knowledge might damage that very same transparency.

Primarily via legal analysis, this book defines and frames environmental information and environmental transparency, analyzes applicable statutes, researches cases in which those statutes were contested or cited in court, investigates whether the statutes in question have been correctly or efficiently observed and enforced, and finally explores the consequences for the protection of America's environment. The conclusion to this book advances arguments on the state of environmental transparency and offers recommendations for improvement.

What is Environmental Information?

In America, the government has been given statutory control over the use of the natural environment. On public lands such as national forests, national parks, federal wilderness areas, Bureau of Land Management territories, and the like, the federal government is the ultimate decision-maker in how the lands are used. Meanwhile, private lands are often owned and used by entities that are regulated by particular agencies within the executive branch of the federal government and which fall under the purview of a variety of federal land use or pollution control statutes. For example, a landowner may wish to allow a telecommunications company to build an antenna tower on his/her land – a transaction that is overseen by the Federal Communications Commission and the Federal Aviation Administration. A farmer may wish to divert a waterway for the irrigation of his/her own fields without considering the needs of other water users in the area – a decision that is overseen by the Department of Agriculture. Actions like these, depending on the circumstances, might also fall under the purview of federal environmental statutes like the Endangered Species Act or the Clean Water Act.

The federal administrative agencies that oversee these actions, as conducted by either the government itself or by regulated private parties, are required by their own governing statutes as well as more general pan-agency statutes (most notably the National Environmental Policy Act) to collect and manage the information that arises from such environmental decision-making processes. In short, environmental law in America is inherently informational.

For the purposes of this book, government-held environmental information falls into two major categories. The first is the information generated during the environmental impact statement process under the requirements of NEPA, which must be completed for any environmentally-relevant activity by any federal government agency or any private party that it regulates. Per NEPA, this voluminous information must be collected by the agency in question, managed by the Environmental Protection Agency, and made available to citizens upon request. Affiliated natural protection statutes like the Endangered Species Act and the Comprehensive Environmental Response, Compensation, and Liability Act (known informally as CERCLA or the "Superfund" Act)[9] are enforced via official government-compiled lists of relevant phenomena (threatened species and toxic dump sites, respectively) that are used as the basis for agency rulemaking and judicial review during citizen suits.

The second category of government-held information comes from statutorily-enforced reporting requirements by industry. These requirements are codified in a variety of statutes that are influenced by the informational and transparency requirements of NEPA. For example, the Clean Water Act requires immediate reporting, to the Environmental Protection Agency, of any accidental or unpermitted discharge of pollutants into waterways. The Toxic Substances Control Act[10] requires the government to maintain an official list of such substances, and requires industrial operators to submit to the government regular reports on their use of those substances. Another instructive example is the Emergency Planning and Community Right-to-Know Act,[11] which requires industrial operators to proactively report the quantities of any pollutants they have discharged (permitted or otherwise) into the surrounding air, water, or land.

These environmental statutes and others engender the creation of vast amounts of information that can be used by the public in its efforts to check government environmental abuses or protect the health of their communities. This documentation is in the hands of a variety of federal government agencies and is managed under the requirements of many different statutes. The existence of this information in large quantities is not in dispute. However, its availability to the citizenry and its ultimate usefulness for true environmental protection will form the basis of the upcoming legal and political analysis.

The Significance of Studying Access to Environmental Information

The general philosophy of the National Environmental Policy Act and its affiliated environmental statutes is regulation through administrative procedure and the management of the resulting information. The requirements of the environmental impact statement process under NEPA, and the informational requirements of many other environmental statutes, were meant to discourage wanton destruction of the natural world by mandating sound management of the information gathered during the planning and permitting of government projects.[12] The transparency provisions of NEPA and subsequent environmental statutes have the potential to encourage a great amount of natural protection through the collection and disclosure of information, if those provisions are observed by all parties to the fullest extent possible. Whether or not such revelations are occurring to their greatest potential will be the major theme of the upcoming discussion.

The arguments herein are constructed from the standpoint of federal government information policy. While environmental statutes are discussed fairly intensively, some details of environmental jurisprudence are left out for the sake of brevity, and this book is not meant to provide an in-depth analysis of American environmental law. Instead, the theme is the management and disclosure of government-held information in the public interest, the resulting effects on the natural world, and how well citizens can review and check the environmental abuses committed by government agencies and the parties they regulate.

The strengths and weaknesses of the National Environmental Policy Act are regular topics of research in environmental/natural resources law journals. A search of the HeinOnline database reveals 167 articles in legal research journals (in all disciplines) featuring "National Environmental Policy Act" in their titles between 1969 (the year the act was passed) and early 2009. Notwithstanding articles that simply describe the act itself, the majority of these articles discuss the viability of NEPA in the face of particular environmental crises or controversies, and in recent years many NEPA-related articles have recommended updates or improvements to the statute. A more targeted search of environmental/natural resources law journals in particular reveals well over a thousand articles during the same time period that mention NEPA and analyze it to varying degrees, illustrating the statute's influence on all matters of environmental jurisprudence.

The presence of environmental information in the American regulatory sphere is a matter of some discussion in environmental/natural resources law journals, and such articles tend to focus on the use or abuse of that information by regulators and the parties they regulate.[13] However, legal research into the transparency of this environmental information and its accessibility for citizens, particularly the transparency provision of NEPA, is rare to nonexistent in environmental/natural resources law research. Meanwhile, in communications law research (the discipline that typically tackles the general topic of government transparency) the matter has barely been discussed at all.

A HeinOnline search for the relevant transparency language of NEPA reveals just nine mentions in environmental/natural resources law journal articles from 1969 to the present. None of those articles dealt with the NEPA transparency provision in detail, merely referencing it in passing, and only two of those articles made significant use of the provision to corroborate substantive arguments.[14] The National Environmental Policy Act overall is almost never addressed in communications law journals, with just ten mentions in articles found in HeinOnline between 1969 and early 2009. There is little reason for concern here, because an environmental statute obviously has little practical relevance for research in telecommunications or media law. Most of those ten articles mention NEPA only briefly, usually as a brief citation in a discussion of a dispute surrounding an environmental impact statement filed by the Federal Communications Commission for telecommunications tower construction projects. Only one of the articles discusses the quality (though not the transparency) of environmental information arising from telecommunications regulation.[15] Most importantly for this book, a thorough HeinOnline search reveals that the NEPA transparency provision has *never* been mentioned in a communications law journal.

This book seeks to fill that gap in the academic and legal research literature, which is likely due more to a lack of academic interest in (or knowledge of) the laws discussed herein, rather than a lack of relevance. According to a LexisNexis search of federal and state court cases, the National Environmental Policy Act was either cited in, or was the primary basis of, 154 lawsuits in 2008 alone. These cases typically involved citizen challenges toward faulty or insufficient procedures followed by government agencies when compiling environmental impact statements. Since the EIS process involves the creation of considerable amounts of information that is then held by the government and (presumably, per NEPA) reviewable by citizens, this represents a significant aspect of government transparency in America that has never received a robust analysis in either environmental law or communications law.

Public Participation in Environmental Decision-Making

The environmental statutes discussed herein not only attempt to enforce transparency at government agencies, but to also encourage public participation in government and industrial decision-making processes. Basic theories of democracy and civil society argue that citizens are well-served by access to government-held information, while disclosing information adds legitimacy to the operations of the government and its leaders. At a more specific level, researchers have found that access to government-held information concerning the environment can lead to greater equity in environmental protection and greater accountability for the American government as a whole.

Due to the forces of nature, environmental problems do not observe geographic borders, pollution can be spread from a single source to a wide area, deleterious effects can take many years to manifest themselves, and the citizens most in need of environmental protection can be difficult to identify. Scientific assessments of environmental risks can also be quite different from the opinions of citizens who must live in polluted neighborhoods, or with the effects of industrial processes that were approved by regulators but not by themselves. For these reasons, public participation is essential for the effective drafting of environmental regulations and their subsequent enforcement.[16]

Citizens must be given access to environmentally-relevant information, they should have opportunities to participate in decision-making processes, and they should be provided with legal remedies and redress procedures when disclosure of environmental information is denied by officials.[17] These are the basic precepts of government transparency, and they are especially relevant for environmental protection. When a citizen is denied any of these principles of government transparency, true protection of the natural world is compromised because citizens will be unable to check abuses by government officials.[18]

Democratic theorists have long contended that public participation is crucial to a functioning democracy, which is made possible when citizens have access to information about (and held by) their government and the opportunity to participate in political discourse. Such participation is dependent on both the effective distribution of information by the government and its equitable reception by citizens. The distribution side of this equation can be made more effective by a reduction of bureaucracy and politicking within government agencies. The reception side of the equation is especially important because citizens are better able to make informed decisions and check the actions of their government when they have been exposed to a variety of opinions, including those that may not correspond with their previous notions. Only then can the public counter the domination of political discourse by elites who enjoy greater access to political decision-makers and communication channels.[19] In the words of democratic theorist Thomas I. Emerson:

The crucial point... is not that freedom of expression is politically useful, but that it is indispensible to the operation of a democratic form of government. Once one accepts the premise of the Declaration of Independence – that governments derive "their just power from the consent of the governed" – it follows that the governed must, in order to exercise their right to consent, have full freedom of expression both in forming individual judgments and in forming the common judgment.[20]

At a lower level, in the American system of governance environmental decisions made by the government usually come from administrative agencies in the executive branch. While public participation in American governance dates back to the colonial era, in modern times citizens have had to interact much more often with specific federal agencies. This phenomenon dates back to Franklin D. Roosevelt's New Deal, in which the President encouraged the Department of Agriculture to collaborate with farmers when making decisions affecting agricultural policy; while the Tennessee Valley Authority was encouraged to gauge the opinions of local residents toward river damming and hydropower projects.[21] This model has been extended to environmental matters in the modern administrative state, in which unelected agency employees rather than elected political leaders are the most involved in how the government takes action.[22] According to a study sponsored by four federal government agencies with a hand in matters of environmental protection:

When done well, public participation improves the quality and legitimacy of a decision and builds the capacity of all involved to engage in the policy process. It can lead to better results in terms of environmental quality and other social objectives. It also can enhance trust and understanding among parties.23

The report goes on to examine the crucial importance of direct public participation in environmental decision-making by the government, especially from local residents in the areas most affected by agency decisions, and not just government-employed scientists and regulators. In other words, those who must live with the consequences of an environmental decision should have some influence on that decision:

> Substantial evidence shows that effective public participation can help agencies do a better job in achieving public purposes for the environment by ensuring better decisions and increasing the likelihood that they will be implemented effectively. Good public participation also helps build capacity in agencies and among participants and the scientific community for future environmental decision making.24

The benefits of public participation are maximized if the information to be discussed, and the process itself, are transparent. The government and public participants in the decision-making process should be fully informed on the purpose and objectives of each decision, and citizens should be made aware of the processes followed by the federal agency in question.[25] For the best results from public participation, government agencies should seek broad citizen involvement across the entire decision-making process, invite a broad range of citizens from scientific experts to community representatives, clearly inform citizens on how their input will be utilized, and exercise flexibility in the deliberative process.[26]

The aforementioned government study concludes that public participation, not just for environmental matters but in general, usually leads to better results – at least in terms of inclusion of different ideas, the legitimacy of decision-making processes, and the quality of ultimate decisions by government agencies. However, public participation in government decision-making can sometimes lead to undesired results that may be worse than what would have resulted from less participatory processes. Unfavorable outcomes are often the result of inflexible processes at particular agencies that have their own bureaucratic traditions of disregarding citizen input, and differences in each party's true understanding of the science and uncertainty behind the environmental issue at hand.[27] As will be seen throughout this book, agency utilization of the public participation process, or lack thereof, is at the root of many inefficiencies and inequities in environmental decision-making by the American government.

Of course, the true foundation of public participation is information that the citizen can truly use. For environmental matters, the most useful information should describe not just the particular issue at hand, but also the environmental decision-making process of the relevant government leaders and the potential environmental implications of such decisions. For example, the members of a community must know if their local leaders have permitted the release of waste into their water supply, or if hazardous industrial processes are permitted nearby. Without this type of knowledge meaningful public participation is impossible, indicating the need for statutory protection of access to government-held information.[28] The knowledge required for true public participation is much more intensive than that gained from traditional environmental volunteerism and stewardship, such as community clean-up efforts or tree-planting projects. Instead, the public must be involved in the environmental assessments, plans, monitoring programs, and ongoing evaluation efforts that are conducted by government agencies. This involvement can range from advising agencies on matters of public opinion to actual collaboration with agency decision-makers.[29]

Even if citizens have access to information on decisions that were already made by the government, and how and why those decisions were made, that knowledge is meaningless unless citizens can participate in the actual process that leads to those decisions. For the best environmental governance, citizens should be able to give input and attempt to influence the actions of their leaders. Public participation in government decision-making has been known to increase the accountability of officials, educate those officials on the local impacts of their decisions, bring all stakeholders into the discussion, and inspire officials to shape ultimate decisions in the public interest.[30] Given the complexity of potential environmental damage, which may affect entire poorly-understood ecosystems, the stakeholders must include not just the government and the private businesses involved in development projects, but also citizens and community organizations. The effects are also not just economic but can also be political, social, and cultural. This makes true public participation imperative for environmental decision-making, in which many different groups of stakeholders have differing interests in the environmental question at hand.[31]

Participation should extend from specific government actions like the licensing of a resource retraction operation (such as logging or fossil fuel drilling) to general processes of policy design and regulatory enforcement.[32] Secrecy of any kind during any part of the process restricts effective political decision-making, as it is impossible for any small group of leaders to consider all the facts and opinions that are relevant to a given issue. On the other hand, participation by citizens allows for stronger review of political decisions and a more robust debate before those decisions are finalized.[33]

Meanwhile, environmental information, and the opportunity to participate in decisions, must usually be provided by government leaders and at special request from citizens. The process of information disclosure becomes meaningless if citizens are not offered redress procedures when information is denied by government officials. Secrecy and non-disclosure of requested information can be rightfully seen by citizens as signs of bad intentions, while openness can build public support for government leaders.[34] For example, a government agency may refuse to disclose environmentally-relevant information due to its possible national security implications. Or the agency may achieve *de facto* secrecy by simply ignoring citizen requests for information or by imposing excessive fees or bureaucratic requirements.[35] In such events of non-disclosure of environmental information, the citizen should have access to legal remedies, such as an appeal to higher agency officials or to the courts, in order to overcome the denial of access to desired documents.[36]

In highly technical or scientific matters, including environmental protection, citizen access to information can encourage more public participation, by creating a network of knowledgeable citizens who strengthen the democratic process and increase their community's knowledge of government operations and opportunities for legal relief. Unfortunately, the reverse is also true. Citizens who are left out of political decision-making become isolated, alienated, perhaps hostile to government institutions, and unable to access social services in a time of need.[37] In a modern world of increasing environmental crises, it is impossible to hold a meaningful public debate on complex issues unless citizens have access to all pertinent information and the ability to participate in public forums in which they can express their views.[38]

Much of the preceding discussion can be applied to public participation and transparency at all levels of government. But the transparency of government-held information concerning the environment carries its own benefits for both natural protection and public participation in government decision-making. For environmental decision-making processes, citizen access to information adds equity, legitimacy, and accountability for government leaders and their processes, and self-protection for citizens who are affected by those processes.[39]

Transparency and public participation are essential for the equity of justice and self-government among people in all tiers of society.[40] This is relevant in the natural world given the environmental justice phenomenon, in which citizens have resisted the placement of landfills, factories, and other sources of pollution near poorly-represented communities. Equity is a key factor in democratic theory, as representation in government and the transparency of that government are both believed to ensure fairness in the distribution of resources[41] (such as relief efforts after incidents of severe pollution). In terms of effectiveness, government equity has been defined as a desirable distribution of goods and services among the members of society,[42] and the transparency of government operations is crucial for how well citizens can review if such equity has been achieved.

The equity aspect of government transparency is becoming more important in the era of increased agency influence and power within the federal government, especially those agencies with a direct impact on the environment. With greater citizen oversight of such agencies, government becomes not just more knowledgeable about the needs of the citizenry, but also more open to citizen demands for greater equity in decision-making processes.[43] Equity in political decision-making, in turn, allows citizens to effectively argue about just what has gone wrong when their leaders allow environmental damage, and citizens are in a better position to recommend viable solutions.[44]

Transparency and public participation also lend legitimacy to government decision-making of all types, as citizens are less likely to support lawmakers who operate under a veil of secrecy.[45] An excessively secretive government will find itself unpopular with citizens and unable to win their trust or support. Under-informed citizens may resort to rumor-mongering and conspiracy theories about the motivations of their political leaders, and those citizens may become suspicious and overly critical of the government.[46] Such legitimacy is crucial for large government projects with significant environmental impacts and competing constituencies, like a dam construction project in which a river used by fishermen and boaters is altered for the use of agricultural and residential water consumers, with many different government agencies involved in permitting and planning. By providing information on such projects to the public, government leaders can manage serious conflicts among constituencies and reduce the chance of illegitimate decisions being made by politicians working behind closed doors.[47]

One of the most fundamental aspects of democratic theory is that transparency and public participation provide the government with accountability, because politicians will be less likely to act in extreme ways if they know their motivations are plainly visible (through transparent documents and processes) for all to see. For the environment, this applies not just to government agencies but also to the private industries and other actors regulated by those agencies.[48] Government officials enjoy greater accountability if they act transparently when making decisions on policy, regulation, or distribution of resources. If citizens disagree with any such decision, public participation increases the chances of those citizens being able to find out who made the decision, with an increased ability to demand justification or reconsideration from that decision-maker.[49]

Government accountability is further strengthened by transparency practices themselves, because leaders who exhibit a commitment to the passage and enforcement of transparency statutes (like the Freedom of Information Act) will be considered more accountable by citizens. Hence, accountability becomes not just a quality of a transparent government, but an incentive to maintain that transparency as well.[50] Politicians who give the impression of handing over information at citizen request and lending a hand in effectively implementing and enforcing transparency laws will also enjoy greater accountability in the eyes of citizens who desire open government and access to information.[51]

And finally, transparency adds self-protection to the democratic process, particularly when it comes to environmental protection. When citizens know (through transparent documents and processes) beforehand that they may face threats to their health or livelihoods, they are better able to take proactive steps toward amelioration rather than wait for the government to fix problems after the damage has been done.[52] Knowledgeable citizens with full access to government-held information, and the ability to participate in government decision-making, may be able to detect environmental problems before they become disasters, putting them in a better position to agitate for amelioration beforehand. These citizens may also become less dependent on government after an environmental calamity and more able to review the efficacy of the government's response to the crisis.[53]

The Convergence of Environmental Protection and Government Transparency

Until the early 1970s, environmental law was split into two basic categories that were not always compatible – statutes that attempted to conserve natural resources and statutes that attempted to control pollution. For example, the creation of national parks like Yellowstone and Yosemite were federal efforts to preserve areas of great natural beauty from economic exploitation, but those efforts showed little direct concern for pollution and public health.[54] Conversely, early pollution control laws, enacted by cities and states as early as the 1880s, were focused on public health but showed no interest in conserving natural resources.[55]

These two strains of environmental jurisprudence began to converge in the early 1970s when Congress enacted the Clean Air Act[56] and the Clean Water Act.[57] Both of these statutes, and others passed during that time period, were inspired by recent scientific knowledge of the trans-border nature of air and water pollution, and the long-distance effects of subsequent problems like acid rain, with natural resources and scenic areas being affected by pollution originating far away.[58] Thus for the first time, these two major statutes combined a desire to control pollution with the preservation of natural resources that are or could be impacted by that pollution. Pollution was now regulated not just at the original source, but also at the location of impact.[59] And most importantly for the present discussion, the new era of environmental protection came with a special focus on the management and accessibility of environmental information.

Since the early 1970s, the former philosophical dichotomy between natural resource preservation laws (focused on the public interest or public trust) and pollution control laws (focused on public health) has largely disappeared. This is due to changing philosophies of environmental protection as well as emerging scientific evidence of the widespread effects of pollution and degradation. For instance, laws pertaining to mining have evolved into regulations of mining techniques and extraction levels at the source, as well as the impacts on bordering ecosystems downwind or downstream.[60] This converged philosophy also inspired a new information-intensive focus on permitting and reporting. In particular, the Clean Water Act introduced stringent permitting requirements for entities (usually in industry and agriculture) that release contaminants into waterways, and these entities are required to deliver specific and robust information to the government when applying for permits. Also included were strict reporting requirements, forcing polluters to provide information on discharge levels and their efforts to conform to the statute's limits on pollutants. Any discrepancies in the reported information, or a lack of reporting altogether, empower government enforcement efforts and provide ammunition for citizen lawsuits.[61]

Requirements for permit applications and reporting by the entities that create pollution represented a new era in environmental law. The Clean Air Act and Clean Water Act also represented the first large-scale efforts to regulate environmental protection through the use of information that industry is required to supply to the government. This new emphasis on information, statutorily required from polluting entities and delivered to the government, represented a new era not just for environmental protection but for the transparency practices of government and the parties it regulates.

Whether these processes work, and how well, has a major impact on the health of the natural world in America and raises important issues of government transparency and democracy. The need for access to government-held information and environmental protection naturally indicates the need for access to government-held information *about* environmental protection. When citizens have access to this kind of information, they have the ability to check abuses of the environment by their political leaders. Citizen oversight of government actions toward the natural world is a powerful tool for those concerned about both the environment and government transparency.[62]

As will be seen throughout this book, American environmental law is largely based on information that is submitted by actors within the government or from parties that the government regulates, and this information is managed in turn by those same government agencies. Most of this information is in the form of environmental impact statements and permit applications. Since the enactment of the National Environmental Policy Act in 1970, American environmental law, at the philosophical level, has been leaning toward the convergence of government transparency and protection of the natural world, with supposed enhancements to both. This combined regulatory focus has become particularly successful (or at least viable) in the American political arena.[63]

Unfortunately, the fundamentally administrative and reactive characteristics of American law, and environmental law in particular, have prevented this convergence from truly coming to fruition. Government actors are required by law to follow certain procedures, and citizens are only offered the opportunity to counter government decisions by arguing over improperly-observed procedures. A successful citizen argument over government malfeasance often comes too late to prevent the environmental destruction that has resulted from a regulatory decision that was already made, even if that decision was made incorrectly according to the law.[64] This is especially ironic because many American environmental statutes are proactive in spirit, such as the Endangered Species Act, which strives to prevent the Earth's creatures from disappearing into extinction.[65]

A brief comparative focus can shed light on the chances of achieving true convergence of government transparency and environmental protection in America. Different legal traditions can lead to different results in the effort to achieve environmental protection through the effective management of government-held information on the subject. The convergence of government transparency and natural protection, with evident enhancements to both, has been attempted with greater success outside of the United States, particularly in Europe and other regions where the body of law is less focused on administrative procedures and reactive punishment, and more focused on rights-based goals and proactive encouragement.[66]

In many countries outside of the First World, citizens have increasingly demanded the acknowledgement of environmental protection and access to government-held information as basic human rights. A right of access to information about the environment is a logical outgrowth of these trends in human rights activism. For example, in 1994, the United Nations drew up the Draft Declaration of Principles on Human Rights and the Environment,[67] an attempt to encourage a binding resolution that would elevate environmental protection to the level of an enforceable and justiciable human right around the world.[68] Most importantly for the present discussion, the Draft Declaration states:

> All persons have the right to information concerning the environment. This includes information, howsoever compiled, on actions and courses of conduct that may affect the environment and information necessary to enable effective public participation in environmental decision-making. The information shall be timely, clear, understandable and available without undue financial burden to the applicant.[69]

The Draft Declaration of Principles on Human Rights and the Environment (though it is not yet binding on the world's nations at large) highlighted a relatively new and certainly emergent philosophy of human rights that could redefine the relationship between government transparency and environmental protection. But for the time being, in the American legal regime access to government-held information and solutions to environmental crises are not proactive and rights-based as they are in some other countries, but reactive and procedural. Citizens are sometimes able to participate in government decision-making before environmental decisions are made, but in most cases citizens must react to those decisions by requesting documents and demanding mitigation of damage that often has already been done.[70]

Government transparency and environmental protection are not mentioned in the Bill of Rights like freedom of speech or the right to due process. Instead, in America these are statutory protections only, and as such are dependent on practical enforcement by government actors and oversight by other government actors under the system of checks and balances. Citizens must keep an eye on whether government actors are following proper procedures, but are then required to argue charges of malfeasance in court. The ramifications of this legal focus on administrative procedures will be the basis for most of the upcoming discussions on both government transparency and environmental protection.

Chapter 1 Notes

[1] 5 U.S.C. § 552 (1966).

[2] 42 U.S.C. §§ 4321-4375 (1970).

[3] 42 U.S.C. § 4332.

[4] 42 U.S.C. § 4333.

[5] One prominent example is the Endangered Species Act (1973), which requires observance of NEPA for any agency action that may affect the habitat of an endangered or threatened species. A more recent federal statute with specific NEPA-inspired transparency provisions that go above and beyond that statute's intentions is the Emergency Planning and Community Right-to-Know Act (1986). Both of these will be discussed in detail in Chapter 6.

[6] Bradley C. Karkkainen, "Whither NEPA?" *New York University Environmental Law Journal* 12 (2004): 338-343.

[7] 33 U.S.C. §§ 1251-1387 (1972).

[8] 16 U.S.C. §§ 1531-1544 (1973).

[9] 42 U.S.C. §§ 9601-9675 (1980).

[10] 15 U.S.C. §§ 2601-2692 (1976).

[11] 42 U.S.C. §§ 11001-11050 (1986).

[12] James W. Spensley, Esq., "National Environmental Policy Act," in *Environmental Law Handbook*, vol. 14, ed. Thomas F.P. Sullivan (Rockville, Md.: Government Institutes, Inc., 1997), 405-407.

[13] One noteworthy expert on this topic is Bradley C. Karkkainen, several of whose articles are referenced herein.

[14] Michael B. Gerrard and Michael Herz, "Harnessing Information Technology to Improve the Environmental Impact Review Process," *New York University Environmental Law Journal* 12 (2003): 35-42; Don J. Frost, Jr., "*Amoco Production Co. v. Village of Gambel* and *Motor Vehicle Manufacturers Association v. State Farm Mutual Automobile Insurance Co.*: Authority Warranting Reconsideration of the Substantive Goals of the National Environmental Policy Act," *Alaska Law Review* 5 (1988): 28.

[15] Kellen Ressmeyer, "The Information Quality Act: The Little Statute That Could (or Couldn't)? Applying the Safe Drinking Water Act Amendments of 1996 to the Federal Communications Commission," *Federal Communications Law Journal* 59 (2006): 215-235. The Information Quality Act, also known as the Data Quality Act, was enacted by the Office of Management and Budget to improve the "quality, objectivity, utility, and integrity of information (including

statistical information) disseminated by Federal agencies." This statute remains untested but has ramifications for environmental protection. The statute was attached as a rider to an appropriations bill and thus has no official name. The Consolidated Appropriations Act of 2001, Pub. L. No. 106-554, 114 Stat. 2763 (2000) (appendix C of statute, codifying H.R. 5658).

[16] Richard J. Lazarus, *The Making of Environmental Law* (Chicago: University of Chicago Press, 2004), 189-190.

[17] World Resources Institute, *Decisions for the Earth: Balance, Voice, and Power 2002-2004* (Washington: World Resources Institute, 2003), 20.

[18] Vivek Ramkumar and Elena Petkova, "Transparency and Environmental Governance," in *The Right to Know: Transparency in an Open World*, ed. Ann Florini (New York: Columbia University Press, 2007), 282.

[19] Jorge Reina Schement, "Broadband, Internet, and Universal Service: Challenges to the Social Contract of the Twenty First Century," in *...And Communications for All: A Policy Agenda for the New Administration*, ed. Amit M. Schejter (Lanham, Md.: Lexington Books, 2009), 5-6.

[20] Thomas I. Emerson, "Toward a General Theory of the First Amendment," *Yale Law Journal* 72 (1963): 883. Here Emerson used "freedom of expression" not in the First Amendment sense but equated that term with public participation in government decision-making.

[21] National Research Council of the National Academies, *Public Participation in Environmental Assessment and Decision Making* (Washington, D.C.: The National Academies Press, 2008), 36.

[22] Logistically, the public interactions of federal administrative agencies are codified in the Administrative Procedure Act, 5 U.S.C. §§ 500-706 (1946); in particular §§ 553-554.

[23] National Research Council of the National Academies, 226. This quote is from a 2008 study of government agency behavior, conducted by the National Academies, a consortium of nonprofit institutions that provide scientific advice to the American government under a Congressional charter. The federal agencies participating in the study were the Environmental Protection Agency, the Department of Energy, the Food & Drug Administration, and the Department of Agriculture, all of which engage in activities that have an impact on the environment.

[24] Ibid.

[25] Ibid., 231-232.

[26] National Research Council, Committee on Risk Characterization & Commission on Behavioral and Social Sciences and Education, *Understanding Risk: Informing Decisions in a Democratic Society*, ed. P.C. Stern and H.V. Fineberg (Washington, D.C.: National Academy Press, 1996), 4-5.

[27] National Research Council of the National Academies, 76, 86. Critics of public participation in public administration note that intensive involvement by citizens might increase the legitimacy of government decisions but is likely to reduce their quality as leaders strive to score political points with voters.

[28] World Resources Institute, 20-21.

[29] National Research Council of the National Academies, 11-12.

[30] Uma Outka, "NEPA and Environmental Justice: Integration, Implementation, and Judicial Review," *Boston College Environmental Affairs Law Review* 33 (2006): 607.

[31] National Research Council of the National Academies, 7-8.

[32] World Resources Institute, 21.

[33] Ann Florini, "Whither Transparency?," in *The Right to Know: Transparency in an Open World*, ed. Ann Florini (New York: Columbia University Press, 2007), 339.

[34] Ibid.

[35] Martin E. Halstuk, "When Secrecy Trumps Transparency: Why the OPEN Government Act of 2007 Falls Short," *CommLaw Conspectus* 16 (2008): 444.

[36] World Resources Institute, 21.

[37] Schement, 7.

[38] Ernest J. Wilson III, "Digital Media, Modern Democracy, and Our Truncated National Debate," in *...And Communications for All: A Policy Agenda for the New Administration*, ed. Amit M. Schejter (Lanham, Md.: Lexington Books, 2009), 32.

[39] Ramkumar and Petkova, 283.

[40] Ibid.

[41] Eric E. Otenyo and Nancy S. Lind, "Faces and Phases of Transparency Reform in Local Government," *International Journal of Public Administration* 27 (2004): 289-290.

[42] Edith Stokey and Richard Zeckhauser, *A Primer for Policy Analysis* (New York: W.W. Norton, 1978), 292.

[43] Florini, "Whither Transparency?," 341.

[44] Joseph E. Stiglitz, "Foreword," in *The Right to Know: Transparency in an Open World*, ed. Ann Florini (New York: Columbia University Press, 2007), viii.

[45] Ramkumar and Petkova, 283.

[46] Richard Calland and Allison Tilley, eds. *The Right to Know, the Right to Live: Access to Information and Socio-Economic Justice* (Cape Town, South Africa: Open Democracy Advice Center, 2002), xi.

[47] Ramkumar and Petkova, 283.

[48] Ibid., 283-284.

[49] Otenyo and Lind, 300-303.

[50] Florini, "Whither Transparency?," 344.

[51] Laura Neuman and Richard Calland, "Making the Law Work: The Challenges of Implementation," in *The Right to Know: Transparency in an Open World*, ed. Ann Florini (New York: Columbia University Press, 2007), 191-192.

[52] Ramkumar and Petkova, 283-284.

[53] Ibid., 284-285.

[54] Lazarus, 178.

[55] The country's first local air pollution ordinances were passed in Chicago and Cincinnati, both in 1881. Bill McKibben, ed. *American Earth: Environmental Writing Since Thoreau* (New York: The Library of America, 2008), 983.

[56] 42 U.S.C. §§ 7401-7671 (1970). A predecessor of the Clean Air Act had been passed a few years earlier but that statute did not adequately address its own inconsistencies with various state and local statutes, leading to the 1970 Clean Air Act, which was technically a major expansion of the existing statute. Doyle J. Borchers, "The Practice of Regional Regulation Under the Clean Air Act," *Natural Resources Lawyer* 3 (1970): 62-63.

[57] 33 U.S.C. §§ 1251-1387 (1972). Upon its passage in 1972, this act was known as the Federal Water Pollution Control Act Amendments, and served as a series of amendments to an existing pollution control statute. It was renamed the Clean Water Act in 1977. Ridgway M. Hall, Jr. "The Clean Water Act of 1977," *Natural Resources Lawyer* 11 (1978): 343-345.

[58] Lazarus, 145.

[59] Ibid., 171-172.

[60] Ibid., 180.

[61] Ibid., 175-176. Throughout the 1970s and 1980s, these requirements were unique to the Clean Water Act. The lack of reporting and permitting requirements in the Clean Air Act was a constant source of criticism from environmentalists, so that act was amended in 1990 to include standards similar to those of the Clean Water Act.

[62] Benjamin W. Cramer, "The Human Right to Information, the Environment, and Information About the Environment: From the Universal Declaration to the Aarhus Convention," *Communication Law & Policy* 14 (2009): 103.

[63] Lazarus, 185.

[64] Wendy E. Wagner, "Commons Ignorance: The Failure of Environmental Law to Produce Needed Information on Health and the Environment," *Duke Law Journal* 53 (2004): 1717-1726.

[65] In the words of the Endangered Species Act, "the United States has pledged itself as a sovereign state in the international community to conserve to the extent practicable the various species of fish or wildlife and plants facing extinction..." 16 U.S.C. § 1531(a)(4).

[66] Cramer, 73-74.

[67] United Nations, *Draft Declaration of Principles on Human Rights and the Environment*, 16 May 1994, United Nations, Annex I., E/CN.4/Sub.2/1994/9, http://worldpolicy.org/projects/globalrights/environment/envright.html, accessed 23 June 2010.

[68] Sumudu Atapattu, "The Right to a Healthy Life or the Right to Die Polluted: The Emergence of a Human Right to a Healthy Environment Under International Law," *Tulane Environmental Law Journal* 16 (2002): 82-83.

[69] *Draft Declaration of Principles on Human Rights and the Environment*, pt. III(15).

[70] Cramer, 103.

Government Transparency: A History

Modern notions of government transparency and access to government-held documents on any subject, including environmental protection, are manifestations of theories and questions that were raised by America's Founding Fathers and the political thinkers who influenced them. Therefore, any understanding of the transparency and usefulness of government-held environmental information requires an in-depth discussion of American government transparency in general.

The term *transparency* generally applies to the ability of citizens to know what their leaders are up to. But in reality, this term carries great weight in many different realms of politics and socioeconomics, and hence has no precise definition. For example, in politics *transparency* often refers to the ability of citizens to check government abuses through the collection of official information.[1] In economic theory, the term has gained an expanded working definition and refers to an intellectual process, in which interested persons can receive information about existing conditions and decision-making that is understandable and useful for their own sociopolitical endeavors.[2] In the security field, *transparency* refers to the distribution of information on military activities and the enactment of international agreements. The term has also been used in various ways in many other policy realms.[3]

Here, the term *transparency* will be applied to the actions of government in the political realm, and particularly environmental protection. Within the American structure of governance, environmental protection is a matter of the interaction between land owners, the users of that land (the general public for government-owned lands; residents and neighbors for privately-owned lands), and parties who would wish to extract resources from or dispose of waste on that land. That interaction is regulated by governments at the local, state, and federal levels in the interests of managing resources and minimizing conflicts among competing interests.[4]

In turn, the government collects and manages great amounts of information during this process, and the transparency and availability of that information can be a crucial matter in citizen oversight of government actions toward the natural world. Despite the eventual focus on environmental matters herein, this is a high-level definition of *transparency* that allows citizens to hold decision makers (both public and private) accountable and allows them to participate in the political and economic processes that affect the health of the natural world. With this level of transparency, decision makers are required to disclose crucial information, voluntarily or involuntarily, retroactively and proactively. In turn, decision-makers will know that disclosure of information is in their best interests and will give them more legitimacy in the eyes of concerned citizens.[5]

Democratic Theory and Government Transparency

Government transparency in America, and the constitutional or statutory protection thereof, is based largely upon the First Amendment freedom of the press and related right-to-know theories. Some rights of access to government documents were also inherited from the common law of England, but such common law rights were not observed uniformly in the early American colonies.[6] These legal matters will be discussed in detail in the next section of this chapter. For now, when it comes to protecting citizen access to government information, American lawmakers have been inspired by wider theories of government transparency and open access to information, which are built upon the earliest conceptions of civil society and democracy.

Theories of open government can be traced back to the Enlightenment, particularly the philosophy of utilitarianism as defined by Jeremy Bentham, who theorized that all persons should tailor their actions toward the greatest good for the greatest number.[7] Bentham influenced future democratic theorists, particularly John Stuart Mill, who expanded utilitarianism by claiming that leaders should act on behalf of their people and work toward the greatest good. Most notably for the present discussion, in his 1859 work *On Liberty*, Mill noted that citizens should have the right to remain free from government oppression, and that political leaders should work toward the ideal of liberty for all citizens of the state.[8] Mill's political philosophy was heavily influential for modern democratic theory, expanding basic theories of representational politics into matters of government legitimacy in the eyes of the people (or in Mill's terms, a rejection of the supposed infallibility of leaders). This requires transparent operations and access to leaders and their decision-making processes.[9]

Mill epitomized a basic idea shared by many early democratic theorists, advocating the need for knowledge as citizens strive to govern themselves through the election of competent representatives.[10] To extend this basic philosophical precept, citizens can be an effective check on government abuses, but in order to do so effectively, citizens require information on what the government is doing. Excessive government secrecy distorts the democratic process by preventing citizens from effectively participating in the decision-making processes of their elected officials.[11]

Governments, by their very nature, tend to operate in secrecy or wish they could exercise more secrecy. This is especially a problem in societies in which secret behavior by leaders is an entrenched value, and even in Western democracies the tendency is toward opacity, not transparency. The implementation of government transparency requires a fundamental change in the worldview of government leaders, who often see the release of information to citizens as a restriction on their own political power.[12] Civil society structures, public participation, and democratic elections can deliver that mind-shift to political leaders. Civil society groups and citizen's coalitions are the single most important source of demand for disclosure of government-held information.[13] When government transparency is properly implemented and enforced, knowledgeable and involved citizens will vote wisely at the election booth.[14]

These are the theories that most influenced the Founding Fathers when they set up the basic structure of the American government. Good governance requires fairness and equity in dealing with citizens, and consistency and coherence in the formation of public policy and the laws to be observed by all citizens. A government that follows these basic principles will be more transparent, accessible, and responsive in its operations.[15]

Traditionally, free press theorists have contended that in a democracy, the press should be the servant of the people and should inform citizens on the operations of their government. As opposed to the uninformed residents of a totalitarian state that controls its press and keeps the public uninformed, the ultimate benefit of a free press is an informed electorate that is capable of governing itself through the election of qualified representatives.[16] Meanwhile, the citizens of a democracy are not well served by mere promises of open government. There must be constitutional protection of the citizen's right of access to information, and if that is not achieved then there should be statutory protection.[17] As will be discussed extensively later in this chapter, Americans do not enjoy unlimited constitutional protection of the right of access to information. Such access is statutorily protected by the Freedom of Information Act and other affiliated laws based on particular policy topics, such as the environment.

In recent decades, transparency activists have expanded their philosophy beyond mere access to information. Inspired by the maxim that knowledge is power, activist groups like Transparency International[18] have reframed the argument into a battle against corruption and collusion among politicians, multinational corporations, non-governmental organizations, inter-governmental organizations, and other parties that wield socioeconomic power. Citizens and activists are making increasing demands on these power players to reveal their decision-making processes in the realms of human rights, public health, allocation of resources, and environmental protection.[19] Access to information, both across the board and in terms of environmental protection, has also been claimed by activists in recent years as a fundamental human right around the world.[20] Indeed, government transparency is becoming a crucial arbiter of the interactions between citizens and their leaders, in any nation, perhaps reflecting an inexorable change in longstanding structures of power and privilege.[21]

This modern philosophy of government transparency, and the need for an informed citizenry in a fully functioning democracy, has slowly spread around the world, with many nations enacting access-to-information statutes in the decades after the passage of America's influential Freedom of Information Act.[22] On the world stage, the push for government transparency can be traced to the formation of the American republic, with the Founding Fathers' revolutionary drive for representative democracy setting the stage for modern practices of government transparency.

A Brief History of the Right to Know in America

America has a rich, though fairly recent, tradition of statutory protection of access to government-held information. In fact, the transparency of the America government has only been statutorily protected for a relatively brief time. In 1966, Congress passed the Freedom of Information Act (FOIA),[23] which provided citizens with access to certain categories of federal government documents. This act is grounded in the philosophy that citizens of a democracy need access to government information in order to participate in self-rule,[24] and the act places a priority on government disclosure of information to the citizen.[25] Meanwhile, the Government in the Sunshine Act (GISA)[26] of 1976 allowed citizens to attend certain types of government meetings. The Sunshine Act arose in an era when distrust toward political leaders was high, due to the Watergate saga and widespread reports of government malfeasance concerning civil rights and the Vietnam War.[27] This act is built upon the then-emergent philosophy that citizens can gain a better understanding of government processes, and the motivations of their elected representatives, by seeing them operate in person.[28]

It is important to note that the Freedom of Information Act, the Government in the Sunshine Act, and related open-government laws are statutory guarantees only, meaning that American citizens do not have a *right* to information from the government. It is also important to note that a statutory protection only outlines a procedure for citizens to follow in the event that a particular piece of information is desired from the government, and a statutory protection is weaker than an inalienable right.

In a series of related cases in the 1970s known as the "Prison Trio," the U.S. Supreme Court ruled that there is no constitutional right to government information in America. In that decade three landmark First Amendment disputes reached the high court. *Pell v. Procunier*[29] and *Saxbe v. Washington Post*[30] both reached the high court in 1974 and arose from disputes in which journalists requested access to federal prisons in order to interview inmates about prison conditions. *Houchins v. KQED*,[31] which reached the high court in 1978, was a similar dispute, with the addition of an attempted independent investigation by journalists into an inmate's suicide. In all three cases, the journalists' requests for access were denied by prison officials, prompting the journalists to sue on First Amendment grounds, under the rationale that their free press rights were violated. In all three cases, the Supreme Court ruled that the First Amendment, via the free press clause or any other clause, does not provide an absolute right of citizen access to government facilities.[32] While seemingly specific to prisons and inmates, these three cases have served as precedents regarding any kind of government-held information and the lack of a constitutional right to it.

The "Prison Trio" shed light on a possible oversight by America's Founding Fathers, because the Constitution does not directly address the issue of whether access to government information should be an inalienable right of the people. Government transparency theory dates back to the earliest years of the American republic, and is closely related to the theories of a free press and self-government that inspired the Founding Fathers. In fact, early theoretical support for a right to transparent government and access to government-held information was usually delivered by the same thinkers who advocated for a free press. But while free speech and a free press were ultimately included in the Bill of Rights, access to government information, *per se*, was not.

In America, the origin of a citizen's right to know about government activities dates back to 17th Century England, where an emergent press struggled to investigate the official secrecy of Parliament. These journalists were often condemned as "radicals" by the British authorities, and were occasionally imprisoned until agreeing to cease and desist in their investigations. This pattern continued in early America, with the British-controlled colonial government exercising the same hostility to the disclosure of official information.[33] For example, in 1671 Governor William Berkeley of Virginia expressed a common attitude among the pro-British colonial government of the time by stating, "I thank God we have no free schools of free printing... learning has brought disobedience and heresy and sects into the world, and printing has divulged them, and libels against the government."[34]

Another illustrative example occurred in 1722, with an order from Pennsylvania leader John Penn. (The colony was administered during this period by its largest landowner, known officially as the Chief Proprietor, who in 1722 was this eldest son of the colony's founder William Penn.) John Penn ordered an author named Andrew Bradford to stop publishing "anything relating to or concerning the affairs of this government... without the permission of the Governor or Secretary of this province."[35] Note that this order acted as both a prior restraint against the press and as an official policy against the citizen's right to know about government activities.

Official colonial secrecy would eventually inspire America's Founding Fathers to carefully consider the power and effectiveness of an informed citizenry. In particular, British efforts to reform colonial taxation and administration between 1763 and 1775 were not only the primary catalysts for the push toward independence, but they also made the residents of the colonies suspicious of government machinations and desirous of more access to official information.[36] The first noteworthy statesman to address this matter was the young John Adams, who in 1765 published an anonymous essay proclaiming that an informed citizenry would be one of the key antidotes to the inequities of British colonial rule. In Adams's words, "The people have a right, an indisputable, inalienable, indefeasible divine right to that most dreaded and envied kind of knowledge... the characters and conduct of their rulers."[37]

Adams was not alone in promoting a more open government, and in the effort to distance themselves from their imperial masters, local governments in the colonies began to make their proceedings more accessible to the public. For example, in 1764 the Virginia House of

Burgesses voted to allow journalists and members of the public to attend debates, a move that was followed by the local government in Boston two years later.[38] In 1774, the Continental Congress passed the Quebec Declaration, in which it recognized the right to a free press for the first time, adding that the press was imperative for the "diffusion of sentiments on the administration of government [and] ready communication of thoughts between subjects."[39]

The need for a well-informed public received its most historic endorsement with the publication of Thomas Paine's *Common Sense* in early 1776. This originally anonymous pamphlet was a smash hit throughout the American colonies, and its rejection of the British system of government was a direct influence on the Declaration of Independence and the Constitution.[40] Aside from Paine's revolutionary thoughts on democracy and independence, he made a contribution to future right-to-know theory by stating the importance of the free flow of government information for an informed public and a functioning democracy.[41] Paine also addressed the question of who should have control over government information in the soon-to-be American republic. A key line of thought among the Founding Fathers was that the government should be checked by an unencumbered and curious press, as opposed to the reverse situation in which the press is checked (and censored) by the government.[42] There could hardly be a better endorsement of the right of the press, and ultimately the citizen, of access to government information.

However, while a free press was obviously an important value to the Founding Fathers, the rights of the press as enshrined in the First Amendment were seen more as protection from government censorship of a journalist's speech, rather than a requirement for the government to cooperate with the press. James Madison was a noteworthy champion of an unencumbered press and its duty to inform the public of the activities of the government, but he saw freedom of the press as a high-level protection against the cumbersome effects of federal power.[43] Madison is also credited (perhaps inaccurately) with one of the great early American quotations on the need for an informed citizenry, telling a friend late in life that "A popular government without popular information, or the means of acquiring it, is but a prologue to a farce or a tragedy, or perhaps both."[44] This quote has been praised by government transparency activists ever since, and even though Madison was talking more about education than reading newspapers, his thoughts on the matter have been extremely influential.[45]

But for right-to-know theory, the First Amendment does not give the journalist or the citizen the right of access to government information, and does not require the government to furnish such information upon request. America's Founding Fathers, influenced by revolutionary thinkers like Thomas Paine, were certainly proponents of a free press that is unfettered in its investigations of government and can effectively contribute to an informed electorate.[46] But on the other hand, despite popular perceptions of early American history and the supposed theoretical ideals of the Founding Fathers, there is little evidence that government secrecy was a matter of ripe discussion at the Constitutional Convention, according to historian Daniel Hoffman. The Convention itself was a secretive operation, with general disagreement among the delegates over what aspects of the deliberations should be reported to the press or to the political representatives still serving under the structure of the Articles of Confederation.[47]

Total secrecy at the convention was championed by none other than George Washington. After a leak of information by an unnamed delegate to his state representatives back home, Washington berated both his colleague and public rumormongers: "I must entreat Gentlemen to be more careful, least our transactions get into the News Papers, and disturb the public repose by premature speculations."[48] When the Convention entered negotiations for the ratification of the new Constitution, secret negotiations again became an issue, with Alexander Hamilton echoing Washington's sentiments on the need to control uninformed speculation amongst the public. Hamilton added that public speculation would rub off on the delegates and ruin the integrity of the important new document: "Had the deliberations been open while going on, the clamours of faction would have prevented any satisfactory result. Had they been afterwards disclosed, much food would have been offered to inflammatory defamation."[49]

The counterpoint to the secrecy recommended by Washington and Hamilton was the idealistic philosophy of openness championed by Thomas Jefferson. In a diplomatic statement made in Paris during an ambassadorial trip, Jefferson worried about the precedent set by the secrecy of the Constitutional Convention and the poor prospects for openness in the near future of the young American republic.[50] Referring to his fellow conventioneers, Jefferson lamented, "I am sorry that they began their deliberations by so abominable a precedent as that of tying up the tongues of their members. Nothing can justify this example but the innocence of their intentions, [and] ignorance of the value of public discussions."[51]

Despite this fairly active debate over secrecy during the Convention, the new American Constitution contained very little language about the need for openness in the new government structure and practically no discussion of the apparent goods or evils of secrecy. This belies the stereotypical belief in the philosophical ideals of the Founding Fathers, at least at the Constitutional Convention, at which discussions were focused more on institutional design rather than democratic theory.[52] Thus, as the new American federal government got to work there was immediate confusion over how much transparency should be allowed, with debates over what types of information (in the form of congressional journals and executive reports) should be disclosed to the press and the public. James Madison and George Mason were among the Constitutional delegates who favored limited secrecy in military operations and matters of diplomacy.[53] John Marshall represented a vaguely-defined higher-level view, noting that "secrecy is only used when it would be fatal and pernicious to publish the schemes of government."[54] But this view immediately attracted critics, most notably an unsurprisingly vehement Patrick Henry, who feared that the Constitutional Convention had indirectly encouraged secrecy by failing to address the matter properly in its construction of the new government.[55] Henry demanded "at least a plausible apology why Congress should keep their proceedings in secret... The liberties of a people never were, nor never will be, secure when the transactions of their rulers may be concealed from them."[56]

Meanwhile, the young America was involved in a triangular pattern of Cold War-like political tensions with England and France, leading to additional critical feelings about government transparency from America's leaders. As is often the case during political or military crises, leaders found ways to justify greater secrecy in the national interest.[57] The political tensions of the immediate post-convention period, particularly between the Federalists and Anti-Federalists,[58] inspired patterns of government secrecy embodied by the Alien and Sedition Acts of 1798. This pair of laws restricted foreign policy discussion and contradicted any philosophy of open government, throwing into doubt the efficacy of the First Amendment and the protection of political speech in the young republic.[59]

The Founding Fathers enshrined freedom of the press in the First Amendment to the Constitution, under the philosophy that an unhindered press can aid the people in knowledgeable self-government. However, in its own words the First Amendment does not recognize the need for proactive access to leaders and their documents, and the political trends of the revolutionary period inspired many of the Founding Fathers to acknowledge the need for secrecy in at least some government operations. Thus, they did not equate modern notions of government transparency with their own contemporary notions of freedom of the press.[60]

Consequently, the question of whether the Constitution guarantees citizen access to government information, and political speech in general, did not become a practical matter until the early 20th Century. In particular, restrictions against popular dissent during World War I inspired several landmark rulings by the Supreme Court concerning questions of free expression. New statutes like the 1917 Espionage Act and the 1918 Sedition Act, both passed by Congress in the belief that suppression of political dissent was a crucial matter of national security, represented the most worrisome government restrictions on speech since the revolutionary era. Landmark First Amendment disputes like *Schenck v. United States* (1919),[61] *Abrams v. United States* (1919),[62] and *Gitlow v. New York* (1925)[63] showed the Supreme Court transitioning from deference to the wishes of the Founding Fathers to analyses of currently applicable government responses to perceived social problems.[64] These rulings, while more relevant for political speech and the ability of the government to restrict that speech during times of war and other emergencies, inspired the high court to consider possible new interpretations of how the protections of the First Amendment can make a difference in the political knowledge of the American citizenry.

Right-to-know theory thus began to creep into Supreme Court rulings on First Amendment disputes. In *Whitney v. California* (1927), which was also inspired by the World War I-era restrictions on political speech, Justice Louis Brandeis delivered a concurring opinion in which he advocated the need for an informed citizenry, beyond the information that could be unearthed by journalists who continually faced official obfuscation.[65] Though this conception had little or no impact on the high court's ultimate ruling toward the constitutionality of a "criminal syndicalism" law in California, Brandeis planted the seeds of right-to-know theory among his fellow justices. In *Grosjean v. American Press Co.* (1936), Justice George Sutherland, within an opinion that mostly repeated basic American rhetoric about the need for a free and uncensored press, noted in passing that a free press was "a vital source of public information." The insinuation was that public information includes knowledge of government activities, and this knowledge "is the most potent of all restraints upon misgovernment."[66]

With the *Whitney* and *Grosjean* rulings, the Supreme Court, though indirectly, began to free the press not just from government censorship, but also from official revenge when reporting on the most embarrassing secrets of the government. But the question still remained as to whether the First Amendment actually included a right of access for the press (and by extension, the citizen) to government information.[67] A traditional reading of the First Amendment, thanks to the poetic brevity of its text, would conclude that freedom of the press was merely protection from government censorship of what the press reports, with no mention of how a journalist's incoming information was gathered.

Activists for a constitutional right of access to government information were required to embark on creative interpretations of the text of the First Amendment and the intent of the Founding Fathers. The personal writings of James Madison became a useful source on what the Constitution's framers thought about a right to know. Around the time of the First Amendment's ratification in 1791, Madison noted that one of the amendment's primary purposes was to guarantee "the right of freely examining public characters [i.e. government leaders] and measures, and of free communication thereon," with the belief that this right was "the only effective guardian of every other right."[68]

By the middle of the 20th Century, Madison's conception of the right to know became an influence on the theories of free speech activist Alexander Meiklejohn, who advocated an interpretation of the First Amendment as an absolute protection for a citizen's political speech, which in turn must include a right of access to government information. In Meiklejohn's words, "The First Amendment does not protect a 'freedom to speak'... it protects the freedom of those activities of thought and communication by which we 'govern'."[69]

Note that Meiklejohn was really a free political speech absolutist, and right-to-know advocates added their own interpretations to Meiklejohn's interpretation of the First Amendment. Wallace Parks, a legal scholar and staff attorney for the House Government Affairs Committee (which was later involved in drafting the Freedom of Information Act), noted in 1957 that Meiklejohn's conception of the First Amendment included the duty of citizens to properly exercise the responsibilities of citizenship in a free society. Therefore, "it is certainly reasonable to conclude that freedom of the press and speech... includes the right to gather information from government agencies and stands as a constitutional prohibition against all forms of withholding information."[70] Around the same time, prominent news industry attorney Harold L. Cross (an important contributor to later efforts to pass the Freedom of Information Act) offered his own broad interpretation of the First Amendment, concluding that "the language of the Amendment is broad enough to embrace, if indeed it does not require, the inclusion of a right of access to information of government without which the freedom to print could be frittered into futility."[71]

These thinkers may have claimed that a right to know was indeed included in the free speech and free press clauses of the First Amendment (albeit via creative interpretations of the intent of the Founding Fathers), but the absence of such a right in the plain language of the amendment resulted in little protection in the courts. During this period, a right to know was often noted in court opinions, including those from the Supreme Court, but usually in the form of dicta and without the establishment of useful precedents.[72]

In the middle of the 20th Century, some rulings show that the high court may have been influenced by right-to-know theory, but this theory had no real impact on the outcome of any particular case. For example, in *Martin v. City of Struthers* (1943), the high court first recognized the First Amendment right of the citizen to receive information, with Justice Hugo Black noting that the right to receive information was "vital to the preservation of a free society."[73] This right was reaffirmed in two Supreme Court cases from 1965, *Lamont v. Postmaster General*[74] and *Griswold v. Connecticut.*[75] However, the right to receive government information was not germane to the issues of those cases and had no direct influence in the ultimate rulings from the high court.

The Road to the Freedom of Information Act

If the courts could not fashion a constitutional right of access to government information, then perhaps the answer was a federal statute that could be utilized by citizens and investigative journalists. Given the inconclusive jurisprudence on whether the First Amendment truly guaranteed a "right to know," by the 1950s there arose a movement for the statutory protection of access to government-held information. The politically-charged term for this phenomenon, *freedom of information*, first arose as early as 1934, when Carl V. Ackerman, Dean of the Columbia University Graduate School of Journalism, denounced press restrictions in other nations, particularly in Europe after World War I.[76]

During World War II, the American government exhibited the patterns of increased secrecy that are common during military conflicts and other emergencies. The administration of Franklin D. Roosevelt took an expanded view of "national security" and placed greater restrictions on the release of not just military and strategy-related documents, but rapidly-growing categories of other government information as well. Roosevelt authorized the classification of militarily-sensitive information for the first time in 1941, making all documents with such a classification off-limits to the press and the public.[77] This executive order was justified by the need for "national security," and in a phenomenon that would be seen again and again during times of crisis, this crucial term was vaguely defined and often misused to deny access to information for reporters and citizens.[78] As noted by constitutional scholar Zechariah Chafee, "The misuse of this power by the government becomes a more and more serious danger. ...

What is significant is the enormous recent expansion of the subjects which officials are seeking to hide from publication."[79]

As hostilities increased and America formally entered the war, the Roosevelt Administration went so far as to create the Office of Censorship in 1941, a body with the authority to enforce its rules of government secrecy and punish reporters who broke those rules.[80] After a brief period of agreement with the need for secrecy during wartime, the American press became largely dissatisfied with this increased secrecy, and reporters initiated a movement for greater government transparency via the First Amendment rights of the press.[81] At this time, an emerging freedom of information philosophy reflected the desire of the press to gain access to government-held information in the interests of informing the public, with any acts of non-disclosure by the government being considered violations of the First Amendment.[82]

The quantity of government-held information was growing by leaps and bounds by mid-century, largely as a result of the increasing size and authority of the government during the war years. In 1946, Congress passed the Administrative Procedure Act (APA),[83] a wide-ranging statute that governs the processes to be followed by federal administrative agencies when forming and enforcing rules and regulations, adjudicating or arbitrating disputes among regulated parties, and managing the information that arises during such procedures. As noted during Senate debates prior to the passage of APA: "Administrative operations and procedures are public property [that] the general public, rather than a few specialists or lobbyists, is entitled to know or have the ready means of knowing with definiteness and assurance."[84] The APA facilitated an enormous increase in the paperwork generated by federal government agencies, which themselves were growing rapidly in number due to the increasing complexity of federal government operations during the New Deal era and World War II.[85] But this proliferating information was often shuttered in agency archives and was rarely made available to the public.[86]

After the war, the freedom of information movement started picking up steam amongst the American press and the public, with demands for more access to all forms of government-held information and more access to government officials and their meetings. Such demands grew as the government became more secretive with the advent of Cold War tensions with the Soviet Union.[87] Wartime secrecy patterns within the American government continued after the end of World War II, when the administrations of Harry S. Truman and Dwight D. Eisenhower exhibited a military-style animosity toward the disclosure of information, as wartime secrecy extended into peacetime.

In 1951 Truman expanded Roosevelt's wartime authorization for military classification of documents to all nonmilitary civilian agencies within the federal government, once again with justification provided by the vaguely-defined "national security."[88] Truman's action was not well received by the American press, with journalists showing increased support for the freedom of information philosophy. Popular CBS radio host and newsman Edward R. Murrow noted that Truman's order extended secrecy "into vast areas where, by no stretch of the imagination would legitimate security interests be involved."[89] The *Wall Street Journal* summed up this emerging view amongst the press, noting that "A free government lives on the freedom of the people to know what their government is doing."[90]

In 1954, Eisenhower created the controversial Office of Strategic Information (OSI), a new federal agency that was put in charge of managing sensitive information that could lead to national security problems upon falling into enemy hands. The OSI endeavored to keep not just top secret or classified information under wraps, but unclassified information as well. The problem was that there was no official definition of "unclassified," although the OSI adopted the policy of withholding such information from the public and the press regardless.[91]

The investigative press was outraged, with a rash of anti-secrecy editorials appearing in newspapers and magazines across the country. Journalists were not impressed by the government's security rationale, and detected ulterior motives behind the new patterns of secrecy. For example, the editors of *Time* declared: "Such a policy is just the thing for Government officials who want to cover up their own mistakes by withholding 'nonconstructive' news."[92] The major newspapers were also incensed by the government's not-so-covert efforts to encourage the press to join in the secrecy. J.R. Wiggins, editor of the *Washington Post* and an active commentator on press issues, lamented: "The newspapers will not join in a conspiracy with this or any other administration to withhold from the American people nonclassified information."[93]

In addition to the controversial machinations of the OSI, by the 1950s the Administrative Procedure Act was being widely misused by federal agencies. Thanks to APA, the American government was creating more information than ever in the years after World War II, but the proportion of such information being made available to the public was shrinking.[94] One major issue was a poorly-defined phrase that appears throughout APA, "public interest," which was often cited by agency officials as giving them the authority to withhold documents.[95] In the 1950s, this became a common tactic in the Eisenhower Administration, turning a statute that was intended to be a passive encouragement for the management of information into an official justification for government secrecy.[96] By mid-decade this increase in secrecy inspired some members of Congress, such as Senator Thomas C. Hennings (D-Mo.) and Representative John Moss (D-Calif.), to advocate for amendments to, or even a complete overhaul of, the Administrative Procedure Act. Such efforts were initially unsuccessful, though Moss in particular took a long-term interest in the issue and would soon lead a special subcommittee to investigate potential solutions to the problem.[97]

Given inconclusive jurisprudence on whether the First Amendment truly guaranteed a "right to know" (see the previous section), by the mid-1950s a serious legislative movement arose for the statutory protection of access to government-held information. Due to recent patterns of secrecy in the American government and changing public attitudes toward transparency and openness, the time was ripe for statutory protection of the freedom of information.[98] During the Republican Eisenhower Administration, the newly-elected Democratic Congress convened the Special Subcommittee on Government Information to explore government secrecy and the possibilities of a federal statute to restrain that secrecy. Representative John Moss became the chairman, and the group became known informally as the Moss Subcommittee.[99]

Inspired by the recent works on secrecy by investigators like Harold L. Cross[100] and Herbert Brucker,[101] as well as a new interpretation of the information-gathering requirements of the Administrative Procedure Act, the subcommittee advocated statutory protection for the transparency of the federal government's rapidly growing quantities of official information.[102] As one of the most prominent journalists and editors of the day, Cross lead the charge for legislative action in decreasing government secrecy and protecting public access to government-held information. In Cross's words, "The time is ripe for an end to ineffectual sputtering about executive refusals of access to official records and for Congress to begin exercising effectually its function to legislate freedom of information for itself, the public, and the press."[103] In less erudite language Cross also summed up changing attitudes toward government transparency with the classic and oft-quoted maxim "public business is the public's business."[104]

The Moss Subcommittee was a key player, but not the only player, in a slowly changing conception of democratic governance and the availability of government information for citizens. In 1955, the Commission on Organization of the Executive Branch of the Government (known informally as the Hoover Commission) issued a report that was critical of the secrecy of federal agencies, comparing agency obfuscation with the false advertising that was otherwise condemned by the government, and proposed an amendment to the Administrative Procedure Act.[105] The evolution of political thought in Washington was reflected that same year in a comment by Representative William Dawson (D-Ill.), chairman of the House Government Operations Committee and the ultimate approver of the formation of the Moss Subcommittee. "If the pertinent and necessary information on government activities is denied the public, the result is a weakening of the democratic process and the ultimate atrophy of our form of government."[106]

Despite the fact that it had many years of difficult work ahead of it, the formation of the Moss Subcommittee represented a breakthrough in American attitudes toward government secrecy and made that topic a major political issue.[107] For example, at the 1956 Democratic Convention, the issue was added to the party platform. "We condemn the Eisenhower Administration for the excesses practiced in this area [federal government secrecy], and pledge the Democratic Party to reverse this tendency."[108]

The Moss Subcommittee set out to define the categories of government-held information that should be made available to the public and the procedures to be followed by federal agencies upon citizen requests for documents or access to meetings.[109] The subcommittee was in operation from 1955 until the passage of the Freedom of Information Act in 1966, with Moss serving as chairman throughout. The formation of the subcommittee was applauded by the American press,[110] but reporters may have been the only true fans of the subcommittee's work during its early years. Progress was initially slow as the subcommittee attempted to amend the Administrative Procedure Act, only to face stiff resistance from federal agencies that had less faith in the ability of the American public to manage sensitive government information.[111] Some agencies also complained of the increased bureaucratic workload that could be necessitated by requirements to disclose documents to the public.[112]

Meanwhile, upon entering the White House in 1961, the administration of Democrat John F. Kennedy disappointed journalists and government watchdogs with its own patterns of secrecy. Escalation of Cold War hostilities with the Soviet Union, and especially the ill-fated 1961 invasion of the Bay of Pigs in Cuba, resulted in a continuation of secrecy during the Kennedy administration, again justified by "national security."[113] At the height of the Bay of Pigs episode, Kennedy made a pointed request to American journalists to exercise voluntary self-censorship and prevent the disclosure of sensitive military information that could be helpful to America's enemies. In Kennedy's words, "In time of 'clear and present danger,' the courts have held that even the privileged rights of the First Amendment must yield to the public's need for national security."[114]

The press reaction to Kennedy's request for voluntary self-censorship was similar to its reaction to secrecy in the Truman and Eisenhower administrations. For example, the *New York Times* raised the now decades-old question of who had the privilege of defining "national security." In the disdainful words of an anonymous reporter, "These questions illustrate the hazards and ambiguity of the course proposed by the President."[115] Kennedy's policies on information disclosure reenergized the moribund Moss Subcommittee, which had been bogged down by agency resistance to the idea of amending the

Administrative Procedure Act. In a 1962 report, the subcommittee compiled an extensive list of recent acts of government secrecy and finally advocated the need for real administrative or legislative action to control the problem.[116] By 1963 the Moss Subcommittee finally endeavored to create a new federal statute that would ensure citizen access to government information, rather than attempt to amend the Administrative Procedure Act, because that earlier goal had only resulted in years of inconclusive hearings and reports.[117]

In 1964, an early attempt at a comprehensive information-disclosure statute first appeared in the U.S. Congress as Senate Bill 1666, introduced by Senator Edward V. Long (D-Mo.).[118] Various versions of the bill made their way through the House and Senate, until the House finally passed the latest version, now known as the Freedom of Information Act, on June 20, 1966.[119] The bill was signed into law by President Lyndon B. Johnson on July 4, 1966.[120] Despite some personal reservations, especially regarding the perennially touchy topic of national security, Johnson lauded the act in his official statement during the signing ceremony. "This legislation springs from one of our most essential principles: A democracy works best when the people have all the information that the security of the nation permits. No one should be able to pull the curtain of secrecy around decisions which can be revealed without injury to the public interest."[121]

For the first time, Americans received statutory protection for their efforts to obtain government documents, with a detailed procedure to be followed by federal agencies in disclosing documents upon citizen request, and an appeals process available to citizens whose requests for documents are denied. (The Act applied to government documents only. Citizen access to agency meetings, another avenue to government transparency, was not statutorily protected until the passage of the Government in the Sunshine Act in 1976.) The Freedom of Information Act builds upon a positive philosophy of open government, meaning that all documents are presumed to be available to citizens, unless the government can justify withholding a particular document for specific reasons.[122] This was a crucial change in philosophy, because the government now had the burden of proof in denying any citizen request for information.

A Legal History of the Freedom of Information Act

The Freedom of Information Act (FOIA), being the "umbrella" statute offering citizens the right of access to government documents, has been the source of many legal disputes that shed light on the viability of government transparency (or the lack thereof) in America. It must be noted that the Freedom of Information Act has not always enforced ultimate government transparency, because of its vague statutory language and uncertainty among government officials and courts on how to interpret some of the act's provisions and exemptions.

Despite its rather straightforward philosophical language on transparency and open government, its vagueness on matters of procedural detail made FOIA quite difficult to implement smoothly. Due to the size and reach of the American government, the agency resistance faced by the Moss Subcommittee did not dissipate after the passage of the act in 1966. Agency officials (the holders of most government information) were reluctant to change their entrenched disclosure practices, while agencies and departments often lacked the manpower to effectively manage and disclose their voluminous documents.[123] FOIA, like many similar administratively-oriented statutes, can only be successful if passage, implementation, and enforcement are all conducted satisfactorily. Even after a law has been passed, without effective implementation and enforcement that law may become merely an obscure entry in the official records that benefits no one.[124] The implementation and enforcement of FOIA, per its own language and procedural requirements, became the source of citizen dissatisfaction and legal disputes that have resulted in a rather checkered legal history. Ultimately, one may ask how much the act really opens up the operations of the American government.

The Freedom of Information Act requires federal government agencies and departments to release to the public, upon request, information concerning agency procedures and methodologies, forms and reports, and statements of general policy.[125] These procedures are quite detailed, in the interests of not just citizen access but in the preservation of agency rules and rationales for keeping certain documents undisclosed if officials deem it necessary.[126] Also, because of the need to keep certain government information secret or classified,

Congress included nine exemptions to FOIA, which an agency can utilize in denying a citizen request for particular records. These exemptions include matters of national security, personal privacy, law enforcement, and other phenomena that may justify withholding a document in the public interest.[127] These procedural matters have limited the reach of the Freedom of Information Act, and the American courts have been called upon to interpret the act's often troublesome language and to determine how powerful the act should really be in guaranteeing access to government-held information.

FOIA turned out to be rather disappointing in its early years, with citizens largely unable to overcome agency denials, either of the direct variety or *de facto* through the unsupported dismissal of requests or the imposition of steep fines.[128] In its original language, the statute completely lacked any deadlines for meeting citizen requests or penalties for government officials who ignored or inappropriately denied those requests.[129] In 1972, Congress noted a "widespread reluctance of the bureaucracy to honor the public's legal right to know" – a legal right that was supposedly codified in FOIA.[130] Citizens who were denied access to requested documents rarely appealed those denials in court, even though the statutory language of FOIA allowed it, because the courts were unlikely to overturn official agency decisions of any kind, including FOIA denials.[131] Over the next several decades, Congress strengthened FOIA's procedural provisions with amendments in 1974 and 1976 (heavily inspired by the Watergate scandal as well as inconclusive jurisprudence surrounding the act's provisions),[132] and the Electronic Freedom of Information Act of 1996, which closed an inadvertent loophole in the original FOIA that allowed agency officials to avoid disclosure of non-paper documents.[133]

Meanwhile, the case history of FOIA reinforces the view that the basic democratic and civil society values of government transparency in America are consistently under threat from officials who refuse to disclose documents upon request from citizens. By extension, there is a perennial conflict between the public interest in open government and the government's needs to protect national security, law enforcement investigations, trade secrets, and other phenomena that require the close management of sensitive information.[134] This has resulted in a great amount of uncertainty in the courts when FOIA denial disputes are heard. In fact, as the act was being written, so many compromises in statutory language were necessary to get it through its Congressional opponents that the language became vague almost to the point of unenforceability, which has proven to be especially troublesome for citizens who find themselves before judges who demand proof that an agency decision should be overturned.

This has made the act especially vulnerable to creative interpretation by government lawyers who represent agencies charged with unlawfully denying citizen requests for documents.[135] The vagueness was reluctantly acknowledged (with little impact on the ultimate ruling) by the U.S. Supreme Court in *Environmental Protection Agency v. Mink*, a 1973 case that shed light on FOIA's inability to prevent the government from arbitrarily withholding information and using vague statutory language as justification. Amazingly, the case concerned the denial of a FOIA request that was made by members of Congress, who sought information from the Environmental Protection Agency on underground nuclear testing.[136] Meanwhile, the act's basic positive philosophy of open access to government information was not even confirmed by the high court until a decade after its passage. In 1976, the Supreme Court ruled in *Department of the Air Force v. Rose* that "disclosure, not secrecy, is the dominant objective of the Act."[137]

The definition of "agency records" to be disclosed upon citizen request was also left vague in the act's statutory language. This instance of vagueness allowed government agencies to withhold requested information by claiming that the information in question should not be defined as "agency records." This matter was not cleared up by the Supreme Court until 1989, when in *Department of Justice v. Tax Analysts* the high court ruled that to qualify for disclosure, requested documents must have been either created by the agency in question or officially in the hands of that agency at the time a FOIA request is made. The court also ruled that the burden was on the agency to prove that a requested document does not fall under the definition of "agency record" per the statutory language of FOIA.[138] Back in 1980, in *Kissinger v. Reporters Committee for Freedom of the Press*, the high court had determined that the statutory definition of "record" in FOIA was lacking and that the mere physical presence of certain records at an agency did not make them eligible for disclosure by that agency under FOIA.[139] It took several more years, via a series of circuit court and Supreme Court rulings, for the definition of "records" under FOIA to cover all types of reproducible documentary information, from traditional paper documents to computer files, films, and sound recordings.[140]

Government officials also found ways to deny citizen FOIA requests by resisting the vaguely defined term "agency" in the act's statutory language. While prominent government entities like the Environmental Protection Agency or the Department of Energy are obvious examples of "agencies" that must fulfill a FOIA request, it took more circuit court and Supreme Court rulings over several decades to determine that entities like independent regulatory commissions and government-controlled corporations also fall under the FOIA definition of "agency."[141]

The original text of the Freedom of Information Act also contained enough vague language surrounding disclosure procedures to give government agencies considerable leverage in withholding requested documents, while paradoxically using that same procedural uncertainty as justification for denying citizen requests. Once again, the courts had to step in several years after the passage of the act when disgruntled citizens challenged unjustified FOIA denials by agencies. The overall result of the vague language of FOIA was the *de facto* secrecy achieved by government agency officials who (either maliciously or through bureaucratic inertia) exploited loopholes in the act's procedural requirements or lack of enforcement, thus making the act ineffective in achieving open government during its early years.[142]

Imposing *de facto* secrecy via unjustified bureaucratic delays, while nominally illegalized in the language of FOIA,[143] was not declared unlawful by a circuit court until 1976.[144] Granted, citizens must not make requests that are impractical or lacking in specificity – for example, requesting every single record held by a particular government office.[145] On the other hand, government agencies are required to make a reasonable search for requested records, in all relevant filing systems, and to avoid telling the requester without justification that the records cannot be located. This was a common tactic by agencies to achieve *de facto* secrecy, until it was finally declared unlawful by the circuit courts in the 1990s.[146] Another tactic used by government agencies to avoid disclosing requested records was the imposition of unreasonable fees. FOIA permitted "reasonable" charges for document search and reproduction,[147] but once again citizens were vexed by the lack of statutory specificity. In 1994, a circuit court finally ruled that the imposition of unreasonable or unexpected fees could not be used by an agency to discourage a citizen's request for documents.[148]

Fortunately, despite some more imprecise language in FOIA on who exactly can request documents under the statute, the Supreme Court has resisted restrictions on the standing of American citizens or citizens' organizations when requesting documents or appealing agency denials. According to the high court, the identity of the requester and the purpose of the request are irrelevant and not to be used as justification by agencies to deny disclosure of requested documents.[149] In *National Labor Relations Board v. Sears, Roebuck & Company* (1975), the Supreme Court ruled that "Congress clearly intended the FOIA to give any member of the public as much right to disclosure as one with a special interest [in a particular document]."[150] At the philosophical level at least, any American has the ability to request documents from any government agency.

This case history, while restricted to the Freedom of Information Act, is relevant to all matters of government transparency. Environmental statutes that require the reporting of environmental activities by government and regulated parties, and the disclosure of that information to interested members of the public, also have not been completely effective in preventing *de facto* secrecy and unsupported denials by federal agencies. Those information-intensive statutes, like the Freedom of Information Act, represent the culmination of centuries of political theory and changing public attitudes, and they have faced their own resistance from the holders of government information.

Chapter 2 Notes

[1] Ann Florini, "The Battle Over Transparency," in *The Right to Know: Transparency in an Open World*, ed. Ann Florini (New York: Columbia University Press, 2007), 4-5.

[2] International Monetary Fund, *Report of the Working Group on Transparency and Accountability* (Washington: International Monetary Fund. 1998), v.

[3] Florini, "The Battle Over Transparency," 5.

[4] Ibid.

[5] Ibid., 5-6.

[6] Harold L. Cross, *The Right to Know: Legal Access to Public Records and Proceedings* (New York: Columbia University Press, 1953), 55-56.

[7] Frederick Rosen, *Classical Utilitarianism from Hume to Mill* (New York: Routledge, 2003), 28.

[8] John Stuart Mill, *On Liberty*, Penguin Classics ed. (Baltimore: Penguin, 1974), 68.

[9] Ibid., 78-81.

[10] Giovanni Sartori, *The Theory of Democracy Revisited* (Chatham, N.J.: Chatham House, 1987), 134-136.

[11] Joseph E. Stiglitz, "Foreword," in *The Right to Know: Transparency in an Open World*, ed. Ann Florini (New York: Columbia University Press, 2007), vii.

[12] Laura Neuman and Richard Calland, "Making the Law Work: The Challenges of Implementation," in *The Right to Know: Transparency in an Open World*, ed. Ann Florini (New York: Columbia University Press, 2007), 191.

[13] Ann Florini, "Whither Transparency?," in *The Right to Know: Transparency in an Open World*, ed. Ann Florini (New York: Columbia University Press, 2007), 342.

[14] Neuman and Calland, 209.

[15] Organization for Economic Co-Operation and Development, *Open Government: Fostering Dialogue with Civil Society* (Paris: Organization for Economic Co-Operation and Development, 2003), 9-10.

[16] Herbert Brucker, *Freedom of Information* (New York: MacMillan Co., 1949), 5-6.

[17] Cross, xiii.

[18] Transparency International was founded in Germany in 1993 and focuses on reducing government corruption by increasing citizen access to government information. The organization also applies a human rights philosophy to the general subject of open government. Transparency International is perhaps best known for its "Corruption Perceptions Index" that ranks the nations of the world by the level of collusion between politicians and business leaders. Transparency International, *About Us*, http://www.transparency.org/about_us, accessed 23 June 2010.

[19] Florini, "The Battle Over Transparency," 1-2.

[20] Benjamin W. Cramer, "The Human Right to Information, the Environment, and Information About the Environment: From the Universal Declaration to the Aarhus Convention," *Communication Law & Policy* 14 (2009): 78-86.

[21] Florini, "The Battle Over Transparency," 4.

[22] John M. Ackerman and Irma E. Sandoval-Ballesteros, "The Global Explosion of Freedom of Information Laws," *Administrative Law Review* 58 (2006): 109-115. By 2007 there were government transparency laws in nearly seventy nations. The inclusiveness, effectiveness, and viability of these laws vary greatly by nation. For a world map illustrating the enactment and enforcement of freedom of information laws as of 2007, see Privacy International, *National Freedom of Information Laws 2007*, http://www.privacyinternational.org/issues/foia/foia-laws.jpg, accessed 23 June 2010.

[23] 5 U.S.C. § 552 (1966).

[24] Martin E. Halstuk and Bill F. Chamberlin, "The Freedom of Information Act 1966-2006: A Retrospective on the Rise of Privacy Protection Over the Public Interest in Knowing What the Government's Up To," *Communication Law & Policy* 11 (2006): 511-564; Glen O. Robinson, "Access to Government Information: The American Experience," *Federal Law Review* 14 (1983): 37-41.

[25] U.S. Senate Report No. 89-813 (1965), 3.

[26] 5 U.S.C. § 552b (1976).

[27] U.S. House of Representatives Report No. 94-880, part 1 (1976), 2. See also Randolph May, "Reforming the Sunshine Act," *Administrative Law Review* 49 (1997): 416.

[28] Kathy Bradley, "Do You Feel the Sunshine? Government in the Sunshine Act: Its Objectives, Goals, and Effect on the FCC and You," *Federal Communications Law Journal* 49 (1997): 475.

[29] 417 U.S. 817 (1974).

[30] 417 U.S. 843 (1974).

[31] 438 U.S. 1 (1978).

[32] 417 U.S. 834-835; 417 U.S. 849-850; 438 U.S. 15-16.

[33] Herbert N. Foerstel, *Freedom of Information and the Right to Know: The Origins and Applications of the Freedom of Information Act* (Westport, Conn.: Greenwood Press, 1999), 1-3.

[34] Quoted in Thomas Cooley, *A Treatise on Constitutional Limitations*, 8th ed., vol. 2 (Boston: Little, Brown, 1927), 822.

[35] Quoted in Louis Edward Ingelhart, ed., *Press and Speech Freedoms in America, 1619-1995: A Chronology* (Westport, Conn.: Greenwood Press, 1999), 15-16.

[36] Foerstel, 3.

[37] John Adams [anonymous], "A Dissertation on the Canon and Feudal Law," *Boston Gazette*, 30 September 1765, page number unknown.

[38] Foerstel, 3.

[39] Ingelhart, 33.

[40] Richard D. Brown, *The Strength of a People: The Idea of an Informed Citizenry in America, 1650-1870* (Chapel Hill, NC: University of North Carolina Press, 1996), xiv.

[41] Thomas Paine, *Common Sense* (1776), http://www.earlyamerica.com/earlyamerica/milestones/commonsense/text.html, accessed 23 June 2010.

[42] Alan Barth, "Freedom and the Press," *The Progressive*, June 1862, 29.

[43] Foerstel, 4.

[44] Gaillard Hunt, ed., *The Writings of James Madison*, vol. 9 (New York: Putnam, 1900-1910), 103.

[45] Note that in Madison's time, the term "popular information" actually referred to public education as a social tool for creating an informed electorate. Madison's quote therefore does not refer to freedom of the press or a public right to government information, and applying this quotation to government transparency could be considered historical revisionism. Nonetheless, Madison's words are often used conceptually in modern debates on those

subjects. Paul H. Gates Jr. and Bill F. Chamberlin, "Madison Misinterpreted: Historical Presentism Skews Scholarship," *American Journalism* 13 (1996): 38.
[46] This is the origin of the theory of a free press acting as an independent "Fourth Estate" that can check abuses by the three branches of the American government. Brucker, 31-32.
[47] Daniel Hoffman, *Government Secrecy and the Founding Fathers: A Study in Constitutional Controls* (Westport, Conn.: Greenwood Press, 1981), 20-24, 257-258.
[48] Max Farrand, ed. *The Records of the Federal Convention of 1787*, vol. 3 (New Haven, Conn.: Yale University Press, 1911), 86.
[49] Ibid., 368.
[50] Hoffman, 22.
[51] Farrand, 76.
[52] Hoffman, 24.
[53] Ibid., 35-36.
[54] Farrand, 233.
[55] Hoffman, 35.
[56] Farrand, 169-170.
[57] Hoffman, 257.
[58] Martin E. Halstuk, "Policy of Secrecy – Pattern of Deception: What Federalist Leaders Thought About a Public Right to Know, 1794-1798," *Communication Law & Policy* 7 (2002): 61-74.
[59] Brucker, 37-38. The Alien and Sedition Acts were passed by President John Adams, purportedly to protect American security by restricting libelous attacks on the federal government. Scholars later found that the acts were primarily a political tool by the Adams administration to suppress legitimate foreign policy criticism from supporters of his main political rival, Thomas Jefferson. Jefferson abolished the acts when he became President in 1801.
[60] Cross, 224-225.
[61] 249 U.S. 47, 52 (1919). The *Schenck* case involved the First Amendment rights of socialists arrested and convicted for distributing literature under the 1917 Espionage Act. The high court ruled that the Espionage Act did not violate the First Amendment because Congress had the right to restrict speech that presented a "clear and present danger" to the nation. The "clear and present danger" concept was articulated by Justice Oliver Wendell Holmes.

[62] 250 U.S. 616, 624-631 (1919). The *Abrams* case arose from an arrest similar to that under dispute in the *Schenck* case, and the two cases were separated by just six months. In *Abrams*, Justice Holmes changed his mind on the constitutionality of restrictions on political speech. In his dissent to the ruling, Holmes instead endorsed the "marketplace of ideas" theory of free speech, in which unpopular or untruthful ideas can be countered by other ideas in the "marketplace." The ultimate result of the *Abrams* ruling was another endorsement of the constitutionality of the World War I-era restrictions on political speech, though Holmes's endorsement of the "marketplace of ideas" represented an important turning point in First Amendment jurisprudence.

[63] 268 U.S. 652 (1925). The *Gitlow* case involved the First Amendment rights of a socialist arrested and convicted for distributing literature under a state law in New York. The high court found the state law unconstitutional, delivering a ruling that was influential for the jurisprudence of not just the First Amendment but also the Fourteenth Amendment, applying the equal protections of that amendment to state and local laws. This application of the Fourteenth Amendment is now known as the Incorporation Doctrine.

[64] Foerstel, 9.

[65] 274 U.S. 357, 375-376 (1927). The *Whitney* case involved the arrest of a philanthropist who attended a Communist Party meeting, under a California state law that prohibited "criminal syndicalism." The high court ruled that the state law was not a violation of the philanthropist's First Amendment rights.

[66] 297 U.S. 233, 250 (1936). The *Grosjean* case concerned the constitutionality of a politically-motivated tax levied on particular newspapers in Louisiana, which was found by the high court to be a violation of the First Amendment.

[67] Foerstel, 10.

[68] Gaillard Hunt, ed., *The Writings of James Madison*, vol. 6 (New York: Putnam, 1900-1910), 398.

[69] Alexander Meiklejohn, "The First Amendment is an Absolute," *Supreme Court Review* 1961 (1961): 255. While this article was published in 1961, it summarized the free speech theories that Meiklejohn had been articulating regularly since the early 1950s.

[70] Wallace Parks, "The Open Government Principle: Applying the Right to Know Under the Constitution," *George Washington Law Review* 26 (1957): 9, 12.

[71] Cross, 131-132.

[72] Foerstel, 12.

[73] 319 U.S. 141, 146-147 (1943). This case involved a dispute over the arrest of a Jehovah's Witness who distributed leaflets door-to-door.

[74] 381 U.S. 301 (1965). This case concerned a federal statute that allowed the U.S. Postal Service to control and restrict the delivery of Communist Party propaganda through the mail.

[75] 381 U.S. 479 (1965). *Griswold v. Connecticut* was a landmark decision for privacy law, in which the high court struck down a state law restricting the use of contraceptives. For the first time, the high court fashioned a constitutional right to privacy through an interpretation of the First, Third, Fourth, and Fifth Amendments, plus an application of equal protection under the Fourteenth Amendment.

[76] Halstuk and Chamberlin, 519, n.45.

[77] Executive Order No. 8,381, 3 C.F.R. 634 (1940).

[78] Cross, 197.

[79] Zechariah Chafee, Jr., *Government and Mass Communications: A Report from the Commission on Freedom of the Press*, vol. 1 (Chicago: University of Chicago Press, 1947), 12-13.

[80] James Russell Wiggins, *Freedom or Secrecy* (New York: Oxford University Press, 1964), 96-98.

[81] Jeffrey A. Smith, *War and Press Freedom: The Problem of Prerogative Power* (New York: Oxford University Press, 1999), 151-156.

[82] Halstuk and Chamberlin, 519.

[83] 5 U.S.C. §§ 500-706 (1946).

[84] U.S. Senate Report No. 752-79 (1945), 7.

[85] "The Federal Administrative Procedure Act: Codification or Reform?," *Yale Law Journal* 56 (1947): 671.

[86] Gerald L. Hutton, "Public Information and Rule Making Provisions of the Administrative Procedure Act of 1946," *Temple Law Quarterly* 33 (1959): 59-60.

[87] Halstuk and Chamberlin, 520.

[88] Executive Order No. 10,290, 3 C.F.R. 789 (1951).

[89] Quoted in A.M. Sperber, *Murrow: His Life and Times* (New York: Freundlich Books, 1986), 360.

[90] Editorial, *Wall Street Journal*, 27 September 1951, 6.

[91] Foerstel, 18-19.

[92] "Censorship at the Pentagon," *Time*, 4 July 1955, 62.

[93] Ibid.

[94] Just prior to the passage of the Freedom of Information Act, a statute largely intended to ameliorate the misuse of the Administrative Procedure Act by government officials, the U.S. Senate criticized APA as "Full of loopholes that allow agencies to deny legitimate information to the public. Innumerable times it appears that information is withheld only to cover up embarrassing mistakes or irregularities." U.S. Senate Report No. 89-813 (1965), 3.

[95] Foerstel, 35-36. One example among many in the text of the APA is a section on rulemaking procedures at federal government agencies, giving an agency the authority to *not* provide public notice of an upcoming rulemaking hearing if that notice would be "impractical, unnecessary, or contrary to the public interest." 5 U.S.C. § 553(b)(3)(B). The statute contains no useful definitions of any of the terms just quoted, most notably "public interest."

[96] Foerstel, 36.

[97] Ibid., 36-37.

[98] Hoffman, 258.

[99] Foerstel, 21-22.

[100] In his highly influential study, researched over several years and released in book form in 1953, Cross, an influential commentator on the need for press and public access to government records, compiled an imposing bibliographical treatment of then-current state and local laws that either granted or restricted access to records. His ultimate assessment was that these laws overwhelmingly discouraged public access and enabled government secrecy. Cross's compilation of problematic statutes and their consequences takes up the majority of his 1953 book *The Right to Know: Legal Access to Public Records and Proceedings*. Cross's diagnosis of the problem was the proliferation of an incorrect philosophy among the American political leadership that all documents should remain secret unless a citizen can make a convincing case that a particular document should be disclosed – a struggle that few citizens were willing to undertake, though general political attitudes on the subject were changing. Cross, 5-13.

[101] In his influential 1949 book *Freedom of Information*, Brucker, a commentator on the state of the American newspaper business, argued that "freedom of information" could be an American ideal delivered by investigative journalists with unhindered access to politicians and government

documents. This conception of "freedom of information" predated, and differs from, the democratic and civil society ideals later enshrined in the Freedom of Information Act. Brucker, 276-291.

[102] Foerstel, 22.

[103] Cross, 246.

[104] Ibid., xiii.

[105] Halstuk and Chamberlin, 526.

[106] Quoted in Foerstel, 22.

[107] Ibid., 27.

[108] Quoted in "Freedom of Information," *U.S. News and World Report*, 24 August 1956, 114.

[109] Kent Cooper, *The Right to Know: An Exposition of the Evils of News Suppression and Propaganda* (New York: Farrar, Strauss and Cudahy, 1956), 286.

[110] Foerstel, 22.

[111] James T. O'Reilly, *Federal Information Disclosure*, vol. 1 (St. Paul, Minn.: West Group, 2000), 12.

[112] Halstuk and Chamberlin, 527-528.

[113] Foerstel, 37.

[114] "President Urges Limits by Press," *New York Times*, 28 April 1961, 14. Here Kennedy was probably referencing the decades-old U.S. Supreme Court ruling in *Schenck v. United States* (1919), in which the high court ruled that censorship of political speech was acceptable during times of "clear and present danger" to national security. However, recall that the high court had soon abandoned this concept in favor of the "marketplace ideas" theory of free speech, as advocated in a dissent to *Abrams v. United States* (1919), and a concurrence in *Whitney v. California* (1927). Thus, Kennedy's use of "clear and present danger" as a justification for national security-related secrecy, and his reference to the Supreme Court's thoughts on the issue, were outdated by as much as four decades.

[115] "Press is Divided on Kennedy Talk," *New York Times*, 30 April 1961, 68.

[116] Foerstel, 38.

[117] Halstuk and Chamberlin, 530.

[118] U.S. Congressional Record, 17,666 (1964).

[119] U.S. Congressional Record, 13,661 (1966).

[120] There was no symbolism behind the signing date of July 4. This was merely the result of scheduling, as the following day was the signing deadline. O'Reilly, 14-15.

[121] Quoted in Halstuk and Chamberlin, 531.

[122] U.S. Senate Report No. 813-89 (1965); U.S. House of Representatives Report No. 1497-89 (1966).

[123] Neuman and Calland, 183.

[124] Ibid., 183-184.

[125] 5 U.S.C. §§ 552(a)(1)(B)-552 (a)(1)(D). The phrase "each agency" appears in almost every clause of FOIA, with the term "agency" describing any administrative agency or cabinet-level department.

[126] 5 U.S.C. §§ 552(a)(6)(A)(i)-552(a)(6)(F).

[127] The exemptions are codified at 5 U.S.C. §§ 552(b)(1)-552(b)(9).

[128] Halstuk, "When Secrecy Trumps Transparency," 444.

[129] Foerstel. 44-45.

[130] U.S. House of Representatives Report No. 92-1419 (1972), 8.

[131] This problem was pointed out by a vociferous early critic of the Freedom of Information Act, law professor and future Supreme Court Justice Antonin Scalia, who belittled FOIA as "a relatively toothless beast" and as "the Taj Mahal of the Doctrine of Unanticipated Consequences." Antonin Scalia, "The Freedom of Information Act Has No Clothes," *Regulation* 6 (1982), 15.

[132] Halstuk and Chamberlin, 532-533.

[133] Halstuk, "When Secrecy Trumps Transparency," 468. The 1974, 1976, and 1996 (eFOIA) amendments are codified at Pub. L. No. 93-502, 88 Stat. 1561 (1974); Pub. L. No. 94-409, 90 Stat. 1241 (1976); and Pub. L. No. 104-231, 110 Stat. 3048 (1996) respectively.

[134] Halstuk, "When Secrecy Trumps Transparency," 431.

[135] Ibid.

[136] 410 U.S. 73, 84 (1973). This case involved a request by several members of the House of Representatives for documents from the Environmental Protection Agency and other agencies, upon hearing that President Richard Nixon had received contradictory advice on the safety of underground nuclear testing.

[137] 425 U.S. 352, 361 (1976). This case involved a FOIA denial for reasons of privacy, and the conflict between personal privacy and the public interest.

[138] 492 U.S. 136, 142-145 (1989). This case involved the denial of a FOIA request by the tax division of the Department of Justice, which claimed that the

requested documents on recent judicial decisions in tax law, to be used by the organization Tax Analysts in legal research and advising, were merely compiled by that division but originated in other government agencies and courts. This was the justification used by that division of the federal agency – not being the originator of the records – to claim that the requested documents were not its own "agency records" under the language of FOIA.

[139] 445 U.S. 136, 157 (1980). This case involved the denial of a journalist's FOIA request made to Henry Kissinger, then National Security Advisor, for phone records. Kissinger denied the request under the rationale that phone records did not fall under the definition of "records" in FOIA.

[140] C. Thomas Dienes, Lee Levine, and Robert C. Lind, *Newsgathering and the Law*, vol. 2 (Charlottesville, Va.: Lexis Law Publishing, 1999), 420. Noteworthy cases include Long v. Internal Revenue Service, 596 F. 2d 363 (9th Cir. 1979) and Burka v. Department of Health and Human Services, 87 F.3d 508 (D.C. Cir. 1996) for computer records; Weisberg v. Department of Justice, 631 F.2d 824 (D.C. Cir. 1980) for photographs; and Forsham v. Harris, 445 U.S. 169 (1980) for sound recordings.

[141] Dienes et al., 421. Important precedents include Dobronski v. Federal Communications Commission, 17 F.3d 275 (9th Cir. 1994) for independent regulatory commissions and agencies (such as the FCC, which is technically independent from the executive branch but not exempt from the requirements of FOIA); and Rocap v. Indiek, 539 F.2d 174 (D.C. Cir. 1976) for government-controlled corporations (such as the Federal Home Loan Mortgage Corporation, known colloquially as Freddie Mac).

[142] Halstuk and Chamberlin, 532-533.

[143] 5 U.S.C. § 552(a)(6)(A)(i). The act requires agencies to respond to a citizen request for documents within twenty business days, but there is no statutory language on procedures to be followed if the agency in question is unable to satisfy this requirement or simply ignores it.

[144] Open America v. Watergate Special Prosecution Force, 547 F.2d 605 (D.C. Cir. 1976). This case stemmed from the investigation of the Watergate scandal, and the citizens' group's attempt to obtain documents on one of the officials being investigated, former Acting Director of the FBI L. Patrick Gray.

[145] American Federation of Government Employees v. Department of Commerce, 907 F.2d 203 (D.C. Cir. 1990). Here the circuit court shot down an appeal of a denied FOIA request due to unreasonableness and impracticality, as

the labor group requested "every chronological office file and correspondence file, internal or external, for every branch office."

[146] Nation Magazine v. United States Customs Service, 71 F.3d 885 (D.C. Cir. 1995); Citizens Commission on Human Rights v. Food & Drug Administration, 45 F.3d 1325 (9th Cir. 1995); Campbell v. Department of Justice, 164 F.3d 20 (D.C. Cir. 1998). In each of these cases, the agencies denied FOIA requests due to a supposed inability to locate the documents in question, but failed to prove that committed searches had actually been performed.

[147] 5 U.S.C. § 552(a)(4)(A)(ii).

[148] Strout v. United States Parole Commission, 40 F.3d 136 (6th Cir. 1994). Here the agency attempted to charge not just an excessive fee to the requester, but also demanded prepayment before attempting to search for the requested documents.

[149] Dienes et al., 422-423. Important precedents include Department of Justice v. Reporters Committee for the Freedom of the Press, 489 U.S. 749 (1989); and Department of Defense v. Federal Labor Relations Authority, 510 U.S. 487 (1994).

[150] 421 U.S. 132, 149 (1975). This case concerned a denied request for internal agency documents surrounding an agency investigation of allegedly unfair labor practices.

CHAPTER 3

Environmental Law: A History

The preceding discussion of government transparency in America is necessary for an understanding of environmental information, because the passage of the Freedom of Information Act in 1966 was a crucial influence on not just the transparency of the American government at large, but also on the far-reaching environmental laws that arose in the early 1970s. The revolution in government transparency in the 1950s and 1960s inspired revolutions in many specific areas of public policy, with the management and availability of government-held information leading to new trends in lawmaking that emphasized the reporting of information to the government, and consequently, an increase in the knowledge levels of concerned citizens. Environmental law was among the first areas of public policy to experience an information-intensive overhaul, inspiring a new type of federal lawmaking in which politicians collaborated with public interest groups (i.e. environmentalists and conservationists) for new types of aspirational statutes that attempted to overhaul agency decision-making processes via increased public participation and management of information.[1]

Most notably, the National Environmental Policy Act of 1969 broke new ground in both environmental protection and the management of the information accumulated during protection efforts. The openness and effectiveness of this information will be the focus of much of the remainder of this book, but first it is necessary to review the history of environmental protection in America, and how concerned citizens came to realize the importance of government-held information about the natural world.

A Brief History of American Environmental Thought and Activism

While this book deals with modern environmental protection in America, particularly from the statutory angle, current law has a long historic heritage. Environmental activism has gone through several cycles of popularity and a variety of prevailing philosophies, and environmentalism itself is neither new nor exclusively American.

In the ancient world, the effects of pollution on the human condition, if not necessarily individual health, were noticed in the earliest organized human societies. For example, citizens of the Roman Empire complained about poor sewage and insufficient public sanitation. Air pollution was a noted problem in almost all early civilizations, due to the burning of wood and manure for fuel.[2] Ancient civilizations in China, India and Peru noted the effects of manmade soil erosion on farming and food supplies, and farmers were encouraged to try to prevent the problem.[3] Ecological side-effects were noted in Europe in the Middle Ages, as the loss of forests from excessive timbering forced a general switch to coal as a fuel source, replacing one type of air pollution with a more dangerous one.[4]

In America, environmental concerns have been known since the beginning of the colonial era, though early colonists usually exercised the biblical view of nature as an opponent to be conquered for the benefit of mankind. For instance, in 1620 William Bradford, a passenger on the Mayflower, viewed unspoiled Cape Cod as "a hideous and desolate wilderness, full of wild beasts and wild men."[5] But the intact and untrammeled wilderness of eastern North America did inspire a new type of appreciation from at least some of the early colonists. For example, in 1681 William Penn, in his charter for his new colony of Pennsylvania, included the requirement "in clearing the ground, care be taken to leave one acre of trees for every five acres cleared."[6]

Benjamin Franklin was an early observer of the public health problems created by patterns of pollution and garbage disposal in revolutionary society, and raised concerns about the state of the Philadelphia drinking water supply. This inspired one of Franklin's more enduring quotations: "when the well's dry, we know the worth of water" – a tidbit of wisdom in the venerable *Poor Richard's*

Almanack.[7] In 1739, Franklin's *Pennsylvania Gazette* editorialized on a public controversy over Philadelphia's tanneries, from which "many offensive and unwholesome Smells do arise," and lobbied for local regulation of the trade, which was soon enacted, thus creating one of America's first public interest-oriented pollution statutes.[8]

Early American environmentalism was also heavily influenced by two observant authors. John James Audubon became a fairly famous birdwatcher in the 1820s, but really made an impact on American thought with the staggered publication (in several portions) of the first edition of *Birds of America* from 1827 to 1838 – a visually stunning collection of full-color, life-size engraved prints of several hundred American bird species.[9] Meanwhile, it took a Frenchman, Alexis de Tocqueville, to tell the rest of the world about the natural wonders to be found in early America. In the second volume of his seminal observation of emerging American society, *Democracy in America*, de Tocqueville criticized the new nation's lack of regard for its natural wonders, which were largely viewed as impediments to manifest destiny. de Tocqueville's vivid descriptions of the vastness of these natural wonders indirectly alerted American citizens to the need for preservation.[10]

Modern environmentalism has its philosophical roots in transcendentalism, a school of thought defined in the 19th Century by American philosopher and poet Ralph Waldo Emerson, who was influenced by then-recent philosophical advances made possible by European philosophers, who at the time were expanding the basic precepts of idealism.[11] Idealism is a basic category of western philosophy, dating back to the ancient Greeks, and maintains that the external world is inseparable from consciousness and intellect. Or in other words, the external world is observable and understandable but is dependent on the mind.[12] By the time of the Enlightenment, Immanuel Kant expanded the concept and held that the mind shapes our perceptions of the outside world, and it is thus impossible to determine if the outside world exists independently or if it is created by our minds.[13] Kant continued this line of thought into the new philosophy of transcendental idealism, holding that human experience is based upon observations of phenomena not necessarily as they are in reality, but as they appear to us. This makes all human experience subjective rather than objective, so one's inner thought processes are essential for observing the outside world.[14]

A product of rural New England and its unique culture of stewardship for the natural world, Ralph Waldo Emerson created the largely American philosophy of transcendentalism[15] by combining Kant's transcendental realism with the then-popular poetry of naturalistic authors like Samuel Taylor Coleridge and William Wordsworth.[16] American transcendentalism, as defined by Emerson and his followers, held that the world is made up of both matter and of mind, each reflecting and inspiring the other. But they also believed that mind "transcends" matter and is more powerful, and that matter is created by the mind.[17] So far, this line of thought is quite similar to Kant's transcendental idealism, but Emerson added a couple of crucial twists, proclaiming that there is a mind dwelling behind nature, while the individual perceives nature in his/her own unique way.[18] Emerson later summed up the emerging philosophy of natural appreciation in America in one of his more enduring quotations: "Adopt the pace of nature. Her secret is patience."[19]

Though Emerson was actually a philosopher and poet who occasionally exercised an appreciation of nature, he became an immense influence on America's first noteworthy environmentalists (or "conservationists," which was the more widely used term at the time). The American style of natural appreciation was largely defined by Henry David Thoreau, a bit of a misanthrope who experimented with a return to nature, with himself as his own experimental subject. A disciple of Emerson and a proponent of American transcendentalism, Thoreau expanded the individualistic tendencies of that philosophy by rejecting society, embracing solitude, and exercising a visceral love for his natural surroundings.[20] From 1845 to 1847, Thoreau spent several extended periods in a secluded cabin near Concord, Massachusetts in woodland owned by Emerson and next to a natural lake called Walden Pond. Thoreau's sojourns at this cabin are often mischaracterized as rough and self-sufficient living, but in reality the site was less than two miles from town and Thoreau often walked in for supplies or to dine with friends and relatives.[21]

Regardless, his 1854 book on his experiences in the cabin, *Walden*, became a classic of environmentalism and espoused the then-emergent

American themes of low-cost living, appreciating the sounds and sights of nature, and enjoying solitude. In his words, "I went to the woods because I wished to live deliberately, to front only the essential facts of life. ... I wanted to live deep and suck out all the marrow of life."[22] One of this book's most noteworthy quotations reflects Thoreau's merging of transcendentalism and natural appreciation, thus cementing his place in the development of American environmentalism: "The wind that blows... is all that any body knows."[23]

Shortly after Emerson and Thoreau helped define American conservationist philosophy, scientists defined the discipline of ecology, or the study of the interconnectedness of nature. In 1864, lawyer and former Congressman George Perkins Marsh published the seminal *Man and Nature,* which is widely acknowledged as the first noteworthy scientific examination of the degradation of the earth's ecosystems by human activity.[24] Marsh's study was largely based on diplomatic visits to Greece and Italy, where he observed the ecological effects of deforestation, but his analysis was readily accepted as an omen for what could happen in America, where the large-scale clear-cutting of forests was already getting underway. In Marsh's rather stilted prose, the purpose of his study was "to point out the dangers of imprudence and the necessity of caution in all operations which, on a large scale, interfere with the spontaneous arrangements of the organic or the inorganic world."[25] Fortunately, unlike many of his fellow scientists Marsh was able to spruce up his language a bit when commenting on humanity and society, with the plea "Let us restore this one element of material life [natural resources] to its normal proportions, and devise means for maintaining permanence."[26] Marsh's thesis was very influential on modern American environmental law, as he succinctly combined natural appreciation, scientific analysis, and the precautionary/preventive principle on which most modern pollution control statutes are based.[27]

During this time period, American citizens were beginning to appreciate the remaining natural bounty of the settled areas of the republic, while explorers were still discovering the wonders of the interior. Most notable was the disabled Civil War officer John Wesley Powell, who in 1869 led a precarious three-month rafting expedition down the Green and Colorado Rivers in Wyoming, Utah, and Arizona, exploring the arid desert country as well as the interior of the Grand Canyon.[28] The highly publicized adventure opened the public's eyes to the unique natural wonders of the American southwest.[29] In a later report to the Department of the Interior, Powell maintained a utilitarian view of the region's scarce water resources and recommended government-subsidized irrigation projects.[30] However, Powell's actual recommendation was for irrigation assistance to small farmers and landholders to prevent domination of the region by absentee corporate interests – a prescient warning that was largely forgotten as the region was settled.[31]

The combined influence of the above philosophers and scientists spawned America's first noteworthy conservationist with political connections and the inspiration to strive for true protection of the nation's natural wonders. John Muir was an immigrant from Scotland who moved as a child with his family to a Wisconsin farm. As a young adult in the 1860s, Muir caught the rambling bug, walking thousands of miles and camping out from Canada to Florida and eventually ending up as a ranch hand in California's then little-explored Sierra Mountains, where he rambled thousands of miles more and climbed several of the area's highest peaks. In the process, he forged an intense love for nature and an awareness of the threats that it faced from modern American industrialism and manifest destiny.[32]

Through a variety of popular books and magazine articles starting in the 1870s, Muir tried to convince Americans that the protection of nature was an ethical issue, and not just an issue of the aesthetics of scenic beauty. In Muir's view, the protection of nature (and perhaps more importantly, natural resources) was a matter of enlightened self-interest for each American, and a counterpoint to the greed and rush for profitability as exercised by those in power.[33] Most of Muir's writing on such matters took place in the 1870s through the first decade of the 1900s, roughly concurrent with the period dubbed the "Gilded Age" by historians. During this period American capitalism and industrialism grew rapidly, the government greatly expanded its geographic control, and inequalities of wealth became a major social problem. As Muir commiserated in a letter to a friend on the urbanization of American wilderness: "The gross heathenism of civilization has generally destroyed nature, and poetry, and all that is spiritual."[34] Rapid industrialization took a noticeable toll on the availability of natural resources and created pollution at levels that were noticed by large numbers of Americans for the first time.[35]

The Gilded Age spawned many social reform movements that were concerned with checking the abuses of political and economic power and preventing unfair distribution of wealth. Examples include the populists, who strove for more political and economic power for the general population rather than the elites;[36] and the progressives, who sought a vast array of social and economic reforms.[37] The burgeoning conservationist movement, spearheaded by Muir's writings, shared with the populists and progressives an abhorrence of unchecked greed and inequality, but transcended those movements by worrying less about the problems faced by people during that time and more about the future impoverishment that could result from exploitation of the natural world. For the well-being of both present and future Americans, the conservationists protested the despoliation of rivers, the destruction of forests, the overhunting of wildlife, and the pollution of cities.[38]

These movements spawned community activism by concerned citizens for the amelioration of a variety of social problems, including environmental degradation. In 1886, naturalist and writer George Bird Grinnell founded the National Audubon Society, which was inspired by the works of John James Audubon to bring attention to the plight faced by America's birds and to fight for their protection. The new organization immediately collapsed logistically when 39,000 people attempted to join.[39] In 1892, John Muir founded the Sierra Club to rally for protection of his beloved Sierra Mountains in California.[40] Other important early conservation organizations ranged from the philosophically-oriented National Conservation Association, formed in 1910, to the locally-focused Save the Redwoods League, formed in California in 1918.[41] These early conservation organizations, particularly those with thousands of volunteer members like the National Audubon Society and Sierra Club, would grow to national influence and would inspire the formation of countless other groups up to the present day.[42]

The progressive and populist movements also spawned a president, Theodore Roosevelt, who for a time expressed concern about the problems championed by the conservationists. Roosevelt was more widely known for being belligerent and jingoistic, but he is also remembered as the most significant environmental president in American history, with a writer's regard for natural beauty and an appreciation for its protection.[43] During his time in office (1901-1909), Roosevelt set aside more than 200 million acres (more than all of his predecessors combined) for national parks, national forests, national wildlife refuges, and national monuments; and greatly expanded the levels of statutory protection for all these types of federal lands.[44] In 1903 Roosevelt, already known as a lover of wildlife and outdoor adventure, exemplified the emerging American philosophy of conservationism in a speech at the Grand Canyon. In an ode to the canyon that could have been applied to all of America's natural wonders, Roosevelt entreated citizens to "Leave it as it is. You cannot improve on it. The ages have been at work on it, and man can only mar it."[45]

Also in 1903, Roosevelt went on a celebrated hiking and mountain-climbing trip with John Muir through the Yosemite area of northern California. Muir invited Roosevelt on the three-day sojourn to personally lobby the President for federal protection of the unique Yosemite Valley and its surrounding highlands.[46] Three years later Roosevelt made Yosemite the first large national park to be removed from the oversight of an existing state, thus lending greater power and legitimacy to the system of national parks.[47]

However, all was not well in the new Yosemite National Park, as the rapidly growing city of San Francisco, about 160 miles away and all downhill, coveted the area's water resources. Disregarding the park's federal protection, San Francisco authorities and their federal allies proposed damming the Hetch Hetchy Valley within the park's borders to create a long-term municipal water supply.[48] Near the end of his life, John Muir rallied his Sierra Club to protest the plans for Hetch Hetchy Reservoir.[49] The battle against Hetch Hetchy Reservoir was the Club's, and the nation's, first large-scale grassroots conservation effort. The campaign was unsuccessful, with the construction of the dam being approved in 1913.[50] But in the process, Muir and the Sierra Club largely defined grassroots environmental activism and organizing, with methods that are still followed to the present day by many, if not most, citizens' activist groups from all areas of interest.[51]

As America became a major industrial power and began to make use of its vast natural resources, particularly the forests, minerals, and hydropower of the west and southwest, conservationists stepped up their efforts to both protect wilderness and inform their fellow citizens about the need for that protection. In 1935 noteworthy conservationists formed two prominent consortiums – the National Wildlife Federation and the Wilderness Society.[52] These organizations dedicated themselves to achieving major enhancements in federal environmental laws, which did indeed happen over the next several decades. In 1949, Aldo Leopold practically invented environmental ethics with the publication of *A Sand County Almanac*, a Thoreau-like work of secluded natural observation in which Leopold added a pragmatic and ethical proclamation that mankind should preserve the environment, because "a thing is right when it tends to preserve the integrity, stability, and beauty of the biotic community."[53] Throughout the 1950s, Sierra Club led the way in publicizing the need for wilderness preservation with highly contentious campaigns against large dams along the Colorado River and its tributaries in the American southwest,[54] complete with popular books of photography for the coffee tables of nature lovers back in the cities.[55]

During this time period, American conservationists were typically upper class and were dedicated to the preservation of their favorite unspoiled natural areas. One prominent example is Russell Train, who grew up in a rural area in northern Virginia, and in the 1950s fought to protect the fields and streams of his boyhood home from encroaching residential development.[56] Train founded the prototypical American land stewardship organization, the Conservation Foundation, and represented the politically well-connected and financially well-funded breed of conservationist. By the 1970s, Train continued to represent the lingering political presence of this school of environmentalism by becoming Secretary of the Interior and later the first Chairman of the Council on Environmental Quality, both under appointments from President Richard Nixon. In these positions Train exemplified the established American philosophy of the preservation of wilderness for its natural and scenic values[57] – a philosophy grounded in Emerson and Thoreau, as well as Muir in his less spiritual moments.

But while Russell Train and his like-minded establishmentarians were ascending to politically powerful positions, and exercising a conservative political philosophy, the American attitude toward nature would soon experience a radical shift from beauty to illness. The public health effects of environmental degradation first became a widespread concern with the publication of Rachel Carson's *Silent Spring* in 1962. This groundbreaking work extended research on the effects of pollution on plants and animals to its potentially life-threatening effects on people. In a study of ecological side-effects and after-effects, Carson described how the pesticide DDT, intended to control insects, ended up being ingested by birds that ate those insects. The result was health problems for the birds and ultimately the people who ate the birds.[58]

While citizens and their leaders had long known that environmental degradation could have indirect effects on the quality of life, thanks to *Silent Spring* a healthy environment became a matter of public and individual health, and even human rights. Carson emphasized that one of the most basic human rights should be the "right of the citizen to be secure in his own home against the intrusion of poisons applied by other persons."[59] Carson's work revolutionized the outlook of the American environmental movement, which realized the need for not just statutory protection of natural wonders, but also statutory protection against pollution for the sake of the health of citizens. This new outlook was exemplified by the formation of Environmental Defense Fund in 1967 – the first environmental volunteer group to be founded by attorneys and scientists. This group immediately agitated for the legal prohibition of DDT,[60] which was officially banned by the American government in 1972.[61]

Meanwhile, the civil rights movement in America inspired an explosion in grassroots environmentalism. The new concern for environmental issues amongst the public was in turn noticed by lawmakers. Senator Gaylord Nelson (D-Wis.) and his intern Denis Hayes organized a series of public gatherings across the nation to discuss environmental issues, which gathered momentum and inspired the first Earth Day on April 22, 1970. Earth Day is still observed in communities and college campuses on that date every year.[62] At the inaugural gathering in San Francisco, Hayes laid out the difference between personal and institutional environmentalism: "We will not appeal any more to the conscience of institutions because institutions have no conscience. If we want them to do what is right, we must make them do what is right." Hayes then recommended strategies borrowed from the civil rights movement – including lawsuits, demonstrations, boycotts, and various types of civil disobedience – that have defined the techniques of grassroots environmentalism ever since.[63]

After the first Earth Day, the rise in popular grassroots activism (not just in environmentalism but in many other realms) and the concurrent political trends resulted in a schism in the environmental community. A divide opened up between law-oriented conservationist politicos like Russell Train, who often came from elite social and educational backgrounds, and a new breed of grassroots environmentalists who were either from disadvantaged constituencies or strove to bring attention to the environmental problems faced by such constituencies.[64] The mainstream conservationists were political insiders who were able to achieve statutory protection for areas of natural beauty, but were criticized for ignoring the needs of the urban poor and for seeking preservation of wilderness lands that do not exhibit the problems of pollution and degradation that were caused by, and were benefits to, their own social class.[65]

Thus, a new perception of who caused degradation and who suffered from it became the impetus for a new movement for environmental justice, a uniquely American conception of social problems as caused by environmental degradation, and a philosophy that has since become popular in other nations, particularly in the Third World.[66] The social justice leanings of the new grassroots environmentalism that emerged in the 1970s led to new achievements in organizing and building scientific knowledge. For a couple of decades this movement achieved little change in actual environmental jurisprudence, which was still based on the scenic impulses of the old-school conservationists. But by the 1990s, the two sides of the environmental movement managed to bury the hatchet and ushered in a new philosophy of environmental law, in which the debate shifted to strengthening enforcement and ameliorating the social problems caused by degradation.[67]

Exemplary evidence of social justice in American environmental jurisprudence came from President Bill Clinton in 1994, when he issued an executive order directing all federal agencies to conduct their activities in a fashion that will promote environmental justice.[68] In turn, the federal government has faced pressure to add local concerns to federal environmental law and also to make the regulatory process of natural protection more transparent.[69] Thus, theories of environmental justice have had a great impact on modern developments in environmental law, and the collection, management, and transparency of government-held environmental information.

The Development of American Environmental Law

The above history of American environmental thought and activism is reflected in the development of statutory protections against pollution and degradation, with an inexorable transition from scenic preservation to the enforcement of public health standards. Over time, American environmental law also became more and more information-oriented.

Due to the constitutional structure of the American government, which favors incremental and decentralized lawmaking, in earlier times it was easier to protect small parcels of nature in areas with little state or local authority. This was the case with the majority of conservation-oriented statutes in the 19th and early 20th centuries. Conversely, the public interest goals of modern environmental statutes are at a decided disadvantage in the American lawmaking system, necessitating major changes in jurisprudence and judicial philosophy. Efforts of this magnitude were indeed necessary for the passage and enactment of the far-reaching environmental statutes that started to appear on the federal stage in the early 1970s.[70]

One will also notice the increasing importance of information in the long-term development of American environmental law, with the management and availability of government-held documentation playing a more and more important role in the ability of citizens to review how well their government protects the natural world.[71] This is necessary because of another challenge placed on environmental lawmaking by the American constitutional and political structure. Environmental problems are difficult to assess with the degree of scientific certainty usually demanded by elected officials, and usually require long-term treatment and precautionary (or proactive) steps that make the quick results demanded by the American political process all but impossible. These phenomena also increase the political controversy surrounding any environmental debate, making the collection and management of accurate and useful environmental information all the more important during the lawmaking process.[72]

Early environmental law (or more accurately, natural resources law) in America developed in line with the nation's expansion, the industrialization of the 19th Century, and the consequent exploitation of the interior's vast natural resources. While the majority of Americans cheered the conquest of uninhabited areas in the interests of economic growth and manifest destiny, the wilderness had always had a grip on the American psyche, and the despoliation of especially dramatic wilderness areas in the 19th Century inspired calls for political action. Hence, American environmental law originated with citizen demands for the protection of "natural resources," or the scenic wilderness that inspired spiritual reflection of the type glorified by Henry David Thoreau and John Muir.[73]

Arguably, the first major development in federal environmental law was the establishment of the Department of the Interior in 1849. This executive department was originally instructed to manage matters that did not fit well into other federal agency responsibilities, such as Indian affairs and land management, but it eventually took charge of wildlife conservation and natural resources management on government-owned lands.[74]

This was also a crucial development in environmental jurisdiction, which was becoming national rather than solely the responsibility of states or localities. The nationalization of American environmental law that commenced in the second half of the 19th Century reflected the increasing powers of the federal government, the trans-border nature of environmental problems, and the awareness of those challenges amongst a better-informed electorate. Nationalized environmental jurisprudence also posed a structural challenge on the statutes and federal agencies it engendered, because the Constitution does not give the federal government any enumerated powers over the natural world, so per the Tenth Amendment such powers would fall to the states by default. This Constitutional problem has not yet been fully resolved, subjecting fundamental matters of natural protection to shifting political ideologies and Constitutional interpretations by the judiciary.[75]

With the advent of the progressive and populist eras in American politics, citizens demanded statutory protections for the natural world, while politicians began to notice the ecological impacts of the age of industrialization, even if their focus was originally on threats to economic growth and profitability. In 1871 the U.S. Congress, noting that "the most valuable food fishes of the coast and the lakes of the United States are rapidly diminishing in number, to public injury," authorized President Ulysses S. Grant to appoint a Commissioner of Fish and Fisheries – the first federal officer with an exclusively environmental job description.[76]

A major step was made the following year when Congress authorized the formation of Yellowstone National Park, where a lack of local jurisdiction (the Wyoming, Idaho, and Montana Territories were not yet states) made federal protection a necessity, thus forming a crucial precedent for federally-enforced conservation of natural wonders across the nation.[77] A state-level precedent was also set in New York in 1885, when the state legislature granted statutory "wilderness" protection (actually controlled development through regulation) to a vast area encompassing six million acres in the Adirondack Mountains region,[78] with an amendment to the state's constitution in 1894 decreeing that the parklands be kept "forever wild."[79] The wilderness protection craze had taken hold in Washington as well, with Congress authorizing Sequoia National Park in California in 1890[80] and the General Land Revision Act the following year.[81] That statute allowed President Benjamin Harrison to set aside 13 million acres as forest reserves in the public interest, instituting what would later become the U.S. Forest Service, which now maintains nearly 200 million acres under the national forest system.[82]

Conservation was the leading environmental philosophy of the time, and the public health effects of pollution and despoliation were not yet fully understood. Nonetheless, local anti-pollution ordinances began to pop up during the progressive era, reflecting the social justice ambitions of that period. In 1881 Chicago and Cincinnati enacted America's first air pollution ordinances.[83] Federal courts also started to show some sympathy toward the public health effects of pollution, even in the face of powerful and well-connected industries. In 1884, the Ninth Circuit Court of Appeals in San Francisco issued an injunction against the gold mining industry's practice of filling riverbeds with the vast volumes of silt and gravel extracted from mountains during heavy mining, which caused flooding and disrupted groundwater patterns for California's farmers. In the words of the court, the practice was "a public and private nuisance," indicating concern not just for each private farmer's profitability but also the impact on the public.[84]

In 1899, Congress passed what is widely regarded as the first federal environmental protection statute, or at least the first that was not dedicated to preserving a parcel of land for its scenic or wilderness value. The Rivers and Harbors Act prohibited the construction of bridges, dams, and other structures on navigable waterways without Congressional approval. The original justification for this law, unsurprisingly, was economic, with Congress seeing the need to keep waterways open for the transport of goods.[85] But the Rivers and Harbors Act also included a precedent-setting prohibition of unauthorized filling and dredging of waterways, which was a crucial step forward for natural preservation in the face of industrial expansion.[86]

More federal statutory protection of lands for more than just their scenic value followed at a rapid pace. In 1903 President Theodore Roosevelt established the first federal bird reservation in Florida, and placed the area under the jurisdiction of the U.S. Biological Survey expressly for purposes of wildlife protection.[87] In 1905 Roosevelt established the U.S. Forest Service[88] to manage existing forest reserves as national forests (and later, prairies as national grasslands) in the interests of wildlife habitat protection, recreation, and timber production.[89] Roosevelt built his conservationist legacy even further in 1906, making use of the recently-passed Antiquities Act[90] to set aside millions of acres of wilderness lands for their "historical" interest, including the future national parks at the Grand Canyon (Arizona), the Grand Teton mountain range (Wyoming), Bryce Canyon (Utah), and Death Valley (California).[91]

Another major precedent in environmental law was set in 1918, when American wildlife protection went international with the Migratory Bird Treaty Act (MBTA).[92] This treaty was originally forged in 1916 by the United States and the United Kingdom. During that era, fears of widespread extinction of bird species encouraged the two nations to act for the protection of the migratory birds of the United States and Canada (over which the United Kingdom still had sovereignty in foreign affairs). While primarily aimed at controlling overzealous recreational hunters, the MBTA also codified the aesthetic and environmental values of birds, making the act one of the first in American history to treat the protection of animals as a matter of public interest. It was also one of the first American environmental statutes to consider the transnational nature of environmental protection.[93]

During the Great Depression, the U.S. Government used the national economic crisis as justification for one of the great advancements in American environmental history. In 1933 President Franklin D. Roosevelt established the Civilian Conservation Corps (CCC) as a job creation program.[94] Millions of unemployed young men were assigned to public works projects that were largely conservation-oriented, such as developing parks and planting trees in deforested areas.[95] The majority of CCC workers were transferred to military duty with the advent of World War II, but before that they were responsible for a huge expansion of citizen access to outdoor recreation and a subsequent increase in natural appreciation amongst the public.[96]

While American appreciation for wilderness dated back to early philosophically-minded nature lovers like Thoreau and Muir, by the middle of the 20th Century there was a popular push for not just the statutory protection of pristine areas but the ability to allow damaged areas to return to their natural states. In particular, the growing middle class was becoming more familiar with America's natural wonders thanks to expanding media coverage and car usage, and more and more citizens became concerned about threatened wilderness areas.[97] In 1964 President Lyndon B. Johnson passed the Wilderness Act,[98] a landmark piece of legislation that allowed the immediate designation of millions of acres of undisturbed lands as federal wilderness areas.[99] The legislation, largely constructed by activist Howard Zahniser of the Wilderness Society, included poetic and influential language defining wilderness as "untrammeled by man, where man is a visitor who does not remain." This carefully-tailored language allowed the Wilderness Act to be applied not just to lands that had never felt the hand of man (an extreme rarity in America by 1964) but also lands that had previously been exploited and could return to a natural state with the assistance of statutory protection.[100]

Naturally-minded American citizens were also turning to litigation in order to achieve not just protection for cherished lands, but protection from pollution as well. Such groups now endeavored to defend, via the judicial process, the public interest in environmental protection. A major problem for concerned citizens' groups was the matter of standing, as administrative law allows citizens to bring suit against the government for perceived statutory violations, but requires convincing evidence of personal harms caused by such violations.[101] For environmental matters, the first noteworthy case in which standing became an issue was the *Scenic Hudson* case in 1965.[102] A government agency, the Federal Power Commission, issued a permit for the construction of a new power plant in New York State's Hudson River valley, which was opposed by citizens who claimed a violation of the Federal Power Act.[103] The circuit court found that the Administrative Procedure Act did not restrain standing to those who could demonstrate personal economic injury, and in this case, standing could also be granted to those who could demonstrate "a special interest in the aesthetic, conservational, and recreational aspects of power development."[104] This was a crucial precedent that allowed courts to interpret the standing of concerned citizens, including those with conservation interests, more liberally – and this was especially important with the advent of a series of public interest-oriented environmental statutes in the early 1970s.[105] However, environmentalists still faced challenges at the Supreme Court, as will be seen below.

In response to growing citizen sentiment in the 1960s, by the end of that decade the American government began to pass a variety of federal statutes meant to protect the natural environment in general, and not just selected locations. "Environmental law" under that name did not even exist as an acknowledged category until this time, with the first official use of the term believed to have been at a 1969 law conference.[106] American voters, and their representatives, were thinking along the same lines, as the public became more knowledgeable about environmental problems and the need for legislation to address such challenges.[107]

The first noteworthy such statute was the National Environmental Policy Act (NEPA) of 1969,[108] Title I of which acted as a "Congressional Declaration of Environmental Policy." The statute established the Council on Environmental Quality, the first federal government entity dedicated exclusively to environmental matters, within the Executive Office of the President.[109] The environmental protection requirements of NEPA were also indirectly responsible for President Richard Nixon's organization of the Environmental Protection Agency (EPA) less than a year after the statute went into effect.[110] Most importantly, NEPA is a procedure-oriented statute that regulates the activities of all government agencies and is not enforced by any one agency, not even the EPA which itself is structured for compliance with NEPA.[111] The Environmental Protection Agency became the primary implementer and enforcer of environmental statutes and regulations in America, with court representation and enforcement assistance provided by environmental specialists in the Department of Justice. Implementation and enforcement by the EPA and the Justice department are handled within the executive branch of the federal government. But it is important to note that like in all other areas of American law, the formation and interpretation of environmental laws are the responsibility of the legislative and judicial branches, respectively.[112] Therefore, environmental protection became the responsibility of the entire American government.

In the following years, Congress passed several more far-reaching statutes aimed at pollution control and waste management that were inspired by, modeled after, and placed under the rubric of, the National Environmental Policy Act.[113] Given the increasing public awareness of environmental degradation in the late 1960s and early 1970s, in line with a new awareness of civil rights issues and other public policy problems, environmental historians consider the influx of new federal environmental regulations to be the "culmination of an era of protest," rather than the abrupt start of a new movement or even an increase in concern among politicians.[114]

Popular concern for the environment also encouraged the American judiciary to uphold the new legislative regime. As early as

1974, the Court of Appeals for the District of Columbia Circuit, which hears the majority of cases involving agency compliance or noncompliance with federal statutes, made environmentalism as American as apple pie by declaring that environmental interests touched on "fundamental personal interests in life, health, and liberty," and that those interests have a "special claim to judicial protection."[115] By the late 1970s the legitimacy of the new environmental law regime no longer seemed to be a matter of dispute in the courts. In 1978, the D.C. Circuit Court declared that NEPA and its affiliated laws reflected "the widely shared conviction that the nation's quality of life depended on its natural bounty, and that it was worth incurring heavy cost to preserve that bounty for future generations."[116]

However, the legitimacy of environmental law did not guarantee the ability of citizens to take the government to task for compliance with the new statutes. In fact, as will be discussed in the upcoming chapters, the true effectiveness of American environmental law for concerned citizens is held back by procedural minutiae and matters of standing and jurisdiction. It was not long before the National Environmental Policy Act inspired a key Supreme Court precedent on the standing of citizens' groups to sue federal government agencies, in the public interest, for the violation of regulations (environmental or otherwise). The procedure-based ruling by the Supreme Court would set the scene for environmental law, and citizen access to environmental information, up to the present day.

In *Sierra Club v. Morton* in 1972,[117] John Muir's large membership-based conservation group attempted to make use of the Administrative Procedure Act (APA) to oppose the construction of a large resort in California's Sequoia National Forest, which had been approved by the U.S. Forest Service. Sierra Club believed that the agency had violated environmental and administrative procedures as required under NEPA. The government respondents raised questions of whether Sierra Club had standing to sue, on whose behalf they had brought the suit, the extent of the injury suffered, and who suffered it.

The Supreme Court made use of more general precedents in which matters of standing were argued, because environmental standing had not previously been an issue under intensive review.[118] According to the high court, Sierra Club was not able to demonstrate injury in fact or direct personal standing in the dispute, and the club was unable to prove that it had suffered an injury itself, because it was a membership organization whose widespread members exercised a general interest in environmental issues across the nation.[119] In the Court's words, a mere "interest in a problem, no matter how longstanding the interest and no matter how qualified the organization is in evaluating the problem, is not sufficient by itself to render the organization 'adversely affected' or 'aggrieved' within the meaning of the APA."[120]

The important outcome of this case is that any public interest organization has the standing to bring suit against a federal agency for violations of environmental statutes, as long as at least one of the group's members can claim an interest in the locality affected by the government activity.[121] However, this seemingly simple requirement is not easy to achieve in the uninhabited areas that are prone to destructive new developments. Citizens who are concerned about pristine natural areas usually do not live in them, and aesthetic or philosophical concern for the health of those areas does not qualify as an economic interest.

This was certainly a setback for environmental groups and other citizens' groups working in the public interest, but the issue of standing would become a bit less distinct over the coming decades. Future attempts to achieve standing for environmental public interest groups built upon a lengthy dissent to *Sierra Club v. Morton* by Justice William O. Douglas. Within a litany of environmental problems that he personally abhorred, Douglas disagreed in principle with the majority ruling that Sierra Club did not have standing just because it could not show direct personal injury from the destruction of a certain section of Sequoia National Forest:

> Those who hike it, fish it, hunt it, camp in it, frequent it, or visit it merely to sit in solitude and wonderment are legitimate spokesmen for it, whether they may be few or many. Those who have that intimate relation with the inanimate object about to be injured, polluted, or otherwise despoiled are its legitimate spokesmen.[122]

Here Douglas was building upon a belief that NEPA placed primacy on the protection of America's environment, and logistical matters like economic harm should be given secondary consideration.

After Morton, Douglas's dissent quickly gained influence not just among outdoor lovers but among other justices. Hence, it did not take long for the Supreme Court to relax the "injury in fact" doctrine that had tripped up Sierra Club. *United States v. Students Challenging Regulatory Agency Procedures* featured a convoluted dispute involving Interstate Commerce Commission tolls on railways, which the citizens' group believed promoted discrimination against the shipment of recycled materials, which in turn created more garbage and the attendant environmental degradation. The high court (in a ruling heavily influenced by *Morton*) dismissed the government's contention that the public interest group had no standing to sue, regardless of its very tenuous arguments about environmental harms. This was supported by provisions in NEPA that prohibited discrimination by government agencies against recycled materials. Consequently, the high court used the softer public interest rationale of NEPA rather than the strict "injury in fact" requirements of APA, and standing for the citizens' group was not disallowed just because the litigants themselves may not have suffered injury personally.[123]

The issue of standing would become unclear over the coming decades, with groups of concerned citizens sometimes able to convince courts of "injuries in fact" but with the U.S. Supreme Court not always sympathetic. In turn, citizens were more often required to prove direct government violations of distinct provisions within the plethora of new environmental statutes that arose in the wake of the National Environmental Policy Act.

American environmental law became a contentious political issue with the 1973 passage of what is arguably one of the most controversial statutes of any kind in the country, the Endangered Species Act (ESA). This act prohibits any agency of the federal government or the parties it regulates from damaging the habitat of a species falling under very precise definitions of "endangered" or "threatened," under the rationale that it is in the public interest to save such species from extinction.[124] ESA soon became the basis of a bitter legal feud that defined a still-ongoing conflict over the public interest in natural preservation and the

public interest in economic development, further delineating the now
politicized role of environmental law in America.

The Endangered Species Act was first disputed in a highly
controversial Supreme Court case involving a small fish called the snail
darter, an endangered species inhabiting streams in eastern Tennessee.
A government agency, the Tennessee Valley Authority, announced
plans to build Tellico Dam on the Little Tennessee River in 1966,
several years before the enactment of ESA. Environmentalists had long
opposed the project, but with little statutory recourse until the snail
darter was listed as endangered (under ESA) in 1975. This finally gave
dam opponents a statutory basis for court action in their efforts to derail
the construction process, and in *Tennessee Valley Authority v. Hill* the
Supreme Court ruled that the project was in violation of ESA. This
ruling shut down the project until a less destructive alternative was
found that ameliorated the risks to the snail darter and its habitat.[125]

The highly contentious nature of endangered species habitat
protection erupted again in the early 1990s, when environmentalists
who opposed logging in the American northwest attempted to utilize
the Endangered Species Act due to the regional presence of a possibly
endangered species, the northern spotted owl. Logging opponents
lobbied politicians for the listing of the northern spotted owl as an
endangered species, with proponents then clamoring for the bird's
delisting, in an illustration of the modern politicization of
environmental protection.[126] Such machinations are heavily inspired by
the Endangered Species Act in particular, because that statute's
restriction on land use and development make it seriously unpopular
with many business leaders, private property activists, and other
conservative political constituencies.[127]

The National Environmental Policy Act and the Endangered
Species Act are two particularly crucial indicators of the new direction
of American environmental law in the early 1970s. In addition to the
aforementioned transition in environmental law from a primary interest
in natural resource protection to an increased effort to control pollution
and despoliation, by this time the body of law had also begun to reflect
new popular conceptions of environmental rights, or the notion that
humans have the right to a healthy and protected environment. In 1968,
Wisconsin Senator Gaylord Nelson (who two years later promoted the

first Earth Day, as described above) made history by proposing a constitutional amendment to guarantee an "inalienable right to a decent environment" and to require all levels of government to protect that right.[128] Environmental rights eventually gained some temporary currency in the courts, exemplified by a 1989 ruling by the Court of Appeals for the Ninth Circuit. In a case concerning the construction of a new superhighway through ecologically sensitive areas in Hawai'i, the Circuit Court wrote that it is "difficult to conceive of a more absolute and enduring concern than the preservation and, increasingly, the restoration of a decent and livable environment."[129] The concept of environmental rights had made some political headway in the 1970s and 1980s, but in practical terms, a rights-based focus tends to force policy into extremism and inflexibility.[130]

Meanwhile, the many categories of activism inspired by the civil rights era were falling before the shifting winds of American politics. The passage of new federal environmental regulations slowed down significantly during the conservative presidential administrations of the 1980s. Just before Ronald Reagan took office, there was one crucial breakthrough with the first federal regulation that added significant liability for polluters, rather than try to proactively encourage better behavior prior to the creation of pollution. In 1980, Congress passed the Comprehensive Environmental Response, Compensation, and Liability Act (CERCLA).[131] Popularly known as the "Superfund" statute, CERCLA was aimed at not just cleaning up environmental disaster areas (in particular, those in urban areas and/or caused by industry), but tracking down and charging the guilty parties. CERCLA was a breakthrough in environmental law not just for its enforceable fines and other punishments for polluters,[132] but also for instituting the collection and management of information on who those polluters are and how they conduct their business.[133]

Unfortunately for environmental activists, starting in the 1980s a newly conservative Supreme Court began to roll back public interest-oriented environmental protections in favor of a new focus on private property rights. A key turning point at the high court came with the *Lucas* case in 1992, in which the court ruled in favor of a landowner who argued that the enforcement of federal environmental requirements (land use restrictions in particular) on his property amounted to an

uncompensated and unconstitutional taking.[134] The newfound
conservative promotion of private property rights is reflected in this
constitutional interpretation by the high court, which does not bode
well for the public health goals of federal environmental law.[135]

In addition to the constitutional aspects of the argument in *Lucas*,
the landowner also claimed that the environmental restrictions at issue
caused economic harms – another argument that the high court found
persuasive. For activists, this was perhaps even more troubling because
environmental protection became less a matter of non-economic public
interest and would only gain legitimacy if it could deliver economic
benefits of its own.[136] This distinction has become especially vexing for
the enforcement of the Endangered Species Act, which requires the
protection of habitat that often falls within private property; while other
pollution control laws like the Clean Air Act and the Clean Water Act
quite often have an impact on the economic activities of private
industry.[137] These developments were also a reflection of the push for
utilitarian cost/benefit analyses of regulatory disputes that swept
through the federal government during the Reagan years.[138] The
outcome of *Lucas* indicates that in the new conservative era, the public
interest is bound to fall behind private property rights and economic
development, and this presents a fundamental conflict with the aims
and goals of most federal environmental legislation.

During this time period the Supreme Court also began to roll back
the legal standing achieved by citizens' environmental groups in the
wake of the 1972 *Morton* case. With Justice Antonin Scalia displaying
a particular animosity toward standing for citizens' groups, the high
court made matters more difficult for environmental activists in *Lujan
v. National Wildlife Federation* (1990)[139] and *Lujan v. Defenders of
Wildlife* (1992).[140] These two initially unrelated cases, known
respectively as *Lujan I* and *Lujan II*, were brought by wildlife
protection groups contesting the suspected disregard for environmental
statutes by government agencies, and shed light on shifting judicial
interpretations of the procedural requirements of NEPA. In these cases
the high court instructed the citizens' groups to satisfy laborious
requirements from the Administrative Procedure Act and to justify
citizen action against government agencies that carry out their legally-
mandated responsibilities.[141] The contradiction among *Morton* and the

two *Lujan* cases remains unresolved, with no firm precedent in place for whether or not citizens' groups with general memberships will be able to achieve standing in suits against the federal government for distinct statutory violations.[142]

By the turn of the millennium, a conservative era push for deregulation, both in the courts and in the halls of Congress, further damaged the effectiveness of federal environmental statutes. For example, a study of rulings by the D.C. Circuit Court in environmentally-relevant cases found a significant decrease in support for federal environmental regulations from the late 1980s to the late 1990s (in line with an ideological trend toward deregulation). The study also detected a drive to reduce judicial oversight and review of government agency decisions, even when those agencies were charged with violating federal statutes, and especially if the remedy would inflict damage on private property rights or economic development.[143]

But despite political posturing to the contrary, powerful conservative lawmakers have been unable to dismantle America's federal environmental protection regime because of continued public support for that protection, and the emergence of constituencies that had not previously shown much concern for environmentalism (or whose concerns were ignored). A new movement to address the problem of environmental racism, inspired by the proximity of polluting industries and landfills to poor and politically powerless communities, has restored and continued the political legitimacy of America's environmental protection regime. Continuing citizen activism and public engagement has allowed American environmental law to persevere in the face of hostile legislators and unsympathetic courts, albeit in a procedurally weakened state.[144]

However, environmentally-oriented rulings by the Supreme Court in the new millennium indicate a trend toward stringent reading of the statutes, with the literal letter of the law trumping wider concerns for the public interest in environmental protection.[145] Hence, federal environmental law has been swept up in the modern ideological drive for less intrusive government intervention in private affairs and for the reduction of regulations that promote non-economic benefits.[146]

In modern America, political and judicial trends have resulted in many hurdles for environmental law and for citizens who wish to make use of those laws. But the laws are still in place by popular demand, and the continual public passion for a clean natural world and its public health benefits will always be noticed by politicians. Regardless of ideological trends, environmental law has shown an ability to evolve and react to changing politics and new problems in the natural world, and the pragmatic nature and long-term focus of environmentalism will allow federal statutes to persevere.[147] Unfortunately, as will be seen in the upcoming chapters, the procedural focus of American administrative jurisprudence will continue to complicate and even reduce protection when environmental disputes end up in court.

Chapter 3 Notes

[1] E. Donald Elliott, Bruce A. Ackerman, and John C. Millian, "Toward a Theory of Statutory Evolution: The Federalization of Environmental Law," *Journal of Law, Economics, & Organization* 1 (1985): 333-338.

[2] J. Donald Hughes, *Pan's Travail: Environmental Problems of the Ancient Greeks and Romans* (Baltimore: Johns Hopkins University Press, 1994), 73-90.

[3] J. Donald Hughes, *Ecology in Ancient Civilizations* (Albuquerque, N.M.: University of New Mexico Press, 1975), 14, 35, 132.

[4] Barbara Tuchman, *A Distant Mirror: The Calamitous 14th Century* (New York: Knopf, 1978), 24, 55.

[5] Bill McKibben, ed. *American Earth: Environmental Writing Since Thoreau* (New York: The Library of America, 2008), 978.

[6] William Penn, "Concessions to the Province of Pennsylvania," 11 July 1681, http://www.teachingamericanhistory.org/library/index.asp?document-2271, accessed 23 June 2010. Whether Penn was more concerned with scenic beauty or the preservation of profit-making trees (such as mulberry and oak) is a matter of some historical dispute.

[7] Benjamin Franklin, *Poor Richard's Almanack* (Waterloo, Ia.: U.S.C. Publishing, 1914), 59. This book was originally published as a pamphlet in 1733.

[8] McKibben, 978.

[9] John James Audubon, *Birds of America* (Self-published, 1827-1838).

[10] Alexis de Tocqueville, *Democracy in America* (New York: The Library of America, 2004), 557. de Tocqueville's comments on this matter were in the second volume of his original manuscript, first published in 1840.

[11] Donald Worster, *A Passion for Nature: The Life of John Muir* (New York: Oxford University Press, 2008), 209.

[12] Philip Stratton-Lake, "Classical Idealism: An Introduction." *The Edinburgh Encyclopedia of Continental Philosophy*, ed. Simon Glendenning (Edinburgh: Edinburgh University Press, 1999), 23.

[13] Immanuel Kant, *Critique of Pure Reason*, trans. J.M.D. Meiklejohn (New York: P.F. Collier & Son, 1901), 139-140. This work was originally published in Germany in 1781.

[14] Henry E. Allison, *Kant's Transcendental Idealism: An Interpretation and Defense* (New Haven, Conn.: Yale University Press, 2004), 20-23.

[15] Worster, 209. Note that this philosophy is sometimes called "American transcendentalism" to distinguish it from the European-oriented transcendental idealism and other related schools of thought.

[16] Coleridge and Wordsworth were more closely associated with the Romantic movement in British literature, but were also members of a group known as the Lake Poets who composed a quantity of philosophically-minded poems that were vaguely influenced by the natural surroundings of the Lake District in northwestern England. The works of the Lake Poets were popular in America (especially New England) in the first half of the 19th Century. Thomas de Quincey, *Recollections of the Lakes and the Lake Poets: Coleridge, Wordsworth, and Southey* (Edinburgh: Adam and Charles Black, 1862), v-vi.

[17] Worster, 209.

[18] Ralph Waldo Emerson, *Nature* (New York: Duffield & Co., 1909), 46, 52-53. This short work originated as an anonymous essay published in 1836.

[19] Ralph Waldo Emerson, *Selected Writings of Ralph Waldo Emerson*, ed. William H. Gilman (New York: Signet Classic, 2003), 482.

[20] Milton Meltzer, *Henry David Thoreau: A Biography* (Minneapolis, Minn.: Twenty-First Century Books, 2007), 30-33.

[21] An early critic was author Robert Louis Stevenson, who found Thoreau's burgeoning philosophy of natural appreciation to be insincere and not really based on a full return to nature. Robert Louis Stevenson, "Henry David Thoreau: His Character and Opinions," *Cornhill Magazine*, June 1860, page numbers unknown.

[22] Henry David Thoreau, *Walden, or: Life in the Woods* (New York: Thomas V. Crowell & Co., 1910), 118.

[23] Ibid., 53.

[24] Lazarus, 5.

[25] George Perkins Marsh, *Man and Nature: On Physical Geography as Modified by Human Action* (New York: Charles Scribner, 1864), iii.

[26] Ibid., 328-329.

[27] Lazarus, 5.

[28] For the full travelogue of the journey, see John Wesley Powell, *The Exploration of the Colorado River and Its Tributaries* (New York: Penguin Books, 2003). Powell's original travelogue was published by the U.S. Government under the title *The Exploration of the Colorado River and Its Canyons: Explored in 1869, 1870, 1871, and 1872 Under the Direction of the*

Secretary of the Smithsonian Institution. Powell's exploits were not hampered by the loss of his left arm at the battle of Shiloh during the Civil War.
[29] McKibben, 981.
[30] John Wesley Powell, *Report on the Lands of the Arid Region of the United States*, 2nd ed. (Washington: Government Printing Office, 1879), 40, 141.
[31] McKibben, 982.
[32] Worster, 118-208; Frederick Turner, *John Muir: Rediscovering America* (Cambridge, Mass.: Perseus Publishing, 2000), 131-219.
[33] Worster, 306.
[34] Steven Fox, *The American Conservation Movement: John Muir and His Legacy* (Madison, Wis.: University of Wisconsin Press, 1985), 13.
[35] Worster, 306-307.
[36] Francisco Panizza, "Introduction," *Populism and the Mirror of Democracy*, ed. Francisco Panizza (New York: Verso, 2005), 4-5.
[37] Lewis L. Gould, *America in the Progressive Era, 1890-1914* (New York: Longman, 2001), 7-13.
[38] Worster, 306. It should be noted that during this era, these were largely philosophical arguments, though future scientific discoveries in ecology and other fields would shed light on the potential public health and economic impacts of environmental degradation.
[39] McKibben, 983. After this unsuccessful attempt at a national organization, several state Audubon Societies formed, which by 1902 had merged into a true National Audubon Society.
[40] Worster, 328-330. In the decades after its founding in 1892, Sierra Club moved away from its focus on the Sierra Mountains of Northern California and is now a nationwide volunteer environmental organization with several hundred thousand members.
[41] McKibben, 986-987.
[42] Philip Shabecoff, *A Fierce Green Fire: The American Environmental Movement* (Washington: Island Press, 2003), 186.
[43] McKibben, 129-130.
[44] W. Todd Benson, *President Theodore Roosevelt's Conservation Legacy* (West Conshohocken, Pa.: Infinity Publishing, 2003), 67-123.
[45] Theodore Roosevelt, Speech at Grand Canyon, Ariz., 6 May 1903, in *A Compilation of the Messages and Speeches of Theodore Roosevelt, 1901-1905*, ed. Alfred Henry Lewis (Washington: Bureau of National Literature and Art,

1905), 327. Though Roosevelt promoted the permanent protection of the Grand
Canyon in this 1903 speech, the area did not receive protection as a National
Monument until 1908. The area was designated a National Park (with greater
protection of natural resources) in 1919.

[46] Worster, 366-368. What is today Yosemite National Park is a large territory
of mountainous highlands, though the vast majority of tourists visit Yosemite
Valley, a glacier-carved canyon about seven miles long and one mile wide and
surrounded by steep cliffs. This outstandingly scenic area received state
protection from California as early as 1864, but Muir and other activists
believed that the state was not doing enough to protect the small canyon from
tourism and agricultural interests – thus Muir's personal entreaty to Roosevelt.
The surrounding highlands that now make up most of the national park were
traditionally used for livestock grazing, and despite their own scenic and
natural wonders, received little to no protection until Roosevelt's action in
1906.

[47] Ibid., 399. The first national park was Yellowstone, established by the U.S.
Congress in 1872 to protect its scenic and natural wonders. The area was
eligible for federal protection because it was not part of any state, with
Wyoming, Idaho, and Montana not being admitted to the Union until nearly
two decades later, thus making state sovereignty a non-issue. Yosemite was the
first sizeable national park to be made up of lands formerly under the control of
a state and then transferred to federal jurisdiction.

[48] Ibid., 403-404. Hetch Hetchy Valley lies a few miles from Yosemite Valley
and is a similar long and narrow glacier-carved canyon with a river that could
be easily dammed to create a large reservoir. The same could be true of
Yosemite Valley, but that valley was easily reached and was a thriving tourist
destination, while Hetch Hetchy was more remote and less well-known
amongst the public.

[49] Ibid., 328-330.

[50] Ibid., 453. Via a long system of aqueducts and canals, today Hetch Hetchy
Reservoir is still the primary water source for most of the San Francisco Bay
area. The dam is formally named O'Shaughnessy Dam after its chief engineer,
who had extensive political connections in San Francisco.

[51] Ibid., 433.

[52] McKibben, 989. The National Wildlife Federation was called the General
Wildlife Federation during its first year. This group would have a major impact

on federal environmental law by calling for statutory protection of state and federal wildlife refuges, which began to be set aside in earnest in the 1960s. The Wilderness Society was created by, among others, noted Alaska explorer Robert Marshall, writer Aldo Leopold, and Appalachian Trail founder Benton MacKaye. This group inspired the protection of various state and federal wilderness preserves during its early decades of existence, and was directly involved in the passage of the federal Wilderness Act of 1964.

[53] Aldo Leopold, *A Sand County Almanac* (New York: Oxford University Press, 2001), 189. This is an illustrated commemorative edition of Leopold's original 1949 publication.

[54] McKibben, 990-991.

[55] The most noteworthy example was a book featuring photos by the celebrated photographer Ansel Adams, depicting many of the scenic wonders of the American west. Ansel Adams and Nancy Newhall, *This is the American Earth* (San Francisco: Sierra Club, 1960).

[56] J. Brooks Flippen, *Conservative Conservationist: Russell E. Train and the Emergence of American Environmentalism* (Baton Rouge, La.: Louisiana State University Press, 2006), 11-28.

[57] Russell E. Train, *Politics, Pollution, and Pandas: An Environmental Memoir* (Washington: Shearwater, 2003), 54-120.

[58] Rachel Carson, *Silent Spring*, 40th Anniversary ed. (Boston: Houghton Mifflin, 2002), 103-128. DDT is the abbreviation for dichloro-diphenyl-trichloroethane, first synthesized for industrial applications in 1874 and used as an insecticide starting in 1939.

[59] Carson made this statement in later testimony before Congress. Linda Lear, "Introduction," in Carson, xv.

[60] McKibben, 993.

[61] U.S. Environmental Protection Agency. "DDT Ban Takes Effect," press release, 31 December 1972. Most nations in the industrialized world have since banned DDT as well, but it is still used extensively in agricultural areas in India and North Korea.

[62] Shabecoff, 105-112.

[63] Denis Hayes, Speech at Sylvan Theatre, Washington, D.C., 22 April 1970. Quoted in McKibben, 482.

[64] Lazarus, 123.

[65] Peter Marcuse, "Conservation for Whom?," in *Environmental Quality and Social Justice in Urban America: An Exploration of Conflict and Concord Among Those Who Seek Environmental Quality and Those Who Seek Social Justice*, ed. James N. Smith (Washington: Conservation Foundation, 1974), 17.

[66] James N. Smith, "The Coming of Age of Environmentalism in American Society," in *Environmental Quality and Social Justice in Urban America*, ed. James N. Smith (Washington: Conservation Foundation,, 1974), 1. Environmental justice quickly gained currency in other areas of civil rights activism. For example, Benjamin Chavis of the NAACP (National Association for the Advancement of Colored Persons) is believed to have coined the term "environmental racism" in 1972. McKibben, 998.

[67] Lazarus, 124-125.

[68] Executive Order No. 12,898, 3 C.F.R. 859 (1994).

[69] James Salzman and Barton H. Thompson, Jr., *Environmental Law and Policy* (New York: Foundation Press, 2003), 39.

[70] Lazarus, 29-30.

[71] Salzman and Thompson, 45-46.

[72] Lazarus, 19-28.

[73] Salzman and Thompson, 4-5.

[74] Act of March 3, 1849 to establish the United States Department of the Interior, 9 Stat. L. 895 (1849).

[75] Lazarus, 31-32. After decades in obscurity, the Tenth Amendment has returned to prominence in conflicts between federal and state regulations, and in 2000 a primarily conservative Supreme Court voted unanimously, per a strict reading of the Tenth Amendment, that the Constitution favors state regulations in the event of such a conflict. The rejuvenation of the power of the Tenth Amendment at the turn of the millennium may reduce the effectiveness of statutory schemes focused on issues that require federal intervention, such as environmental protection. Reno v. Condon, 528 U.S. 141 (2000).

[76] Act of February 9, 1871 to establish an independent United States Commissioner of Fish and Fisheries, 16 Stat. L. 593 (1871).

[77] Act of March 1, 1872 to establish Yellowstone National Park, 17 Stat. L. 32 (1872). Evidence indicates that the "need" for a national park at Yellowstone was promoted by the Union Pacific Railroad, which envisioned a profitable tourist attraction and lobbied strongly for the new park in order to preempt other interested buyers of the land. McKibben, 982. Also, the early national

parks like Yellowstone, Sequoia, and Yosemite were managed on a piecemeal basis until the establishment of the National Park Service in 1916. Act to Establish a National Park Service, 39 Stat. L. 535 (1916). Jenks Cameron, *The National Park Service: Its History, Activities, and Organization* (New York: D. Appleton and Co., 1922), 6-12.

[78] Paul Schneider, *The Adirondacks: A History of America's First Wilderness* (New York: H.H. Holt & Co., 1997), xii.

[79] The Constitution of the State of New York, Art. XIV.

[80] Act of September 25, 1890 to establish Sequoia National Park, 26 Stat. L., 478 (1890).

[81] 26 Stat. L. 1095 (1891).

[82] James L. Huffman, "A History of Forest Policy in the United States," *Environmental Law* 8 (1978): 258-259.

[83] McKibben, 983.

[84] Edwards Woodruff v. North Bloomfield Gravel Mining Company, 18 F9 753 (9th Cir. 1884).

[85] 33 U.S.C. §§ 407-414 (1899). See also McKibben, 985.

[86] Eva H. Morreale, "Federal Power in Western Waters: The Navigation Power and the Rule of No Compensation," *Natural Resources Journal* 3 (1963): 67-69.

[87] George Bird Grinnell, "American Game Protection: A Sketch," in *Conservation in the Progressive Era: Classic Texts*, ed. David Stradling (Seattle: University of Washington Press, 2004), 48. Federal bird reservations and various other land designations for the protection of wildlife were reorganized as national wildlife refuges in 1942.

[88] The U.S. Forest Service was established when Congress transferred jurisdiction over the existing network of forest reserves from the Department of the Interior to the Department of Agriculture, within which the Forest Service became an agency. Transfer Act of February 1, 1905, 33 Stat. L. 628 (1905).

[89] Harold K. Steen, *The U.S. Forest Service: A History* (Durham, N.C.: Forest History Society, 2004), 74-78. The U.S. Forest Service has long been criticized for favoring timber production in the national forests at the expense of natural protections, a perennial political controversy that will be examined in detail in Chapter 5.

[90] An Act for the Preservation of American Antiquities, 16 U.S.C. §§ 431-433 (1906).

[91] Benson, 89-100.

[92] 16 U.S.C. §§ 703-712 (1918). Subsequent treaties with Mexico, Japan, and the former Soviet Union were later added to the Migratory Bird Treaty Act.

[93] Hye-Jong Linda Lee, "The Pragmatic Migratory Bird Treaty Act: Protecting 'Property'," *Boston College Environmental Affairs Law Journal* 31 (2004): 652-653. Soon after the treaty was enacted, U.S. Supreme Court Justice Oliver Wendell Holmes ruled that taking national action to protect migratory birds was in the public interest, because of their aesthetic and environmental value. State of Missouri v. Holland, 252 U.S. 416, 435 (1920).

[94] Act to Establish the Civilian Conservation Corps. 48 Stat. 22-23 (1933).

[95] Joseph M. Speakman, *At Work in Penn's Woods: The Civilian Conservation Corps in Pennsylvania* (State College, Pa.: Pennsylvania State University Press, 2006), 1-2.

[96] Neil M. Maher, *Nature's New Deal: The Civilian Conservation Corps and the Roots of the American Environmental Movement* (New York: Oxford University Press, 2008), 181-210.

[97] Salzman and Thompson, 7.

[98] 16 U.S.C. §§ 1131-1136 (1964).

[99] The first federal wilderness designation was given to a segment of New Mexico's Gila National Forest in 1924. The federal wilderness area system included about nine million acres upon the passage of the Wilderness Act in 1964, and as of 2008 includes more than 100 million acres, with each subsequent presidential administration adding significant amounts of land. Doug Scott, *The Enduring Wilderness: Protecting Out Natural Heritage Through the Wilderness Act* (Golden, Colo.: Fulcrum, 2004), 145-151.

[100] Ibid., 134-136.

[101] These matters are largely codified in the Administrative Procedure Act, which covers the procedures to be followed by government agencies and the recourse available to citizens if those procedures are not followed properly. 5 U.S.C. §§ 553-558, 701-706.

[102] Scenic Hudson Preservation Conference v. Federal Power Commission, 354 F.2d 608 (2nd Cir. 1965).

[103] 16 U.S.C. §§ 791-828. In particular, § 825L(b) of the act grants judicial review of licensing decisions, and whether or not such decisions were made appropriately, upon citizen request. Note that at the time of this case there were not yet any federal statutes that allowed citizen suits for violations of

environmental requirements. The first such statutes, such as the National
Environmental Policy Act, the Clean Air Act, and the Endangered Species Act,
would not arise until the early 1970s.

[104] 354 F.2d 616.

[105] William L. Niro, "Standing to Sue in Environmental Litigation: *Sierra Club
v. Morton*," *DePaul Law Review* 22 (1973): 456.

[106] Lazarus, 47. Previously, the term "natural resources law" was fairly
common, though statutes that preserved natural resources were often
categorized as public health regulations. In the mid to late 1960s, federal
natural resources law began to expand and transition toward the farther-
reaching environmental statutes soon to come. A larger focus is evident in two
of the most crucial natural resources-oriented statutes of the 1960s: the
aforementioned Wilderness Act of 1964 and the National Wild and Scenic
Rivers Act of 1968. George C. Coggins and Robert L. Glicksman, *Public
Natural Resources Law*, 2nd ed., vol. 1 (Eagan, Minn: Thomson/West, 2007),
§§ 2.02-2.04. These trends also inspired the first environmental law journal,
appropriately titled *Environmental Law*, the inaugural issue of which appeared
in 1970.

[107] The increase in public knowledge of environmental issues had many causes,
but was inextricably tied to cultural factors like the political activism and social
criticism of the civil rights era, and a series of highly publicized pollution-
oriented crises in the decades after World War II. Samuel P. Hays, *Beauty,
Health, and Permanence: Environmental Politics in the United States, 1955-
1985* (New York: Cambridge University Press, 1987), 22-26, 260-261.

[108] 42 U.S.C. §§ 4321-4375 (1970). The National Environmental Policy Act
officially went into effect on January 1, 1970, though it has "1969" in its name
because it was passed by Congress in that year.

[109] The structure and responsibilities of this council are codified at 42 U.S.C. §§
4341-4347. The council operates as an advisory and administrative body only.
It should also be noted that this group is made up of political appointees.

[110] The establishment of the EPA was pursuant to a departmental reorganization
of the federal government enacted by the Nixon Administration. Phil Wisman,
"EPA History," U.S. Environmental Protection Agency,
http://www.epa.gov/history/topics/epa/15b.htm, accessed 23 June 2010. Nixon
began his first presidential term in 1969 as a strong supporter of environmental
protection, though he was probably influenced more by public opinion and

political expediency rather than personal belief. Regardless, by 1971 Nixon began to question the increase in government power facilitated by NEPA and related statutes, and by the beginning of his second term in 1973 he had actively joined a conservative backlash against environmentalists and environmentalism. Lazarus, 75-79.

[111] Unlike some large federal agencies that have been allowed to independently interpret and enforce their relevant statutes, like the Federal Communications Commission, the Environmental Protection Agency is responsible for the enforcement of so many environmental statutes that the agency is subjected to considerable and continuous congressional oversight. Lazarus, 80.

[112] Thomas L. Adams, Esq., "Enforcement and Liability", in *Environmental Law Handbook*, vol. 14, ed. Thomas F.P. Sullivan (Rockville, Md.: Government Institutes, Inc., 1997), 55, 58.

[113] Lazarus, 49. Relevant examples of these laws are discussed in detail in the upcoming chapters.

[114] Hays, *Beauty, Health, and Permanence*, 53.

[115] Environmental Defense Fund v. Ruckelshaus, 439 F.2d 584, 597 (D.C. Cir. 1974). This case was inspired by Rachel Carson's *Silent Spring*, with the citizens' group filing for judicial review of a Department of Agriculture decision to allow continued use of the pesticide DDT despite the presence of internal agency documents describing the dangers of DDT to people and animals.

[116] Weyerhauser v. Costle, 590 F.2d. 1011, 1043 (D.C. Cir. 1978). This case was brought by a number of logging and paper companies against the Environmental Protection Agency and regarded a dispute over the classification of certain industrial effluents under the Clean Water Act. The "heavy cost" referenced by the court was the requirement for the companies to upgrade their industrial operations in order to ameliorate the release of effluents into nearby bodies of water.

[117] 405 U.S. 727 (1972).

[118] Supreme Court precedents concerning the standing of public interest groups, found to be relevant in Sierra Club v. Morton, included Baker v. Carr, 389 U.S. 186 (1962); Association of Data Processing Service Organizations Inc. v. Camp, 397 U.S. 150 (1970); Barlow v. Collins, 397 U.S. 159 (1970); and Citizens to Preserve Overton Park, Inc. v. Volpe, 401 U.S. 402 (1971).

[119] 405 U.S. 735-736, 738-739.

[120] 405 U.S. 738-739.

[121] Niro, 452-453.

[122] 405 U.S. 744-745.

[123] 412 U.S. 669, 684-688 (1973).

[124] 16 U.S.C. §§ 1531-1544 (1973). As will be discussed in Chapter 6, there was little controversy surrounding the passage of the Endangered Species Act, but a great amount of controversy would erupt a few years later as the act started to be enforced. The U.S. Fish and Wildlife Service published the nation's first list of endangered species in 1967. See also McKibben, 993.

[125] 437 U.S. 153 (1978). Unfortunately for the opponents of Tellico Dam, it was eventually built anyway, because Congress reacted to the *Tennessee Valley Authority* decision by adding an amendment to ESA in 1978 that allowed particular government development projects to be exempted from the act's requirements by vote of a special committee. Pub. L. 93-632, 92 Stat. 3751 (1978). This 1978 Amendment authorized the special cabinet-level committee and added that authorization to ESA at 16 U.S.C. § 1536(a)(2), with the procedures for finding an exemption codified at § 1536(h). The special committee, known colloquially as the "God Squad," will be discussed in more detail in Chapter 6. In another interesting historical development, biologists later found more snail darter habitats, so the creature's existence was not threatened by Tellico Dam after all, at least not to the point of possible extinction.

[126] Oliver Houck, "The Endangered Species Act and Its Implementation by the U.S. Departments of Interior and Commerce," *University of Colorado Law Review* 64 (1993): 295-307. The saga of the northern spotted owl will be discussed in more detail in Chapter 6.

[127] Philip Weinberg, "Endangered Statute? The Current Assault on the Endangered Species Act," *Villanova Environmental Law Journal* 17 (2006): 390-394.

[128] Salzman and Thompson, 27. Nelson's proposal was unsuccessful, but the idea of environmental rights caught on at the state level. In the coming years Hawai'i, Massachusetts, Montana, and Pennsylvania would add environmental rights to their state constitutions. However, environmental ethicists have argued that environmental rights as proposed by Nelson and protected in those state constitutions reflect an *anthropocentric* focus on the comfort and leisure of humans. Ethicists have also called for a *biocentric* focus on the rights of

existence and protection for plants and animals. The most noteworthy example of this ethic in American environmental law is the Endangered Species Act. A more expansive category of environmental rights would embody an *ecocentric* focus, which calls for an Aldo Leopold-style land ethic in which all natural proccsscs are allowed to function without human disruption. *Ecocentric* environmental rights have not yet appeared in federal environmental law. Ibid., 29-30.

[129] Stop H-3 Association v. Dole, 870 F.2d 1419, 1430 (9th Cir. 1989). The superhighway in question was Interstate H-3 on the island of Oahu, which was designed for national defense purposes and routed to connect two naval bases by road. The environmental dispute and resulting lawsuit resulted in a temporary halt to construction. The freeway was completed in the late 1990s (25 years behind schedule) after Hawai'i Senator Daniel Inouye, in a then-unprecedented move, declared that the H-3 project was exempt from all federal environmental laws and all future environmental lawsuits. Inouye's action perhaps illustrates the fragility of federal environmental law in the face of executive orders. Bruce Dunford, "Danny's Highway to Finally Open in Oahu, Hawaii," *Los Angeles Times*, 14 December 1997, 34.

[130] Salzman and Thompson, 28.

[131] 42 U.S.C. §§ 9601-9675 (1980).

[132] Lazarus, 107.

[133] Michael P. Healy, "Direct Liability for Hazardous Substance Cleanups Under CERCLA: A Comprehensive Approach," *Case Western Reserve Law Review* 65 (1992): 104-128. The informational requirements of CERCLA will be discussed in detail in Chapter 6.

[134] Lucas v. South Carolina Coastal Council, 505 U.S. 1003 (1992).

[135] Lazarus, 133.

[136] Joseph L. Sax, "Property Rights and the Economy of Nature: Understanding *Lucas v. South Carolina Coastal Council*," *Stanford Law Review* 45 (1993): 1454-1455.

[137] Lazarus, 135-136.

[138] Salzman and Thompson, 30-31. Note that upon organizing the Environmental Protection Agency in 1970, President Richard Nixon instructed that agency to exercise cost/benefit analyses when formulating or enforcing environmental regulations. This type of requirement had spread to all areas of regulation during the Reagan administration. In the 1990s, President Bill

Clinton continued the trend with an executive order that required cost/benefit analyses, whenever feasible, at all federal agencies. Executive Order No. 12,866, 58 C.F.R. 51,735 (1993).

[139] 497 U.S. 871 (1990). Here a consortium of wildlife interest groups objected to a decision by the Bureau of Land Management to remove certain parcels of land from federal oversight.

[140] 504 U.S. 555 (1992). Here a different consortium of wildlife interest groups petitioned for judicial review of a decision by the Secretary of the Interior concerning the applicability of the Endangered Species Act to activities conducted by U.S. government agencies in other nations.

[141] The ultimate result of the two *Lujan* rulings was that citizens' environmental groups do have standing in administrative disputes, if they can prove via the Administrative Procedure Act that they participated in the process or decision that is the basis of the dispute. 504 U.S. 570-577. However, this requirement added a significant burden of proof for citizens' groups, given the intricate procedural requirements of APA.

[142] Adrienne Smith, "Standing and the National Environmental Policy Act: Where Substance, Procedure, and Information Collide," *Boston University Law Review* 85 (2005): 658-661.

[143] Richard Revesz, "Environmental Regulation, Ideology, and the D.C. Circuit," *Virginia Law Review* 83 (1997): 1717-1719.

[144] Lazarus, 137-139.

[145] In several cases before the high court, the rulings did require that certain environmental protections be enacted, but whenever the statutory language of an environmental statute conflicted with a strict reading of the Constitution or any non-environmental statute at issue, the effectiveness of the environmental statute was typically undermined, Examples include South Florida Water Management District v. Miccosukee Tribe of Indians, 543 U.S. 805 (2004); Norton v. Southern Utah Wilderness Alliance, 542 U.S. 55 (2004); Department of Transportation v. Public Citizen, 541 U.S. 752 (2004); and Engine Manufacturers Association v. South Coast Air Quality Management District, 541 U.S. 246 (2004).

[146] Lazarus, 245.

[147] Ibid., 254.

The National Environmental Policy Act

The National Environmental Policy Act (NEPA)[1] regulates the environmental activities of the entire American government, and most subsequent environmental statutes are based on it. As will be seen in this chapter, NEPA also revolutionized the collection and transparency of government-held environmental information, and made information the lynchpin of natural protection in America. The case history of NEPA, whenever environmental information (or lack thereof) inspired a court dispute, indicates the general state of America's natural protection efforts and also larger matters of government transparency.

NEPA was the first comprehensive, policy-oriented environmental law in the world.[2] The statute administers the major actions of all agencies and departments within the federal government and requires an environmental impact statement (EIS) for any action, by a government agency or the parties it regulates, with potential consequences for the natural world.[3] Unlike other federal statutes that attempt to force environmental protection through technological standards or the conservation of resources, NEPA relies primarily on information. This information must also be disclosed to all American citizens, making NEPA a groundbreaker in matters of subject matter-oriented government transparency.[4]

The act requires government agencies to consider the environmental impacts of their activities and to report on them – often and in great detail. This approach is emblematic of the civil rights era in which NEPA was passed, illustrating the belief that government will do the right thing if it can properly consider and address issues that are important to the people.[5] NEPA also addresses the need for an omnibus federal environmental policy and encourages the government to respond proactively to the nation's growing environmental problems.[6]

Public participation and the transparency of government-held information are crucial to the philosophy of NEPA. The act was one of the first of the civil rights era's statutes to clearly delineate public participation, with requirements for federal agencies to interact with the public, not just adding the citizen's voice to environmental decision-making but altering the very way that agencies make those decisions. NEPA requires agencies to inform each other and the public about their environmental decision-making processes, which reduces bureaucratic secrecy and increases public accountability.[7]

Shortly after the act was passed, President Richard Nixon expanded NEPA's public participation goals by ordering federal agencies to:

> Develop procedures to ensure the fullest practicable provision of timely public information and understanding of Federal plans and programs with environmental impact in order to obtain the views of interested parties. These procedures shall include, whenever appropriate, provision for public hearings, and shall provide the public with relevant information, including information on alternative courses of action. Federal agencies shall also encourage State and local agencies to adopt similar procedures for informing the public concerning their activities affecting the quality of the environment.[8]

In 1979 the Council on Environmental Quality (CEQ), the executive branch advisory board that was itself created by NEPA, continued to promote the benefits of public participation under the act. When introducing new regulations that strengthened the consensus-building public participation provisions of NEPA, the CEQ general counsel noted that:

> [T]he new NEPA regulations will involve all those who are interested. The regulations make them part of the process. If all are part of the process, the Council believes, the process

will be better. The results will be both more environmentally sensitive and less subject to disruptive conflicts and delays. ... [I]nvolve all the necessary people from the beginning to see that the [environmental] impact statement analyzes the information most significant to the ultimate decision. If the important issues receive attention at the outset, later squabbles about the need for more study and new information can be avoided, along with increased costs and substantial delay. ... Real opportunities exist for those skilled in facilitating consensus to aid diverse participants in exploring the issues and agreeing on those to be studied. Then, when a decision is made on a particular proposal, it can at least be agreed that the analytical groundwork was complete and developed fairly.9

NEPA promotes public involvement not just in final decisions but in all aspects of the environmental decision-making process, starting with the original scoping of a government development project or any other action with potential environmental consequences. This can encourage new approaches that are outside the experience or interests of the controlling agency and can increase the understanding of all parties in assessing and dealing with future consequences.[10] Public participation in the environmental decision-making process works best if agencies are actually committed to citizen involvement and take the results seriously. If this is the case, then the resulting decisions are more likely to be satisfactory to parties other than the government agency and those who will benefit from the development project in question.[11]

Unfortunately, NEPA does not ensure that all ultimate government decisions are right for the environment, or how much influence the public really has on the process. As will be discussed throughout this chapter, NEPA promotes decision-making procedures at the expense of the substance of those same decisions. This is the act's major weakness, and a crucial factor on whether there is truly freedom of environmental information in America.

A General History and Overview of NEPA

In the late 1960s and early 1970s, the U.S. Congress passed an array of sweeping new statutes that reflected popular demand for solutions to longstanding social problems, from consumer rights to civil rights. For example, thanks to in-depth media coverage of pollution, the expansion of state and national parks and wilderness areas, and a burgeoning transportation infrastructure, the percentage of Americans professing concern for the environment grew from practically zero in 1960 to twenty-five percent in 1970.[12] Amidst a plethora of public interest statutes like the Federal Meat Inspection Act, the Flammable Fabrics Act, the Child Protection Act, and the Fair Packaging and Labeling Act, the Democratically-controlled Congress passed the National Environmental Policy Act under the then-prevailing notion that the federal government should directly regulate phenomena of concern to citizens.[13]

An omnibus American environmental policy was advocated in the halls of Congress as early as 1959. Existing pollution-control statutes were deemed sufficient until about a decade later, when Senator Henry Jackson (D-Wash.) and Representative John Dingell (D-Mich.) teamed up to develop a comprehensive environmental policy statute.[14] In particular, Jackson had been swayed by arguments that the heretofore piecemeal nature of American environmental legislation created enough uncertainty and gaps in enforcement to enable the very same environmental degradation that those laws attempted to prevent, and it was time to "break the shackles of incremental policy-making in the management of the environment."[15] In Jackson's words on the floor of Congress, "no agency will be able to maintain [in the future] that it has no mandate or no requirement to consider the environmental consequences of its actions."[16]

Records show that Congress believed a true national environmental policy, to be enacted across the operations of the entire federal government, was necessary for improving the state of the natural world in America. Members of the House of Representatives noted that "There may be controversy as to how close to the brink we stand, but there is none that we are in serious trouble."[17] According to the Senate committee that designed the bill that would eventually be passed as the National Environmental Policy Act:

> It is the unanimous view [of the committee] that our Nation's present state of knowledge, our established public policies, and our existing governmental institutions are not adequate to deal with the growing environmental problems and crises the nation faces. ... [I]mportant decisions concerning the use and shape of man's future environment continue to be made in small but steady increments which perpetuate rather than avoid the recognized mistakes of previous decades.[18]

By the time NEPA came up for debate and ratification in late 1969, a Republican, Richard Nixon, occupied the White House while the Democrats maintained control in the House and Senate. Despite threats of partisan gridlock, the early years of Nixon's first term were still conducive to sweeping legislative mandates. The nation was reeling from contentious popular protests surrounding civil rights and the Vietnam War, and the shocking assassinations of Martin Luther King and the Kennedy brothers. By 1969 America was hungry for political consensus and remedies for seemingly unsolvable social problems. Nixon saw the political capital in supporting the rising environmental movement, as did many of his allies in industry.[19] Both political parties took the opportunity to act on behalf of the latest public passion – protection of the natural world and the amelioration of environmental pollution and degradation.[20] The language of NEPA is clear: "The Congress recognizes that each person should enjoy a healthful environment and that each person has a responsibility to contribute to the preservation and enhancement of the environment."[21]

The beginning of the 1970s was a remarkable time for environmental law in America, especially because of the political compromise that was involved. NEPA inspired federal lawmakers to bring together a wide variety of disconnected pollution-control statutes into a new comprehensive American philosophy of environmental protection, with many states leading the way with statutory weapons against their own unique pollution problems.[22] President Nixon personally complied with NEPA by forming the Council on

Environmental Quality within the White House to advise his administration on environmental matters.[23] While the act's text is deceptively simple in declaring a fundamental American environmental policy, the action-forcing procedural requirements of NEPA fundamentally changed the way the federal government does business.[24]

The National Environmental Policy Act, as its name implies, was envisioned by Congress as a vast restructuring of agency policy and procedure that requires all actors in the federal government to make policy decisions with environmental protection in mind.[25] The act essentially orders the federal government to achieve an omnibus environmental policy by "all practical means"[26] and proclaims that government officials must:

1)   fulfill the responsibilities of each generation as trustee of the environment for succeeding generations;
2)   assure for all Americans safe, healthful, productive, and aesthetically and culturally pleasing surroundings;
3)   attain the widest range of beneficial uses of the environment without degradation, risk to health or safety, or other undesirable and unintended consequences;
4)   preserve important historic, cultural, and natural aspects of our national heritage, and maintain, wherever possible, an environment which supports diversity, and variety of individual choice;
5)   achieve a balance between population and resource use which will permit high standards of living and a wide sharing of life's amenities; and
6)   enhance the quality of renewable resources and approach the maximum attainable recycling of depletable resources.[27]

This was lofty rhetoric for a federal statute and a clear attempt to radically reorganize government attitudes toward the natural world. The framers of NEPA intended to substantively transform the decision-making apparatus within federal agencies so that the nation as a whole would recognize environmental protection as a national interest.[28]

Nevertheless, for practical and legal reasons to be discussed below, this all-purpose American policy never came about. Less dramatically, the courts have interpreted NEPA as requiring certain procedures to be followed when agencies make environmentally-relevant decisions, and for the proper management and disclosure of the resulting documents. According to the courts, the primary use of government-held information under NEPA is the mitigation of potential legal disputes and not necessarily the amelioration of unintended environmental damage.[29] Following its introductory policy rhetoric, the statutory text of NEPA inexorably tends toward procedure rather than substance.

The act's informational requirements, at first glance, appear to be dedicated to the prevention of environmental damage. NEPA contains five clauses describing the required language to be used when discussing expected environmental impacts, which impacts cannot be avoided, alternate plans to avoid preventable impacts, the relationship between the short-term human uses of the project vs. the long-term health of the environment, and the resources that will be required to implement the project.[30] The document resulting from this five-part decision-making process is now known as the environmental impact statement (EIS). This informational process must also be made transparent to all other government agencies and to the public.[31] However, while NEPA broke new ground in informational requirements, it also condemned that information to the procedural focus of American jurisprudence rather than the substance of decisions made with that information.

The statutory and judicial focus on procedural matters has become a disadvantage for citizens wishing to utilize NEPA when challenging poor environmental decisions by government actors.[32] Technically speaking, the public can be invited to comment at various stages of the environmental impact statement process, from initial review of the proposed project all the way through to the final draft of the EIS.[33] But in practical terms, the public is not invited to make truly viable comments on agency environmental decisions until relatively late in the process, after significant decisions have already been made by the government agency in question.[34]

The practical neglect of timely outreach to the public, even though NEPA requires more public participation, tends to force citizens to react to environmental damage after it occurs through lawsuits challenging the agency's procedural compliance during that same decision-making process. This phenomenon was criticized by the Court of Appeals for the Third Circuit, which in 2000 chastised the Department of Housing and Urban Development for this injustice while ultimately deciding that on purely procedural grounds, NEPA did not require any change to the ultimate agency decision based on the environmental impact statement in question, which itself was restricted by that same lack of public participation.[35] This unfortunate aspect of administrative law will be discussed in greater detail throughout the remainder of this book.

This is a severe limitation on the ability of NEPA to give citizens proactive opportunities to resist environmentally damaging government projects before development commences. NEPA may only allow affected citizens to fight for remediation of environmental damage after it occurs, and even this is not guaranteed when a dispute over alleged NEPA violations makes it to court.[36] Indeed, like much of American administrative law, the judiciary's procedural focus has made NEPA more reactive than proactive.

A Legal History of NEPA: Information and Reporting

The National Environmental Policy Act is best known for its requirement of an environmental impact statement (EIS) for any action by a government agency or regulated party that will have an impact on the natural environment.[37] The main purpose of an EIS is to help public officials make informed decisions based on an understanding of environmental consequences and reasonable alternative courses of action. These documents must be "supported by evidence that agencies have made the necessary environmental analyses."[38] Although enforcement of this process and the management of the resulting documents were not codified in the original text of NEPA, this responsibility is now under the purview of the Environmental Protection Agency.[39]

Any government agency must ask itself two questions when determining whether NEPA requires an investigation of the environmental consequences of a proposed activity. First, is the proposed activity a "major federal action?" Second, are the environmental impacts likely to be "significant?"[40] The second question, regarding potentially significant environmental impacts and the analysis thereof, has been the basis for much of the case law surrounding environmental impact statements.

Despite the statute's relatively terse text, the EIS process has become quite elaborate, with many decision-makers acting on behalf of one or several federal agencies whenever the government embarks on or regulates any development or construction project. Great amounts of information naturally accumulate during this process, including scientific reports and correspondence among experts and administrators at the agencies involved.[41] The procedural requirements of the environmental impact statement process were meant to discourage wanton destruction of the natural world by parties who now found themselves exposed to public oversight via reports submitted to the government. In turn, sound management of the information gathered during the project planning and permitting stages would offer citizens greater oversight of environmental protection in America.[42]

The original text of NEPA, as ratified in 1969, is very terse on the requirements of an EIS, and the resulting regulatory uncertainty inspired the Council on Environmental Quality (CEQ) to issue much more specific regulations to govern the process.[43] Per the more recent regulations, to determine whether the potential effects of an action are significant, the agency must first conduct a less-detailed environmental assessment (EA), and if this process concludes with a determination of no significant environmental impact, no further environmental analysis is required.[44] Per CEQ regulations, the environmental assessment must be a "precise public document" that briefly provides "sufficient evidence and analysis for determining whether to prepare an environmental impact statement or a finding of no significant impact." The decision not to continue with a more detailed EIS must also be made with "sufficient evidence."[45]

In order to determine whether an EIS is required (a decision based on the prior conclusion of significant potential environmental impact), the agency must consider the proposed action in the context of its surroundings, including factors like the unique characteristics of the geographic area (historical, cultural, and ecological), the degree of potential political controversy if the development were to commence, the potential impact on endangered or threatened species, or whether any environmental or land use statute (federal, state, or local) will be violated.[46] If any of these factors are present, the government agency must continue its analysis with an environmental impact statement. Judicial review[47] is available for citizens who find any fault at this point in the agency's decision-making process, and the Ninth Circuit Court of Appeals has ruled that NEPA allows the judiciary to require an EIS if an agency has not properly shown that one is unnecessary.[48]

For purposes of the present discussion, NEPA requires public participation in the EIS process. Significantly, the statute recognized that citizens should have input in environmental decision-making by government, but may lack the scientific knowledge necessary for full participation. Therefore, the EIS process is designed to benefit the citizen as much as the regulator.[49] While this matter is discussed at a conceptual level in the text of NEPA, later regulations by the Council on Environmental Quality regulate the public participation process in great detail. For example, all agencies are required to post public notices about relevant meetings in a variety of media, and meetings are to be held in locations accessible to citizens who have expressed interest in the decision at hand.[50] CEQ regulations are even more specific on how information is distributed to the public. For example, agencies must specifically point out portions of an EIS that could be most useful to the public, agencies must affirmatively solicit public comments during all segments of the EIS process, and agencies must invite public involvement even before their official duties during a proposed project commence.[51]

Early in the history of NEPA, some agencies tried to release very vague environmental impact statements and claim that the low level of detail was justified under the act's terse text. The courts were called upon to figure out how much scientific detail was necessary for an EIS, and whether there were any remedies for an insufficient EIS. This uncertainty could be deadly, as seen in the 1971 D.C. Circuit case *Commission for Nuclear Responsibility, Inc. v. Seaborg*, in which the court refused to issue an injunction on a proposed nuclear test even after ruling that the Atomic Energy Commission had violated NEPA upon issuing an insufficiently detailed EIS.[52] The 1977 district court case *Environmental Defense Fund v. Costle* epitomized this conundrum and added a further problem: the appeasement of an agency lacking in scientific knowledge. Here the district court ruled that under the original language of NEPA, the EIS process did not require agency knowledge of all potential environmental impacts,[53] thus letting the agency off the hook for its own decision not to increase the scientific detail or reach of its investigations.

In NEPA's early years, there was also no judicial consistency toward handling citizen disputes with under-detailed environmental impact statements. One district court ruled that "all known *possible* environmental consequences of proposed agency action" should be analyzed in an EIS,[54] and another district court ruled that all "significant aspects of *probable* environmental impact" at least merited discussion in an EIS.[55] But on the other hand, one district court found that a discussion in an EIS of "reasonable alternatives" was sufficient, and that the agency had the discretion to make judgment calls when warranted;[56] while a circuit court ruled that any disputed EIS could be found adequate if it simply included a "reasonably thorough discussion of the significant aspects of the probable environmental consequences."[57]

The new, more specific regulations enacted by the Council on Environmental Quality in 1978 alleviated this legal morass, which was caused directly by regulatory uncertainty in the text of NEPA. A major improvement brought by the CEQ regulations was in addressing how agencies could discuss potential environmental impacts when scientific evidence or other information was lacking or unavailable.[58] Agencies were now required to prepare "worst case" analyses of all *possible* environmental impacts in the event of uncertainty, and to disclose the fact that precise information is lacking.[59] These matters are not found anywhere in the original NEPA text concerning environmental impact statements.

In the years immediately after these regulations were enacted in 1978, the courts muddled with the meaning of "worst case" and created a body of case law that was originally as inconsistent as that which inspired the new regulations in the first place. For instance, one circuit court ruled that a "worst case" analysis did not require a discussion of the potential impacts of an earthquake near the site of a proposed dam, and that the EIS must be thorough, but "need not discuss remote and highly speculative consequences."[60] Meanwhile, a different circuit court ruled that an EIS filed by the city of Galveston, Texas, regarding a proposal to dredge its harbor, must discuss the potential effects of a highly speculative total spill of oil from a crashed supertanker.[61]

Recall that NEPA requires public participation in the EIS process, though the true usefulness or effectiveness of this participation is a matter of some logistical and administrative concern. Within their discretion, agencies may restrict input to the level required by their governing statutes, which tend to be more specific on that issue than NEPA, and upon drafting an EIS agency officials may not have to explicitly discuss whatever ideas or concerns are contributed by the public. This conundrum all but invites ambiguity and misunderstanding over when and how citizens can participate in the process, and how much influence they will have, if any. In turn, agencies and citizens will enter the process with significantly different goals and expectations – a problem that has resulted in significant legal confusion over how the entire EIS process should work.[62]

The "significance" of potential environmental impacts, and the reporting thereof, are also sources of legal and administrative confusion. In early EIS-related legal disputes, citizen plaintiffs added unforeseen complexity by claiming that NEPA required the maximum level of significance and intensity in the creation of an EIS. For example, the significance of an agency action depends on the overall setting, especially if the general area has known environmental value. The intensity of the action includes the potential for controversy and even the emotional trauma of nearby residents. Long-term and short-term impacts are also relevant in determining the intensity of a government action. All of these phenomena are very difficult to quantify and added even more uncertainty to the question of how much detail is required in an EIS.[63] The Supreme Court addressed this particular issue in the *Metropolitan Edison* case, ruling that in an EIS the government agency is only required under NEPA to address physical impacts, rather than try to make judgment calls on possible economic, social, or emotional consequences that would be far removed from the agency action in question.[64]

Due to the inconsistency of the rulings in these early EIS disputes, the level of detail required under NEPA for an environmental impact statement remained an unanswered question, plagued by scientific uncertainty and regulatory vagueness. Of course, an effective environmental investigation should include substantial scientific information found during a collaborative and integrated process in which government scientists, outside scientists, and interested citizens are all involved to the fullest extent possible.[65] But the lofty goals of public participation in the process can become logistically burdensome when the time comes to actually investigate the environmental question at hand. To address these emerging legal difficulties, in 1986 the CEQ adjusted its EIS regulations to place less emphasis on often implausible worst case scenarios, and more emphasis on how to deal with scientific uncertainty, with a requirement that agencies attempt to obtain such information but not to the point at which resources are wasted trying to investigate unlikely catastrophic occurrences.[66]

This new regulation attempted to strike a balance between in-depth investigation of environmental consequences and reasonable concessions to scientific uncertainty. The regulation does away with agency guesswork regarding sensational environmental calamities and allows agencies to move forward in their investigations rather than wait for new scientific data to become available. But still, in a victory for transparency, agencies are not permitted to obfuscate environmental impact statements or to avoid taking action just because information is unavailable.[67] In turn, the Ninth Circuit Court of Appeals, in a case known popularly as *Glacier Bay*, ruled that a government agency cannot decide to avoid a full environmental impact statement (stopping the investigation after the environmental assessment) just because scientific information is unavailable. The missing information does not need to apply to improbable worst case scenarios, but its absence in the investigation of more likely environmental impacts must itself be a point of robust discussion in the EIS.[68]

When some relevant science remains uncertain, the most effective EIS would explicitly disclose what information is still desired and what assumptions have been made.[69] Unfortunately, *Glacier Bay* remains a high-level, conceptual precedent at best because the text of NEPA and the CEQ regulations make an EIS so complex that the facts of any dispute over a case of uncertainty are usually unique enough to inspire drawn-out court battles, with contentious arguments over how to handle uncertainty once it is found to be acceptable within the context of a particular EIS.[70]

A large proportion of environmentally-oriented court disputes in America involve citizen disagreements with particular environmental impact statements. Most such cases revolve around whether an EIS is adequate and whether the agency in question followed proper procedures when putting the document together. Due to the judiciary's interest in reviewing agency procedure rather than substantive decision-making, arguing over procedural compliance has become the only viable option for environmentalists in blocking or delaying unwanted development projects, and the citizen plaintiffs often must ask the court to order the agency to draw up another EIS and to do so correctly.[71] This phenomenon is not necessarily the result of regulatory uncertainty surrounding the EIS process altogether, but the result of the procedural focus of American administrative jurisprudence.

The National Environmental Policy Act, as can be seen in its requirements for environmental impact statements, attempts to reach its policy goals by requiring government agencies to follow specific procedures. The process for collecting the information contained in an EIS and the future use and management of that information has become the most far-reaching of NEPA's ramifications. The EIS requirements were originally viewed by the act's drafters as the promotion of information in the public interest, with little speculation about future practical realities. But this information-management requirement has had the most noticeable impact on the behaviors of government actors. While the EIS process does not require that any particular decision be made by the agency in question, in favor of or against environmental protection, agencies have come to consider environmental ramifications much more carefully in order to avoid future disputes in which violations of NEPA could be contested in court.[72]

However, it is important to note that the environmental impact statement process, under NEPA, has been seen by the courts as a procedural requirement and not a substantive requirement. In other words, citizens can challenge government agencies in disputes over environmental damages by claiming violation of the provisions of

NEPA, but courts will likely only consider amelioration of agency actions if the proper procedures for creating an EIS were not followed. For instance, an agency decision based on an EIS that lacks the required detail or specificity can be ruled in violation of NEPA or can be subjected to a more general ruling of "arbitrary and capricious" decision-making per administrative law,[73] and either of these scenarios can result in a court ruling that the agency in question should mitigate or ameliorate environmental damage. Hence, NEPA requires procedural review by the courts in the event of a dispute over agency action. But on the other hand, courts have not interpreted NEPA to require substantive review, meaning that if all proper procedures have been followed in the creation of the EIS, the agency is then free to proceed with its decision-making process, with or without guidance from the information that ended up in the EIS.[74]

NEPA does not require a government agency to take any particular action based on the information collected in an EIS, be it the approval or rejection of a project or the alteration of project plans. Instead, the act simply requires careful and thorough study of a wide range of potential environmental consequences. The environmental impact statement must be comprehensive, acquisitive, and interdisciplinary, with exploration of alternative courses of action and all the potential consequences in order to give the agency in question viable choices if the original project plans are deemed unacceptable.[75] But note that this analysis does not consider the environmental merits of the ultimate agency decision.

Unlike precise pollution control statutes like the Clean Air Act or Clean Water Act, the effectiveness of which can be assessed by measuring actual pollution, the procedural mandates of NEPA resist measurement. In the eyes of detractors, allowing an agency to conduct an EIS for its own proposed actions, and then disallowing judicial review of whether practical decisions have really been made based on the findings therein, is like putting the fox in charge of the henhouse. From the point of view of the environmentally concerned citizen, there is an ultimate irony to the environmental impact statement process. NEPA does not mandate that the EIS be the most influential factor in an agency's final decision, or that it even enter the final decision at all.[76] A development project can be delayed or halted if proper procedures were not followed when the EIS was put together. But once that procedural requirement has been satisfied, neither courts nor anyone else can counteract the substantive decisions that government actors make after the information has been compiled. In the end, NEPA creates information that is delivered transparently to citizens, but this transparency is of little practical use if the information inspires government decisions that are as opaque as ever.

A Legal History of NEPA: Substance and Procedure

The National Environmental Policy Act features a straightforward requirement that each federal agency examine the potential significant environmental impacts of its actions and propose alternative courses of action. The courts have largely agreed with this general procedural requirement, and whenever agencies neglect to think proactively, environmentalists have seized upon NEPA's procedural requirements in court to challenge the lawfulness of destructive government activities and to ensure mitigation or amelioration. The resulting avalanche of citizen suits has caused substantial delays in a wide variety of development projects.[77]

The National Environmental Policy Act went into effect on January 1, 1970, and it was not long before the fundamental meaning of the statute was argued in court. In 1971, the Court of Appeals for the D.C. Circuit noted in the seminal *Calvert Cliffs* case that Congress's intent in enacting NEPA was to bring an end to the brazen lack of respect for the natural world that was then prevalent throughout the federal government.[78] The circuit court took the opportunity to interpret the statutory meaning of NEPA upon hearing a dispute over the Atomic Energy Commission's refusal to comply with EIS requirements when approving permits for a proposed nuclear power plant in Maryland.

Remarkably, the Atomic Energy Commission actually created a full environmental impact statement per the requirements of NEPA, but in an odd display of bureaucratic inertia, the EIS was compiled by just one sub-department within the Commission's bureaucracy and then was never even read by anyone on the licensing committee. So the licensing committee violated NEPA *de facto* by not making any use of the information required under the act. In a lengthy opinion, Judge

Skelly Wright chastised the Commission for this oversight amidst a great amount of dicta on the spirit of NEPA and the need to protect America's natural environment. First, Wright accurately predicted a flood of new litigation that would seek "judicial assistance [under NEPA] in protecting our natural environment." Wright then declared that NEPA "makes environmental protection a part of the mandate of every federal agency and department." The Atomic Energy Commission and other federal agencies are "not only permitted, but compelled, to take environmental values into account," and NEPA requires agencies "to consider environmental issues just as they consider other matters within their mandates."[79] Wright wrapped up the discussion thusly:

> NEPA requires agencies [to] consider the environmental impact of their actions "to the fullest extent possible." The Act is addressed to agencies as a whole, not only to their professional staffs. Compliance to the "fullest" possible extent would seem to demand that environmental issues be considered at every important stage in the decision making process concerning a particular action – at every stage where an overall balancing of environmental and nonenvironmental factors is appropriate and where alterations might be made in the proposed action to minimize environmental costs.[80]

Despite Wright's passionate prose, the outcome of the *Calvert Cliffs* case was more mundane. The Atomic Energy Commission was merely ordered to revise its internal rules in order to come into compliance with NEPA, and there was ultimately no change in the permitting for the nuclear plant.[81] Regardless, the *Calvert Cliffs* ruling gave NEPA equal prominence among existing federal regulations and Wright's promotion of the act's environmental values brought it to the attention of government agencies that, at the time, were unlikely to reconsider their missions in light of this new environmental statute without some prodding from the courts.[82]

However, since then the courts have tended to appreciate the greatness of NEPA's environmental protections at the philosophical level, while emphasizing its procedural requirements in ultimate rulings in EIS disputes. Most importantly, the Supreme Court has ruled that the act is primarily procedural, rather than substantive. In the *Strycker's Bay* case, concerning an allegedly faulty EIS submitted by the Department of Housing and Urban Development, the high court noted that if an agency has followed proper procedures in formulating an EIS, and the ultimate decision has not been made arbitrarily and capriciously, then the procedural requirements of NEPA are satisfied.[83] NEPA does not give judges the authority to overrule any substantive decisions made by an agency, and an agency can make decisions based on its own expertise as long as the information that forms the basis of a decision has been collected satisfactorily. Thus, NEPA allows procedural review, but not substantive review.[84] In other words, NEPA allows poor environmental decision-making that is based on properly-collected environmental information – a perhaps unintentional interpretation of the act that has blunted its effectiveness in actually protecting the American environment.

NEPA litigation is riddled with administrative roadblocks for the concerned environmentalist. The problem is that, unlike some other environmental statutes, NEPA does not contain a provision that allows private citizens to sue for enforcement of the act's provisions. In other words, if a citizen suspects that a government agency has violated NEPA in any way, that citizen cannot directly sue the agency to force compliance with NEPA itself. Instead, NEPA challenges must be advanced under the Administrative Procedure Act, raising problems for citizen involvement that are unique in American administrative law.[85]

The aforementioned *Lujan I* and *Lujan II* cases (see Chapter 3), in addition to illustrating the judiciary's shifting attitudes toward standing for environmentalists and citizens' groups, also illustrated the procedural burdens placed on citizens who disagree with agency environmental decisions. In *Lujan v. National Wildlife Federation* (*Lujan I*) the wildlife group protested a reclassification of federal land without proper environmental investigation, and the government claimed that the group did not have standing to sue because it could not claim direct injury under the Administrative Procedure Act. The high court addressed the matter somewhat differently, turning the standing issue into a question of ripeness and other procedural matters, using this line of reasoning to reject the wildlife group's complaint.[86]

In *Lujan v. Defenders of Wildlife* (*Lujan II*) the wildlife group contested an agency interpretation of the Endangered Species Act, which itself is observed by government agencies under the procedural requirements of NEPA. In the Court's ruling, not only was Defenders of Wildlife unable to prove direct injury (a reprise of the standing issue), the group was also unable to adequately address two other important administrative law requirements – causation and redressability. No proof was offered that the government agency was directly responsible for the environmental harms alleged by the wildlife group, nor that the agency would be able to correct the problem.[87]

These rulings illustrate longstanding matters of administrative law that come into play whenever an agency decides whether or not to follow federal statutes, such as NEPA, that do not have their own internal enforcement mechanisms. When a dispute arises, courts will typically only rule against an agency if a particularly "arbitrary and capricious" statutory violation can be found – and that term tends to apply to an agency's governing statute rather than non-agency-specific statutes.[88] Consequently, environmental litigation has been complicated by the overlapping regulatory requirements caused by a plethora of statutes with conflicting authority over each other. NEPA and all of its more specific progeny fall under the umbrella of the Administrative Procedure Act, which directly regulates the activities of federal agencies,[89] including their observance of environmental laws.

This administrative overlap has blunted the ability of American environmental statutes to protect the natural world, and has turned NEPA's procedural mandate into an Achilles heel. NEPA revolutionized environmental decision-making by government, but its focus on procedure has attracted criticism from both sides of the environmentalist fence. Nature lovers and community activists have criticized NEPA for requiring data to be filed by government-affiliated scientists and bureaucrats who are out of touch with public concerns and may have a history of poor environmental decisions. Meanwhile, the procedural overlap engendered by the pan-government oversight of the Administrative Procedure Act has caused an insidious pattern of bureaucratic delay in the approval of government-sponsored projects and the assessment of unfavorable environmental consequences – a phenomenon that is criticized by both development interests and environmentalists.[90] And most fundamentally, government watchdogs from all sides of the political spectrum decry the bureaucracy-inducing inefficiencies of American administrative law, including environmental decision-making, in which bad substantive decisions will be upheld simply because proper procedures were followed, and usually with great time and expense.[91]

An exemplary circuit court case about pesticides and birds illustrates the often labyrinthine challenges of administrative law, in the context of agency actions that are disputed by citizens and come up for judicial review under the Administrative Procedure Act or any more specific statute that allows judicial review. In the *Defenders* case in 1989, the Eighth Circuit Court of Appeals handed down a crucial ruling on the procedural requirements of environmental litigation, the broader goals of NEPA, and whether the act can truly achieve proactive environmental protection.[92]

The *Defenders* case involved alleged government violations of a series of environmental statutes that are managed under the purview of NEPA: the Endangered Species Act (ESA);[93] the Federal Insecticide, Fungicide, and Rodenticide Act (FIFRA);[94] the Bald and Golden Eagle Protection Act (BGEPA);[95] and the Migratory Bird Treaty Act (MBTA).[96] The overlapping environmental requirements of these various statutes, and their observance under the Administrative Procedure Act (APA), are illustrative of the procedural quagmire of American environmental jurisprudence. In this court dispute, the citizens group Defenders of Wildlife protested the Environmental Protection Agency's classification of certain fungicides and rodenticides containing strychnine as acceptable for above-ground use, believing the classification to be in violation of the aforementioned environmental statutes. The group in turn asked the court to review the agency's compliance with those statutes as well as the administrative requirements of APA.[97]

The primary issue in the case was the EPA's failure to hold an administrative hearing before its most recent classification of the pest-control products containing strychnine. Here the EPA relied on *Environmental Defense Fund, Inc. v. Costle*, in which the Court of Appeals for the D.C. Circuit ruled that an agency need not hold hearings in which environmentalists are invited, because those citizens would have the option of calling for judicial review later.[98] In Defenders the petitioners argued instead that the agency violated the procedural requirements of APA, and in particular its prohibition against "arbitrary and capricious" decision-making.[99] A secondary issue, argued more vigorously by the petitioners, was that the fungicides and rodenticides under dispute were known to harm other animals (especially birds), and these harms could be claimed under the various environmental statutes. The petitioners compiled evidence that use of the disputed products harmed animals that were protected under ESA, BGEPA, and MBTA.

Meanwhile, when classifying the substances in question, the EPA operates under the provisions of the Federal Insecticide, Fungicide, and Rodenticide Act. In its analysis, the court noted that this statute balances the needs of agricultural pest control with environmental protections, and that use of the regulated products should not create unreasonable and adverse effects on the environment. FIFRA includes a judicial review process that is influenced by, but is more specific than, the provisions in APA. Due to the facts of the case, the judicial review and administrative relief procedures of FIFRA were applicable, and the court found that the EPA had not violated these provisions.[100]

This was a momentary setback for Defenders of Wildlife, but FIFRA was not the only statute relevant to the facts of the case. The court also looked into the relevant provisions of the Endangered Species Act. In the case at hand, while the Environmental Protection Agency was operating under FIFRA, it was still prohibited from violating ESA. That statute includes its own judicial review and administrative relief procedures, and allows any person to initiate a civil suit against any government agency for its violation.[101]

Further support was provided by the Administrative Procedure Act. The court reasoned that BGEPA and MBTA (statutes protecting large groupings of birds) did not include private rights of action, so non-governmental citizens' groups could not sue government agencies for noncompliance with those statutes.[102] This may have seemed like a setback for the petitioners, but the court then applied specific provisions of APA, which allows judicial review of agency action when no other administrative relief is available, and mandates judicial review for injuries suffered within the meaning of a relevant statute.[103] Since

BGEPA and MBTA were relevant to the case but effectively made judicial review unavailable on their own terms, the court allowed APA review to kick in instead. Thus, judicial review of the EPA's disputed actions was allowable under FIFRA, ESA, and APA.[104]

The court's conclusion in the *Defenders* case was that the petitioners could indeed pursue a claim against the Environmental Protection Agency and its contested classification of fungicides and rodenticides. The agency was then enjoined from making the disputed classification until it could prove that doing so would not violate the Endangered Species Act, while the procedures warranted by the Administrative Procedure Act must be followed.[105]

However, in addition to the confusing alphabet soup analysis of many overlapping statutes, the ultimate result of the *Defenders* case is that a great amount of procedural contortion is necessary to achieve environmental protection whenever incompatible statutes overlap. The natural resources and animal species protected by these statutes were still adequately protected after the *Defenders* ruling, but this favorable outcome was concocted by the court in a very convoluted fashion. The ruling demonstrates how American administrative law makes proactive environmental protection nearly impossible, with judicial relief only being found after environmental damage has been done, and often with tortuous statutory interpretation by the courts.

This conundrum is the Achilles heel of American environmental law, and in particular the National Environmental Policy Act, the proactive spirit of which has been subsumed by reactive legal realities.[106] The ultimate lesson is that administrative procedure, under which NEPA has been subsumed, favors judicial deference to agency decisions, and the burden of proof has been handed to citizen plaintiffs in disputes over alleged procedural violations by agencies.[107] Generally, the courts will uphold an agency environmental decision if the agency "has considered the relevant factors and articulated a rational connection between the facts found and the choice made."[108] The Supreme Court has ruled that the role of a court in a NEPA dispute is not to interject itself into the agency's "area of discretion... as to the choice of action to be taken" after all required procedures have observed, but simply to ensure that "the agency has taken a 'hard look' at environmental consequences."[109] Hence, the Supreme Court has indeed determined that NEPA is "essentially procedural,"[110] meaning that the act can dictate procedures to be followed by an agency, but says little about judicial review of the resulting environmental decisions.

The result of this judicial focus on NEPA's procedural structure, rather than on the subsequent environmental effects of those procedures, is that federal agencies are given discretion over how to observe the act. This makes enforcement of NEPA's procedural requirements a *post-hoc* process that will not be considered by the courts until after a violation (and the subsequent environmental damage) has occurred, and after other interested parties have recognized the violation and have initiated the legal process.[111] Even then, the courts can only review whether the precise procedures of NEPA were followed.[112]

This leaves internal agency discretion as the deciding factor in compliance with NEPA, to which the courts have historically deferred.[113] One of the major goals of NEPA is to expose potential environmental damage by the federal government and thus encourage public criticism and legal challenges.[114] But given the judiciary's *post-hoc* procedural view of NEPA, whenever a potentially destructive project is proposed, an agency may be tempted to craft the environmental assessment process for the support of its own mission.[115] Even though NEPA requires an agency to consider environmental impacts in detail, the problem is that the only effects that may be judicially reviewable will be those reported with a degree of detail that will convince the average judge. Even worse, the responsibility for providing those details will belong to potential plaintiffs in hypothetical future lawsuits.[116]

This conundrum has been addressed by one court in a case involving NEPA. The court in *City of Davis* found that making an agency's compliance with NEPA contingent upon hypothetical challenges from future plaintiffs might encourage the agency to evade its environmental responsibilities.[117] Unfortunately, that particular ruling did not solve the problem that it so articulately described. The continuing conundrum is that plaintiffs who suspect that an agency has violated NEPA are forced to compile the information that should have been compiled by the agency *before* the violation took place. Thus, the plaintiffs (who are typically private citizens) are performing the tasks that NEPA requires of the agencies. Meanwhile the agencies are effectively encouraged to ignore their NEPA duties, and take the arguably remote risk of being required to comply more fully with the act *after* citizens have taken on the burden of proof.[118]

In cases involving suspected NEPA violations, the courts have largely tried to avoid intruding on an agency's discretion in its own area of expertise. The agency is thus allowed to make the ultimate choice of whether, and to what degree, it carries out its environmental impact statement obligations under NEPA. As a result, this purely procedural view of NEPA preserves the independent discretion of those agencies toward environmental protection, and severely handicaps the act's ability to require compliance from agencies.[119] Unfortunately, in its current form NEPA is largely powerless in preventing environmental degradation before it occurs, and this severely damages the very spirit of the act.

As this legal history shows, NEPA's central goal of environmental protection is shrouded in generalizations and arcane procedures, leaving much discretion to agencies and courts, who have concocted practically as many different interpretations of the statute as there are agencies and courts.[120] Environmentalists might not be aware of the act's procedural inability to achieve its policy goals of natural protection. If anything, NEPA has succeeded merely in allowing interested parties to talk about possible environmental destruction in the form of voluminous reports, without the need to take any action to prevent that destruction.

The NEPA Transparency Clause

Does the National Environmental Policy Act truly create information that can be useful to citizens in striving for protection of the American environment? The precise procedural requirements of NEPA, and the amount of investigatory detail that has become necessary for an EIS, has greatly improved the transparency of government agencies in their interactions with the environment.[121]

The Freedom of Information Act (FOIA)[122] is the primary government transparency statute in America. Although FOIA was still relatively untested itself at the time NEPA was passed, regulators and government watchdogs had learned that procedural requirements forcing the disclosure of documents were altering the behavior of federal agencies. Chances were that an environmentally specific information disclosure provision in NEPA would be beneficial for both regulators and citizens, who would have greater knowledge during disputes with the government over matters of environmental protection.[123]

When it was passed in 1966, FOIA applied transparency to most of the U.S. Government, and that spirit of openness inspired many statutes that were passed in the next few years, including the National Environmental Policy Act. Perhaps most importantly, FOIA mandates judicially enforceable access to government-held information and operates on a philosophy of full disclosure, thus limiting the discretion of officials to withhold documents requested by citizens.[124] Of interest in the environmental arena are the provisions in FOIA that require agencies to release to the public, upon request, information concerning agency procedures and methodologies, forms and reports, and statements of general agency policy.[125]

FOIA was designed by the U.S. Congress to provide citizen access to government documents from a wide variety of federal agencies, which are the holders of the vast majority of the documents created and managed by the federal government.[126] Also recall that the Administrative Procedure Act regulates the creation and management of documents at federal agencies, resulting in huge amounts of information. By extension, federal agencies are the holders of the vast majority of government-held documents on environmental investigation and protection. Importantly, these disclosure requirements apply to all other laws that agencies follow, including NEPA.

Importantly, NEPA contains a specific provision providing citizen access to the information generated when government bodies proceed through the environmental decision-making process.[127] The act requires that agencies "make available to States, counties, municipalities, institutions, and individuals, advice and information useful in restoring, maintaining, and enhancing the quality of the environment."[128] NEPA also contains a related requirement that proper information on environmental impacts be collected by government officials before, during, and after major agency actions.[129] In other words, American citizens are entitled to information about the government's activities that affect the environment, and that access is statutorily protected by NEPA.

Buried within a section of NEPA that otherwise regulates the EIS process is a transparency clause pertaining to the information accumulated during that process. In turn, this clause is just one portion of a larger paragraph that requires inter-agency cooperation on environmental matters, based on a particular agency's expertise. The relevant portion of the paragraph is stated thus:

> Copies of such statement [EIS] and the comments and views of the appropriate Federal, State, and local agencies, which are authorized to develop and enforce environmental standards, shall be made available to the President, the Council on Environmental Quality and to the public as provided by section 552 of title 5, United States Code, and shall accompany the proposal through the existing agency review processes[.][130]

This transparency provision is strengthened by the Administrative Procedure Act, which requires the collection and management of documents by agencies, and public participation in the processes that engender those documents; while the Freedom of Information Act requires those documents to be made available to the public. Both of those requirements, thanks to the transparency clause of the National Environmental Policy Act, were now applied to environmentally-relevant information held by the federal government.[131]

The U.S. Supreme Court has enforced this procedural connection among the various administrative statutes, ruling in 1981 that any disclosure requirement under the NEPA transparency provision is also governed by the disclosure requirements of the Freedom of Information Act.[132] These interconnected statutes now make it possible for interested members of the public to make informed judgments about government environmental decisions while the agencies are still in the decision-making process, and allow citizens some influence over ultimate agency decisions.[133] Though it should be noted that neither

NEPA, FOIA, nor APA require government agencies to actually *use* public input during the decision-making process, only encourage it; while the documents to be made transparent and accessible later in the process are not required to describe whether or not public input was utilized, and why or why not.

Unfortunately, the NEPA transparency clause has a meager case history and there is no definitive court precedent that confirms the transparency of government-held environmental information. A targeted search reveals that of the thousands of lawsuits involving NEPA from 1969 (the year the act was passed) to 2009, 113 cases mention the NEPA transparency provision. (Most of the rest of the cases pertain to procedural problems related to various stages of the environmental impact statement process.) A quick review of the relevant cases shows that many of them only cite the statutory language of the transparency provision in footnotes. Only a small percentage of those cases discuss in detail the transparency of the government-held information at issue, but this topic was not germane to the ultimate rulings in those cases. Subsequently, access to government-held documents after a final decision has been made, per the NEPA transparency provision, has never been the sole topic of dispute in any case in the federal courts. Also, legal precedent regarding the transparency of the EIS process in general has been confined to a variety of inconsistent rulings from the circuit courts, and the issue has not yet been argued before the Supreme Court.

The earliest case to involve the transparency and public participation provisions of NEPA came before the Fourth Circuit soon after the act went into effect. In a relatively unique ruling that does not reflect the almost purely procedural approach that would be adopted later in the act's career, the court in *Arlington Coalition on Transportation v. Volpe* admonished the government agency for violating the public participation spirit of NEPA by forgetting (or refusing) to file an environmental impact statement for a Virginia highway construction project.[134] Perhaps inspired by the lingering spirit of natural protection that engendered the passage of the act, Judge James Braxton Craven of the Fourth Circuit declared the dispute "an ecology case" and a "value judgment" while quoting the preamble of NEPA in which the nation is instructed to act "as trustee of the environment for succeeding generations."[135] The court ordered a halt to the highway project until after the completion of an adequate EIS, after the document was made available to the public, and after public comments were collected and considered. Of particular note is Judge Craven's emphasis on what type of public comments were required, in particular "information about the social effects of the proposed location, its impact on the environment, and its consistency with the community's urban planning goals."[136]

The spirit of community environmental stewardship, and the government transparency that can make it a reality, appeared in a few other circuit court cases during the first few years of NEPA. Another case involving a federal highway project, brought by a Connecticut citizens' group called I-291 WHY?, inspired a similar ruling from the Second Circuit in 1975. In this case, the court found that the Department of Transportation neglected to include scientific information on the air and noise pollution effects of the highway project in the environmental impact statement, even though there was some knowledge on these matters held by government officials. Furthermore, the absence of this information in the EIS violated the transparency and public participation provisions of NEPA, and prevented citizens from making use of the information. This was another early victory for environmental transparency under NEPA, with an outcome that reflected the environmental spirit of the act, because the Connecticut highway project was halted until the government officials in question improved the EIS and solicited public comments properly.[137]

Unfortunately for environmental advocates, these early circuit court victories were based on an interpretation of the substantive spirit of NEPA that was not adopted by all the circuits. A contemporaneous decision by the Ninth Circuit not only reflected a different view of the spirit of NEPA and its transparency requirements, but was also a harbinger of what would soon become the dominant trend in environmental jurisprudence: the move away from substantive environmental policy and toward the enforcement of proper administrative procedures. This ruling, concerning citizen opposition to an expansion of Honolulu International Airport in Hawai'i, did particular damage to the public's ability to participate during the environmental impact statement process.[138]

The EIS for the airport project was partially researched and written by an engineering firm that had also been awarded a lucrative state contract for runway construction, but the circuit court found no statutory language in NEPA that precluded such arrangements.[139] More fundamentally, a draft EIS was made available to the public and comments were gathered, but these comments were not discussed in the final EIS and apparently did not influence that document in any way. The court's reaction to this problem illustrates a significant turning point in NEPA jurisprudence, in that no evidence was found that the statutory text of NEPA imposed a procedural requirement for the attachment of public comments to a final EIS. It is important to note that while citizen comments were absent from the final EIS for the airport project, the comments of several interested engineering firms, local officials, and the Federal Aviation Administration were present in the document. Regardless, the circuit court did not find any reason to declare the final EIS inadequate under NEPA, after a strict reading of the text of the statute and a focus on procedural requirements. Thus, the airport expansion project was allowed to proceed.[140]

This ruling reflects a proper reading of procedural requirements in the spirit of established administrative jurisprudence. However, the ruling became a dangerous precedent that may have irreparably damaged the transparency and public participation provisions of NEPA. The ruling was short-sighted and assumed that only the citizens and officials involved in the present dispute would ever wish to take action on the issue at any time. In reality, any citizen who might wish to challenge environmentally-relevant events at the expanded Honolulu International Airport, such as fuel leaks or declining local wildlife populations, would make use of the project's environmental impact statement in the future. Thanks to the Ninth Circuit decision, those citizens would only know how engineering firms and government officials felt about the project, and would not know that many citizen comments were collected on matters of noise pollution, water quality, recreation, and wildlife.[141] The public comments, submitted for the draft EIS, are a matter of the public record but would be in the possession of the government agencies in question, and would not be visible in the final EIS that is made much more transparent by the requirements of NEPA. Instead, the existence of such comments would have to be discovered by citizens on their own and would have to be obtained via requests under the Administrative Procedure Act or the Freedom of Information Act.

After the 1970s, circuit court jurisprudence surrounding the transparency provisions of NEPA inexorably turned toward a procedural focus that favored agency action rather than citizen oversight. Recall from the previous section that by 1980 the reigning precedents for NEPA procedural disputes (at a higher level than the transparency and public participation provisions) had been established by the Supreme Court. In the seminal *Strycker's Bay* case the high court declared NEPA to be "essentially procedural" and that the judicial branch should review the act accordingly.[142] Meanwhile, in the *Kleppe* case the high court defined the mission of the judicial branch in reviewing the adequacy of environmental impact statements, declaring that "the only role for a court is to insure that the agency has taken a 'hard look' at environmental consequences; it cannot interject itself within the area of discretion of the executive as to the choice of the action to be taken."[143] This purely procedural focus would come to overwhelm transparency in citizen challenges to the adequacy of the EIS process and the true usefulness of the ensuing government-held information.

In a 1980 case involving the construction of a dam by the Army Corps of Engineers, the Ninth Circuit turned to the Administrative Procedure Act when ruling that the agency had acted in good faith and attempted to comply with NEPA even though it neglected to solicit public comments during a stage of the EIS process, and that the ultimate decision made after this act of forgetfulness was not arbitrary and capricious.[144] In 1982 the Second Circuit briefly (and inconsistently with the other circuit courts) delivered a brief respite for transparency under NEPA, ruling that two different federal agencies had erred in not publicly disclosing some crucial information on the EIS for a New York State landfill and highway construction project. However, here the Second Circuit still avoided the substantive policy goals of NEPA and issued a purely procedural ruling in which the state was instructed to compensate the citizen plaintiffs for their legal costs. The project was not halted, except for an order to the agency to draw up a supplemental EIS, because the court found that the NEPA violation was not an act of bad faith.[145]

Further indicating the lack of consistency among the circuit courts, in 1983 the Seventh Circuit illustrated another challenge of American administrative jurisprudence. The *West Chicago* case concerned a dispute over lack of public participation in the environmental impact statement process. In short, the Nuclear Regulatory Commission did not solicit public comment from the city itself during the drafting of the EIS for the demolition of buildings believed to contain radioactive waste from old industrial processes. The court primarily analyzed the requirements of the agency's specific governing statute while offering almost no analysis of the government-wide requirements of NEPA.[146]

The agency, in accordance with the procedural requirements of the 1954 Atomic Energy Act, offered an informal public hearing with limited notice to citizens and lesser recording of comments than what would be required at a formal hearing.[147] The agency's decision to issue a permit for the project was challenged by the city per the public participation requirements of NEPA, but the court instead analyzed the Atomic Energy Act and found no violations of that statute's procedural mandates.[148] In turn, the court applied the public notice and hearing requirements of the Atomic Energy Act to the more stringent public participation mandates of NEPA, regardless of the differing levels of transparency and participation required. Hence, after a rather convoluted procedural analysis the court found that the agency had not violated NEPA simply because it had not violated its own governing statute. This finding was made even though the agency hadn't even submitted an environmental impact statement, as required by NEPA, because such an action was not required by the Atomic Energy Act and the agency had therefore not acted in bad faith.[149]

The *West Chicago* ruling may or may not reflect proper administrative procedure (via quite twisted judicial analysis), but the conflict between the agency-specific statute and the government-wide goals of NEPA allowed the court to disregard the public participation and EIS requirements of NEPA altogether. While the procedural prerogatives of government agencies are upheld by this ruling, the conflict between NEPA and other statutes is not so uncommon as to allow the total disregard of NEPA, which is what happened in the *West Chicago* ruling. This Seventh Circuit decision does not bode well for environmental impact statements, or for the ability of citizens to become involved in potentially crucial environmental decisions by federal agencies.

The overall lesson to be learned from the legal history of the National Environmental Policy Act, from procedure to substance to its specific transparency provisions, is that the act has not achieved its substantive policy goals of nationwide environmental protection. This is not because those policy goals are unviable, but because the courts have refused to enforce them, or even fully consider them, when traditional administrative jurisprudence calls for exact standards of judicial review of miniscule procedural requirements. In other words, a strict procedural focus blurs the diagnosis of the environmental problems that NEPA seeks to cure.[150]

Chapter 4 Notes

[1] 42 U.S.C. §§ 4321-4375 (1970).

[2] Lynton K. Caldwell, "A Constitutional Law for the Environment: 20 Years with NEPA Indicates the Need," *Environment* 31 (Dec. 1989): 8.

[3] 42 U.S.C. §§ 4332(C)(i)- 4332(C)(v).

[4] 42 U.S.C. § 4332(C). Subsequent non-environmental federal statutes have added special transparency requirements for government-held documents in other subject areas, such as security and finance. Alasdair Roberts, *Blacked Out: Government Secrecy in the Information Age* (New York: Cambridge University Press, 2006), 150-170; Cynthia A. Williams, "The Securities and Exchange Commission and Corporate Transparency," *Harvard Law Review* 112 (1999): 1276-1289.

[5] James Salzman and Barton H. Thompson, Jr., *Environmental Law and Policy* (New York: Foundation Press, 2003), 275.

[6] James W. Spensley, Esq., "National Environmental Policy Act," in *Environmental Law Handbook*, vol. 14, ed. Thomas F.P. Sullivan (Rockville, Md.: Government Institutes, Inc., 1997), 404.

[7] National Research Council of the National Academies, *Public Participation in Environmental Assessment and Decision Making* (Washington, D.C.: The National Academies Press, 2008), 37-38.

[8] Executive Order No. 11,514, 35 C.F.R. 4247 (1970).

[9] Quoted in National Research Council of the National Academies, 38-39.

[10] Ibid., 39.

[11] Ibid., 99.

[12] James McEvoy, "The American Concern with the Environment," in *Social Behavior, Natural Resources, and the Environment*, ed. William Burch, Neil H. Cheek, Jr., and Lee Taylor (New York: Harper & Row, 1972), 214-236.

[13] Richard J. Lazarus, *The Making of Environmental Law* (Chicago: University of Chicago Press, 2004), 53.

[14] Spensley, 405.

[15] Henry Jackson, "Environmental Policy and the Congress," *Natural Resources Journal* 11 (1971): 406.

[16] Hearings on S. 1075, S. 237 and S. 1752 Before Senate Committee on Interior and Insular Affairs, 91st Cong., 1st Sess., 206 (1969).

[17] U.S. House of Representatives Report No. 91-378 (1969), 4.

[18] U.S. Senate Report No. 91-296 (1969), 4-5.

[19] By the time of his 1972 reelection, Nixon had abandoned environmentalism and re-aligned himself with industrial interests that had reacted negatively to the increased regulations, for which Nixon had played an instrumental role just a few years before. This political about-face symbolized the end of civil rights-inspired bipartisanship, which had run out of steam by Nixon's second presidential term. J. Brooks Flippen, *Nixon and the Environment* (Albuquerque, N.M.: University of New Mexico Press, 2000), 199-214.

[20] Lazarus, 53-54. Federal lawmakers were probably also reacting to developments in the states, where 112 pollution control laws were enacted in 1967 alone.

[21] 42 U.S.C. § 4331(c).

[22] Lazarus, 67-68.

[23] The council was officially established at § 4342.

[24] Lazarus, 68.

[25] Samuel P. Hays, *Wars in the Woods: The Rise of Ecological Forestry in America* (Pittsburgh, Pa.: University of Pittsburgh Press, 2007), 6.

[26] 42 U.S.C. § 4331(b).

[27] 42 U.S.C. §§ 4331(b)(1)-4331(b)(6).

[28] Matthew J. Lindstrom, "Procedures Without Purpose: The Withering Away of the National Environmental Policy Act's Substantive Law," *Journal of Land Resources & Environmental Law* 20 (2000): 249.

[29] Hays, *Wars in the Woods*, 6. This is largely a phenomenon of case law, as NEPA contains provisions requiring that the environmental consequences of all federally-approved activities be carefully analyzed *before* those activities are carried out. However, citizen or judicial review of this process is impossible until *after* those activities are carried out. This paradox will be discussed extensively below,

[30] 42 U.S.C. §§ 4332(C)(i)-4332(C)(v).

[31] 42 U.S.C. §§ 4332(C). This rather obscure clause will be discussed in detail later in this chapter.

[32] Uma Outka, "NEPA and Environmental Justice: Integration, Implementation, and Judicial Review," *Boston College Environmental Affairs Law Review* 33 (2006): 607.

[33] Spensley, 422.

[34] Outka, 609-610.

[35] Society Hill Towers Owners' Association v. Rendell, 210 F.3d 168, 183-184 (3rd Cir. 2000).

[36] Sheila Foster, "Environmental Justice in an Era of Devolved Collaboration," *Harvard Environmental Law Review* 26 (2002): 484-485.

[37] 42 U.S.C. § 4332(C). According to the statute, the EIS requirement applies to all agencies of the federal government. The EIS process has since evolved into a two-step process involving a preliminary and less-detailed Environmental Assessment (EA), with greater agency discretion over what constitutes a potential environmental impact. Spensley, 416-424.

[38] 40 C.F.R. § 1500.2(b).

[39] This was the result of an agreement between the EPA and the Council on Environmental Quality. U.S. Environmental Protection Agency, *National Environmental Policy Act: EIS Filing System Guidance*, 1989, http.//www.epa.gov/compliance/resources/policies/nepa/fileguide.html, accessed 23 June 2010.

[40] Salzman and Thompson, 277-278.

[41] 42 U.S.C. §§ 4332 (C)(i)-4332(C)(v). In the statute, the EIS process is described in just five partial sentences, though with enough open-ended terminology (such as "impact", "alternatives," and "relationship") to make the process much more complex during subsequent jurisprudence.

[42] The true extent of the EIS process has been simplified here for ease of discussion. Note that there are a great many procedural requirements and investigative stages not discussed in detail here, starting with scoping meetings with the federal agency that regulates the party proposing the development project, data collection, assessment of potential impacts, a preliminary draft EIS, a draft EIS, collection of public comments, a preliminary final EIS, a final EIS, and a record of the final decision made by the agency. Jacob I. Bregman, *Environmental Impact Statements*, 2nd ed. (Boca Raton, Fla.: Lewis Publishers: 1999), 24-28. See also Spensley, 405-407.

[43] In 1977, President Jimmy Carter increased the CEQ's powers and ordered it to tailor specific regulations for the EIS process. Executive Order No. 11,991, 3 C.F.R. 123 (1977). This order reflected Carter's goal that "impact statements be concise, clear, and to the point." The resulting CEQ regulations are found at 40 C.F.R. §§ 1500-1508 (1978).

[44] 40 C.F.R. § 1501.3(a). In environmental law, the conclusion of insignificant potential effects is known by the acronym FONSI, or "Finding of No

Significant Impact." The FONSI process and its effects will be discussed in more detail in Chapter 7.

[45] 40 C.F.R. § 1508.9(a)(1), defining the content of an EA; 40 C.F.R. § 1501.4(e), defining the process for deciding whether to continue with an EIS; 40 C.F.R. § 1508.13, defining "significant impact."

[46] 40 C.F.R. § 1508.27(b). This particular regulation highlights ten factors that must be considered, when relevant, in assessing the potential intensity of a government development project. The provision about endangered and threatened species is required under the Endangered Species Act, which was passed after NEPA but before the CEQ regulations.

[47] Judicial review, an important component of the legal history discussed in this and the following chapters, is the process by which American courts can overturn a government agency decision if statutorily-required procedures were not followed when the decision was made. In administrative law, the procedures for courts to follow when reviewing an agency decision, considering the agency's statutory duties, and determining how much deference to give to the agency's subject matter expertise were largely laid out by the Supreme Court in Chevron USA, Inc. v. Natural Resources Defense Council, 467 U.S. 837 (1984).

[48] LaFlamme v. Federal Energy Regulatory Commission, 852 F.2d 389, 398 (9th Cir. 1988).

[49] Bregman, 30.

[50] 40. C.F.R. §§ 1506.6(b)-1506.6(c).

[51] 40. C.F.R. §§ 1500.4(f), 1503.1(a), 1501.2(d).

[52] 463 F.2d 796, 798 (D.C. Cir. 1971).

[53] 439 F.Supp. 980, 991-993 (E.D.N.Y. 1977).

[54] Environmental Defense Fund v. Army Corps of Engineers, 325 F.Supp. 749, 759 (E.D. Ark. 1971). Emphasis added.

[55] Environmental Defense Fund v. Army Corps of Engineers, 348 F.Supp. 916, 933 (N.D. Miss. 1972). Emphasis added. These two cases are not the same despite their identical names. Both involved disputes between the citizens' environmental group and the development-oriented Corps, arising from different projects to dam rivers for purposes of navigation and power generation. Projects of this type were a primary source of environmental controversy in the 1960s and 1970s.

[56] Farmland Preservation Association v. Adams, 491 F.Supp. 601, 605, 609 (N.D. Iowa, 1979). This case involved a dispute over the EIS for a segment of an interstate highway.

[57] Trout Unlimited v. Morton, 509 F.2d 1276, 1283 (9th Cir. 1974). This was another case of a dispute over a dam and hydropower project, in which the citizens' group attempted to block the agency decision by petitioning for review of the EIS process as followed by the agency.

[58] Carla Mattix and Kathleen Becker, "Scientific Uncertainty Under the National Environmental Policy Act," *Administrative Law Review* 54 (2002): 1131.

[59] 40 C.F.R. § 1502.22. Emphasis added.

[60] Warm Springs Dam Task Force v. Gribble, 621 F.2d 1017, 1026 (9th Cir. 1980).

[61] Sierra Club v. Sigler, 695 F.2d 957, 974 (5th Cir. 1983).

[62] National Research Council of the National Academies, 43, 45.

[63] Salzman and Thompson, 279-280.

[64] Metropolitan Edison Co. v. People Against Nuclear Energy, 460, U.S. 766, 777-778 (1983). This case concerned a citizen challenge to an EIS that addressed the possible reopening of Pennsylvania's Three Mile Island nuclear facility, which had been shuttered since a radioactive leak in 1979.

[65] National Research Council of the National Academies, 234.

[66] 51 Fed. Reg. § 15,618 (1986).

[67] Mattix and Becker, 1134-1135.

[68] National Parks & Conservation Association v. Babbitt, 241 F.3d 722, 732-736 (9th Cir. 2001). This case is known as *Glacier Bay* because it involved a dispute over an EIS that investigated proposed increases in boating permits at Alaska's Glacier Bay National Park.

[69] National Research Council of the National Academies, 236.

[70] Mattix and Becker, 1164-1165.

[71] Salzman and Thompson, 281-282.

[72] Hays, *Wars in the Woods*, 181-182.

[73] NEPA, of course, applies specifically to environmentally-oriented agency actions. An "arbitrary and capricious" ruling is supported by an often-used provision of the Administrative Procedure Act, which can be applied to any type of agency action. 5 U.S.C. § 706(2)(A).

[74] Hays, *Wars in the Woods*, 182.

[75] Ibid., 6-7.

[76] Bregman, 5.

[77] Lazarus, 68. In 2008 alone, NEPA was mentioned in, or was the primary basis of, 154 cases in the federal court system.

[78] Calvert Cliffs Coordinating Committee v. Atomic Energy Commission, 449 F.2d 1109 (D.C. Cir. 1971).

[79] 449 F.2d 1111-1112.

[80] 449 F.2d 1118. Here Wright was referencing NEPA at 42 U.S.C. § 4332(2)(C), which regulates the environmental impact statement process.

[81] 449 F.2d 1129. Even though the citizens' group was the immediate victor in this case, the Maryland nuclear facility was built and opened four years later, after the Atomic Energy Commission made proper use of its own EIS in light of the court's ruling.

[82] Salzman and Thompson, 276-277.

[83] Strycker's Bay Neighborhood Council v. Karlen, 444 U.S. 223, 227 (1980). "Arbitrary and capricious" decision-making by government agencies is prohibited under the Administrative Procedure Act, 5 U.S.C. § 706 (2)(A). This case offers an intriguing example of how all government agencies, even those that one may think had no impact on the environment, do indeed have impacts that are regulated by NEPA. Here, the Department of Housing and Urban Development was required to submit an EIS for a proposed low-income housing development in Manhattan that was opposed by local residents.

[84] Salzman and Thompson, 277.

[85] Outka, 618.

[86] 497 U.S. 871, 891-894 (1990).

[87] 504 U.S. 555, 568-571 (1992).

[88] The Administrative Procedure Act governs the processes followed by the courts in reviewing regulatory agency decisions, and permits a court to find that an agency has violated a statute if its actions are deemed arbitrary, capricious, or an abuse of discretion; in excess of statutory jurisdiction; or a failure to observe legally required procedures. 5 U.S.C. §§ 706(2)(A), 706(2)(C), 706(2)(D).

[89] 5 U.S.C. § 551.

[90] Wendy E. Wagner, "Commons Ignorance: The Failure of Environmental Law to Produce Needed Information on Health and the Environment," *Duke Law Journal* 53 (2004): 1622-1623.

[91] National Research Council of the National Academies, 9-10.

[92] Defenders of Wildlife v. Administrator, Environmental Protection Agency, 882 F.2d 1294 (8th Cir. 1989). This case should not be confused with *Lujan II* (discussed above) which also involved Defenders of Wildlife.

[93] 16 U.S.C. §§ 1531-1544 (1973).

[94] 7 U.S.C. § 136 (1972).

[95] 16 U.S.C. § 668 (1959).

[96] 16 U.S.C. §§ 703-712 (1918).

[97] 882 F.2d 1296-1298.

[98] 631 F.2d 922, 932-937 (D.C. Cir. 1980). This case also involved a citizen dispute with an EPA decision concerning a substance covered by FIFRA.

[99] 5 U.S.C. §706(2)(A).

[100] 882 F.2d 1298-1299.

[101] 16 U.S.C. § 1540(2).

[102] 882 F.2d 1301-1302.

[103] 5 U.S.C. § 704, 702.

[104] 882 F.2d 1302-1303.

[105] 882 F.2d 1303-1304.

[106] Harvey Bartlett, "Is NEPA Substantive Review Extinct, or Merely Hibernating? Resurrecting NEPA Section 102(1)," *Tulane Environmental Law Journal* 13 (2000): 428-433.

[107] The fact that citizens bear the burden of proof was confirmed by the Supreme Court in Baltimore Gas & Electric Company v. Natural Resources Defense Council, 462 U.S. 87, 105 (1987); and Department of Transportation v. Public Citizen, 541 U.S. 752, 763 (2004).

[108] Baltimore Gas & Electric Company v. Natural Resources Defense Council, 462 U.S. 87, 105 (1987).

[109] Kleppe v. Sierra Club, 427 U.S. 390, 410 (1976). This case stemmed from citizen demands for a comprehensive environmental impact statement for a regional resource development plan, including coal mining permit plans by the Department of the Interior, for a very large region of the American midwest.

[110] Vermont Yankee Nuclear Power Corp. v. Natural Resources Defense Council, 435 U.S. 519, 558 (1978). This case involved citizen disputes over a nuclear plant license, and will be discussed in more detail in Chapter 7.

[111] Nicholas C. Yost, "NEPA's Promise – Partially Fulfilled," *Environmental Law* 20 (1990): 547-549.

[112] Natural Resources Defense Council v. Morton, 458 F.2d 827, 838 (1972). This case involved a question of the how much discussion of alternative plans of action is required in an environmental impact statement. This ruling has since been cited by the Supreme Court in Kleppe v. Sierra Club, 427 U.S. 390, 410 (1976); and Strycker's Bay Neighborhood Council, Inc. v. Karlen, 444 U.S. 223, 227-228 (1980).

[113] Abramson, 282-283.

[114] Susannah T. French, "Judicial Review of the Administrative Record in NEPA Litigation," *California Law Review* 81 (1993): 962-963.

[115] Caldwell, 25-26. For a list of cases in which NEPA's possible obstructions of an agency's primary mission were argued, see French, 962-963, n210.

[116] French, 964.

[117] City of Davis v. Coleman, 521 F.2d 661, 678 (9th Cir. 1975). The impetus for this case was the failure of a variety of federal agencies to solicit public comments when drafting an environmental impact statement for a highway construction project.

[118] French, 965. Emphasis added.

[119] Ibid., 966.

[120] Bradley C. Karkkainen, "Whither NEPA?," *New York University Environmental Law Journal* 12 (2004): 333-334.

[121] Salzman and Thompson, 284-285.

[122] 5 U.S.C. § 552 (1966).

[123] Lazarus, 85-86.

[124] Martin E. Halstuk, "When Secrecy Trumps Transparency: Why the OPEN Government Act of 2007 Falls Short," *CommLaw Conspectus* 16 (2008): 430.

[125] 5 U.S.C. §§ 552(a)(1)(B)-552 (a)(1)(D).

[126] Halstuk, "When Secrecy Trumps Transparency," 430.

[127] 42 U.S.C. § 4332(C).

[128] 42 U.S.C. § 4332(G).

[129] 42 U.S.C. §§ 4332(A), 4332(B).

[130] 42 U.S.C. § 4332(C). Emphasis added. The referenced portion of the United States Code is the Freedom of Information Act.

[131] National Research Council of the National Academies, 38.

[132] Weinberger v. Catholic Action of Hawai'i/Peace Education Project, 454 U.S. 139, 143 (1981). This case involved a dispute over national security, with the U.S. Navy arguing that withholding certain information from the EIS in

question was allowed under the national security exemption to FOIA. The Navy's use of that exemption was permitted by the high court, though the ruling tied together the transparency provisions of FOIA and NEPA. The Council on Environmental Quality allows limited exemptions for the disclosure of sensitive security-related information on an EIS. 40 C.F.R. § 1507.3(c) (1978).

[133] National Research Council of the National Academies, 38.

[134] 458 F.2d 1323 (4th Cir. 1972). One issue of concern in this case was that the project, for Interstate 66 in northern Virginia, was approved before NEPA went into effect. However, the court found that NEPA and its requirements could be applied to ongoing projects with several phases of construction, which was indeed the case for the I-66 project. 458 F.2d 1330-1332.

[135] 458 F.2d 1326. Craven quoted NEPA at 42 U.S.C. § 4331.

[136] 458 F.2d 1339. This ruling was bolstered by similar public comment requirements in the Federal-Aid Highway Act, 23 U.S.C. §§ 101-166 (1956).

[137] I-291 WHY? Association v. Burns, 517 F.2d 1077, 1080-1081 (2nd Cir. 1975).

[138] Life of the Land v. Brinegar, 485 F.2d 460 (9th Cir. 1973).

[139] 485 F.2d 467. The court concluded that NEPA requires the government agency to take final responsibility for the accuracy and adequacy of the EIS, which should inspire the agency to avoid ethical questions before the process begins.

[140] 485 F.2d 468-473. Emphasis added.

[141] These matters, and the public comments about them, were discussed in a fair amount of detail in court, although the court later found them to be procedurally irrelevant. 485 F.2d 472-473.

[142] Strycker's Bay Neighborhood Council, Inc. v. Karlen, 444 U.S. 223, 227 (1980). This ruling was inspired by Vermont Yankee Nuclear Power Corp. v. Natural Resources Defense Council, 435 U.S. 519, 558 (1978).

[143] Kleppe v. Sierra Club, 427 U.S. 390, 410 (1976).

[144] Warm Springs Dam Task Force v. Gribble, 621 F.2d 1017, 1022 (9th Cir. 1980). The Ninth Circuit issued a similar ruling regarding an agency that neglected to solicit public comments, on slightly different procedural grounds, in State of California v. Block, 690 F.2d 753 (9th Cir. 1982).

[145] Sierra Club v. Army Corps of Engineers, 701 F.2d 1011, 1044-1046 (2nd Cir. 1982).

[146] City of West Chicago v. Nuclear Regulatory Commission, 701 F.2d 632 (7th Cir. 1983).

[147] Public hearings held by the Nuclear Regulatory Commission, and the judicial review thereof, are regulated by the Atomic Energy Act at 42 U.S.C. § 2239 (1954).

[148] 701 F.2d 638. These procedural requirements were also found to comply with the Administrative Procedure Act. 701 F.2d 641.

[149] 701 F.2d 647-652. The failure to submit an EIS was found to not be arbitrary and capricious under the Administrative Procedure Act.

[150] Bradley C. Karkkainen, "Toward a Smarter NEPA: Monitoring and Managing Government's Environmental Performance," *Columbia Law Review* 102 (2002): 906.

CHAPTER 5

Agency Compliance with the National Environmental Policy Act

The National Environmental Policy Act was structured by the U.S. Congress as the enactment of a true federal environmental policy to be observed throughout the federal government. At the time of its enactment in early 1970, NEPA required each federal agency to review its internal policies and procedures, and to begin revising those policies and procedures to come into compliance with the act's environmental protection requirements. Consequently, all federal agencies were given eighteen months to closely inspect, and if necessary, overhaul their internal procedures in order to comply with the new national environmental policy. A section of NEPA tersely stated this requirement:

> All agencies of the Federal Government shall review their present statutory authority, administrative regulations, and current policies and procedures for the purpose of determining whether there are any deficiencies or inconsistencies therein which prohibit full compliance with the purposes and provisions of this Act and shall propose to the President not later than July 1, 1971, such measures as may be necessary to bring their authority and policies into conformity with the intent, purposes, and procedures set forth in this Act.[1]

Because of the National Environmental Policy Act's ambitious policy goals and multiple mandates for the overhaul of decision-making processes at government agencies, many of those agencies viewed

NEPA with caution or even unapologetic contempt.[2] Within a few short years, occasionally troubling patterns of agency (non-)implementation of NEPA's requirements became evident. In the analysis of environmental lawyer and activist Richard A. Liroff:

> First, there were those agencies like the AEC [Atomic Energy Commission]... and the FPC [Federal Power Commission] who felt that compliance might interfere with their advancement of their traditional missions. Second, there was a lack of procedural response on the part of environmental agencies like the EPA [Environmental Protection Agency] that saw NEPA as superfluous because their decisions were already infused with environmental considerations. Third, there were a few agencies... in which some concerted efforts to implement NEPA were made. ... Fourth, some agencies showed a lack of interest in NEPA because ecological considerations did not seem germane to their principal missions, and there was little reward to be gained by allocating scarce agency resources to environmental concerns.[3]

The National Environmental Policy Act raises issues of agency autonomy and statutory restraints on decision-making processes in realms in which a particular agency is likely to deem itself the expert authority. Recall that NEPA was passed during an era of far-reaching public interest statutes that tried to rein in government abuses by mandating the observance of specific procedures. Environmentalists hoped that federal agencies that obviously interacted with the natural world, such as the U.S. Forest Service, as well as the government at large, would face a mandate under NEPA to radically restructure their views on environmental protection. As discussed throughout this book, the courts eventually settled into an interpretation of NEPA as a collection of precise procedural requirements rather than a substantive mandate for particular types of decisions.[4] Thus, some agency autonomy has been preserved although NEPA slowly instilled a sense of responsibility toward environmental protection across the many agencies of the federal government.

NEPA is not under the control of any one government agency, not even the agency with direct jurisdiction over environmental matters, the Environmental Protection Agency. Instead, NEPA regulates the environmentally-relevant procedures of all government agencies, which are required to abide by its provisions. What follows is an analysis of selected examples of government agencies and their compliance with NEPA, including its informational and transparency requirements. Included are agencies that obviously have a relationship with natural conservation and pollution control: the Environmental Protection Agency and the U.S. Forest Service. Also included is the Federal Communications Commission, which serves as an interesting example of an agency that has an unlikely and little-known impact on the environment. This illustrates not only the vast reach of the National Environmental Policy Act throughout the federal government, but the many unexpected ways that government agencies and the parties they regulate interact with the natural world.

For many agencies, compliance with NEPA is codified in their own internal regulations, as is the case for the agencies described in this chapter. However, the extent of that compliance is often at the discretion of the agency, which can weaken the environmental protections that the act strives to enhance. The agencies discussed below have been selected as illustrative examples of agency compliance with NEPA, and the ways some agencies have been able to skirt the policy goals of NEPA due to procedural conflicts with their own internal regulations or governing statutes.

The Environmental Protection Agency

President Richard Nixon authorized the creation of the Environmental Protection Agency (EPA) in December 1970, acting upon inspiration from the National Environmental Policy Act.[5] It is important to remember that the EPA is not the overseer of that act. Instead, the act oversees the activities of the EPA as it administers all federal environmental laws. The EPA indeed describes itself as the guardian of environmental protection laws as enacted by Congress.[6] Since its formation the EPA has also been the primary instigator for new federal regulations, especially when new sources of pollution and previously unknown environmental challenges come to light.[7]

Before Nixon authorized the formation of the EPA, responsibility for various federal pollution control and natural resources laws was dispersed throughout several federal agencies and departments. The scattering of authority directly contradicted the comprehensive goals of the National Environmental Policy Act. The Nixon Administration, for a variety of political and logistical reasons (including a magnanimous desire to avoid the "capture" of environmental administrators by industrial and development interests), chose to create a non-cabinet agency to focus exclusively on the general mandate of NEPA and to administer America's growing slate of environmental statutes.[8] Interestingly, like all other federal agencies the EPA must observe the provisions of NEPA during its own regular activities, including research and development projects and facilities construction.[9] While the EPA does enjoy some specific exemptions from direct compliance with all of the provisions of NEPA,[10] this has been the structure and orientation of the EPA ever since its formation.

The EPA has acted upon powers granted to it under various environmental statutes by giving itself final review authority over any environmental impact statement (EIS). This gives the EPA extra oversight powers over most other federal government agencies concerning their interactions with the environment. The EPA's policy is to conduct a detailed review of any EIS, prepared by any agency, that raises issues that EPA reviewers find important (often as the result of public controversy). This power of ultimate review allows the EPA to act as an arbiter of currently important environmental issues and to interact with citizens in determining the acceptability of actions proposed or permitted by any agency in their communities.[11]

In commenting upon the environmental impact statements submitted by other agencies, the EPA has a potentially wide-ranging ability to shape and influence federal environmental policy. However, reflecting a pattern discussed throughout this book, the EPA does not have the power to substantively alter another agency's environmental decisions or its actions after the EIS has been completed.[12] When an agency makes a final decision that is deemed harmful for the environment, the EPA can get the President's Council on

Environmental Quality (CEQ) involved, and the EPA's comments in the public record can be used against the offending agency in court, perhaps influencing the judicial review process.[13] But in reality, the EPA can enforce the procedures of the EIS but can only provide unbinding advice on the actual environmental decision that is made after procedures have been followed properly. Substantive referrals to the CEQ are very rare, averaging less than one per year.[14]

As required under federal regulations, the EPA can become involved in another agency's EIS process as early as the project planning stage, during which the EPA can advise on what topics should be discussed in the forthcoming documents. This involvement can be at the request of the other agency, though sometimes the EPA may invite itself to discussions.[15] At this point in the process, the EPA adds substantive expertise on potentially significant environmental impacts, while if necessary the CEQ can address any procedural issues. This active consultation can possibly allow the EPA to advance the policy goals of the National Environmental Policy Act, but in the rare event that the EPA raises an issue with the ultimate decision made by an agency after the EIS process is complete, the courts will be less concerned with the substance and more with the procedure.[16]

The rarely-used authority to preclude agency environmental impact statements has been litigated even less. Thus, the EPA enjoys little support from case law in exercising its mandated responsibility to critique any EIS for poor environmental decision-making. In one exemplary case involving the politically-charged topic of oil and gas drilling in the pristine lands of Alaska, the Court of Appeals for the D.C. Circuit made some oblique references to the need for environmental protection as promoted by the EPA, but stuck with a strictly procedural and administrative focus when considering remedies.[17]

When the EPA reacted negatively to the EIS in question, and the matter ended up in court, the Circuit Court noted in dicta that an unsatisfactory review from the EPA created a "heightened obligation" to the originating agency (in this case, the Department of the Interior) to "explain clearly and in detail its reasons for proceeding." However, the court did not define this burden in any way, and the ultimate outcome of the case was a remand to the Secretary of the Interior for the inclusion of additional information in the EIS.[18] In effect, the procedures were redone but the ultimate environmental decision remained the same, reducing the EPA's review power to a matter of procedural bureaucracy rather than active environmental protection.

There is one more possible avenue of environmental mitigation if the EPA's critical review of an EIS leads to no substantive change in another agency's ultimate decision. The EPA does not have the authority (or the resources) to monitor the post-EIS implementation of any project, though the EPA does have the authority to conduct targeted follow-up reviews to determine if an agency has implemented the recommended mitigation measures.[19] However, the Supreme Court has also declared this follow-up process to be unbinding, even if the mitigation measures recommended by the EPA are discussed in the EIS. In *Robertson v. Methow Valley Citizens Council*, the high court noted that "it would be inconsistent with NEPA's reliance on procedural mechanisms – as opposed to substantive, result-based standards – to demand the presence of a fully developed plan that will mitigate environmental harm before an agency can act."[20] In other words, since the mitigation measures were recommended before the project actually commenced, they became merely part of a developing plan rather than authoritative standards to be acted upon. Here the high court largely eliminated any substantive uses for NEPA, and the EPA's influence on its policy ramifications, by referencing a previous case in which it ruled that "NEPA does not require agencies to adopt any particular internal decisionmaking structure."[21]

Once again, it is important to note that the EPA has only been instructed to review whether other agencies observe the National Environmental Policy Act's mandates and procedures regarding environmental impact statements. While the EPA does have substantial authority in enforcing the mandates against pollution and toxicity as granted in other environmental statutes,[22] the procedural focus of American administrative jurisprudence has actually allowed the agency to exercise little direct influence over federal environmental policy. While the EPA can impose sanctions on non-governmental polluters, it has little ability to encourage its fellow federal agencies to exercise sound environmental decision-making, regardless of the policy goals of NEPA.

The U.S. Forest Service

The American government saw the need to protect forests during the first wave of popular conservationism in the late 19th Century. The General Land Revision Act of 1891 allowed President Benjamin Harrison to set aside 13 million acres of land as the first national forests.[23] The U.S. Forest Service (USFS) was set up within the Department of Agriculture in 1905,[24] under the rationale that America's vast (yet shrinking) forests could be a source of revenue and that forests should be managed for maximum economic value. The Forest Service's mission has since expanded into wildlife protection and ecosystem services, though timber production remains an important matter of policy. The management of timber for economic purposes was codified in the statute that currently administers the management of national forests, the National Forest Management Act of 1976.[25]

The Forest Service has long been criticized for favoring timber production in the national forests at the expense of natural protections – a perennial political controversy.[26] The USFS also attracts controversy over its legally-mandated management of the extraction of minerals and fossil fuels from beneath national forest lands.[27] For purposes of the present discussion, the USFS is a federal government agency that certainly affects the natural world in almost all of its regular activities, but which can still sometimes evade the substantive policy goals of the National Environmental Policy Act by arguing that procedure should trump substance. This happens because the USFS is engaged in economic and industrial activities with influence from competing interests, belying the agency's stereotypical image as a protector of pristine natural areas of scenic beauty.[28]

The USFS, due to the concerns of environmentalists over the loss of forests and the influence of the powerful logging and fossil fuels industries, has inspired some of the most heated and drawn-out administrative controversies of recent decades, while the agency has had great difficulty in managing public participation and the transparency of its decision-making processes.[29] The USFS is also hampered by a vague agency mission, as its various organic statutes and Congressional mandates have sent mixed messages about the need for natural preservation vs. resource development.[30] This dilemma has even been noted by the federal courts, with one judge observing that the Forest Service's role is a "nearly impossible task of serving many different interests."[31]

The seminal case (and political aftermath) that illustrates the conflicting policy goals of American forest management was heard in the Court of Appeals for the Fourth Circuit in 1975. The Izaak Walton League sued the USFS, claiming that a plan to allow clear-cutting (which strips a forest bare of all trees) in a section of West Virginia's Monongahela National Forest violated the 1897 Forest Management Act. The circuit court agreed, ruling that the statute issued a clear directive that trees under federal management should only be cut "if they are dead, matured, or large growth and then may be sold only when the sale serves the purpose of preserving and promoting the young growth of timber on the national forests."[32] This ruling was disagreeable to the powerful logging industry, which initiated political efforts for the repeal of the 1897 act. These efforts were successful, leading to the repeal of some of that act's more specific anti-clear-cutting provisions via the 1976 National Forest Management Act,[33] which in turn gave the USFS sole administrative authority in decisions regarding the management of national forests. This new administrative focus reflected the contemporaneous trend in the courts to view environmental statutes as procedural in nature, with a decreasing regard for the policy mandates of the National Environmental Policy Act. That statute was now essentially irrelevant in disputes over decisions by the USFS.[34]

One potentially positive ramification of the 1976 act was that the managers of each national forest were required to compile 15-year plans with detailed descriptions of logging and resource extraction policies, alternative plans of action, and justifications for final decisions. These plans naturally create a great amount of information for public consumption, and citizens are invited to attend planning meetings and provide comments throughout the process.[35] Industry proponents had initially endorsed this process in the belief that political controversy could be avoided. But this was not the case in reality, as environmentalists took inspiration from NEPA and demanded full environmental impact statements for all resource management decisions by the USFS for any particular national forest.[36] The result was an explosion of litigation in which the Forest Service's use of public participation and the transparency of the resulting information was almost always the source of dispute.[37]

While such suits are numerous, most fall into matters of judicial review and deference to agency decisions, given the modern procedural view of NEPA and other federal environmental statutes, including the National Forest Management Act.[38] One important circuit court precedent usefully illustrates this procedural point of view. In a dispute involving a Forest Service decision to deny wilderness protection to 47 forested areas in California, the Court of Appeals for the Ninth Circuit ruled that the USFS decision must be made under the environmental impact statement process as required by NEPA. But in accordance with a theme seen throughout the case history of NEPA, the court did not enjoin the ultimate USFS decision but merely instructed the agency to redo its environmental impact investigation and include matters that had been neglected the first time around. The USFS was instructed to perform a local investigation for each of the areas in question, whereas the original decision was focused regionally. In the court's view, as long as this procedural error was rectified, it would take no stand on whether or not the forested areas in question should receive wilderness protection.[39]

During the George W. Bush Administration, the president's Healthy Forests Initiative aggressively promoted "forest thinning" and "fuels reduction," which were framed as methods to make forests healthier by reducing the risk of fires, but which really allowed for more commercial logging. Interestingly, when this initiative became law in 2003, the statute included a mandate for increased public participation in development plans and ecological projects to enhance forest health.[40] Environmentalists saw through the euphemistic language, but were stymied in their efforts to resist new logging projects by the procedural focus of the National Environmental Policy Act. Ironically, NEPA also decelerated the logging projects, as forestry personnel were bogged down in investigations for environmental impact statements. In a strange paradox, the Healthy Forests Initiative inspired both the proponents and opponents of increased logging in national forests to bemoan the laborious procedural requirements of NEPA.[41]

The Healthy Forests Initiative gave the USFS its own initiative to exempt itself from some of the informational requirements of NEPA. One of these new self-imposed exemptions was quickly challenged in court by the Sierra Club, and the resulting ruling was a rare victory for environmentalists even though the court took the established view of procedure over substance.[42] Under the Bush administration's stance that removing old timber promotes the health of a forest, the USFS enacted a program of controlled burns in some national forests to reduce the risk of large forest fires, and declared that controlled burns under a certain acreage did not require an environmental impact statement. This was named the Fuels CE Exemption.[43]

Via a procedural analysis per the Administrative Procedure Act, the Ninth Circuit ruled that the Fuels CE Exemption was an arbitrary and capricious evasion of the requirements of the National Environmental Policy Act.[44] However, whereas the environmentalists wanted the court to invalidate the Fuels CE Exemption as a violation of NEPA, the court once again allowed only a pyrrhic victory for the natural world, by merely instructing the USFS to perform a more robust investigation and add detail on why the Fuels CE Exemption would not be a violation of NEPA, and to do so while following the procedures mandated by the Administrative Procedure Act.[45] At the time of writing, the Fuels CE Exemption is still up in the air, but chances are that the exemption would be found in compliance with NEPA if the Forest Service follows the proper procedures in any new investigation into the need for the regulation, and once again substantive environmental protection goals would take a back seat to procedure.

After a contentious history of controversy over its transparency (or lack thereof) and its attitudes toward public participation, in 2005 the USFS issued new regulations attempting to clarify its goals under the informational provisions of the National Environmental Policy Act and affiliated environmental statutes. Regarding public comments on disclosed documents, the Forest Service exempted itself from NEPA requirements at all stages of its planning process except for the stage in which ultimate land use and resource management decisions are made.[46] Within language that appears to reflect NEPA's philosophy of public participation and transparency, these new regulations free the Forest Service from its previous attention to detail, perhaps reducing costs and controversy but substantially reducing citizen oversight of the agency's decisions on resource extraction in national forests.[47] At the time of writing, this 2005 initiative has been critiqued by irate environmentalists but not yet challenged in court.

The Federal Communications Commission

The Federal Communication Commission (FCC) is an interesting example of a federal agency that is required to observe the National Environmental Policy Act and its affiliated environmental statutes, even though such statutes seemingly have little to do with the agency's mission. But the FCC is involved in one regulatory matter that certainly has environmental consequences – the placement and construction of antenna towers. The ensuing regulatory conflicts are illustrative of the challenges of administrative and procedural jurisprudence in America.

Per its governing statutes,[48] the FCC has a statutory mandate to foster an efficient nationwide telecommunications network, which in turn requires the construction and maintenance of infrastructure for antennas, transmitters, and related equipment. The FCC also has a statutory mandate to determine whenever the public interest would be best served by the expansion of the network infrastructure.[49] This mandate is relevant whenever environmental questions arise during a communications tower construction project. Additionally, the FCC is not a land planning or environmental agency, and it defers environmental responsibilities to its licensees and applicants – the parties who design and construct the towers. Regardless, as a federal agency the FCC is required to observe the environmental responsibilities that are required of all agencies, particularly the environmental impact statement (EIS) requirements of the National Environmental Policy Act.

The FCC provides licenses to private parties for the building of new communications towers, and an EIS is often required, per NEPA, for the construction site. Like most other federal agencies, the FCC has codified NEPA compliance regulations into its internal rules.[50] On its website, the FCC states: "As a licensing agency, the Commission complies with NEPA by requiring our licensees to review their proposed actions for environmental consequences."[51] However, upon exercising the doctrine of agency discretion,[52] the FCC has found many reasons not to comply with NEPA to the letter.

For instance, the internal regulations state that the FCC "has found no common pattern which would enable it to specify actions that will thus automatically require EISs."[53] In other words, the FCC has decided that not all of the activities of its licensees can be categorically described as "major federal actions" under the language of NEPA. Subsequently, the internal regulations "categorically exclude from environmental processing" all actions except for those specifically identified within those same internal regulations.[54] This creates a catch-22 in that the FCC has defined its own compliance with an outside statute (NEPA) with which it is required to comply. The language of NEPA includes all "major federal actions," but the lack of definition surrounding that term has allowed the FCC (and other federal agencies as well) to determine what exactly those major actions are, and more importantly to decide internally that some actions are *not* "major."

The FCC's internal regulations still contain a great amount of detail concerning licensing and construction projects deemed to be "major" and therefore subject to the requirements of NEPA. However, the lack of self-enforcement within NEPA allows even more internal discretion by both the agency and its licensees. When reviewing applications for the construction of new communications towers, the FCC makes a primary determination of whether the construction will have a significant effect on the environment.[55] Here it is important to note that there is no higher federal entity overseeing this determination, because per NEPA such a body does not exist.

According to the FCC's internal regulations, "significant impact on the environment" falls into eight possible categories of damage, and if some or all of those categories of damage are expected to occur during the construction of a tower, the licensee is required to submit an environmental assessment (the less-detailed precursor to a full EIS) that describes the possible damage.[56] Of interest in this regard is a provision that allows any "interested person" to petition the agency to request an environmental assessment for any tower construction project that would not otherwise require one.[57] But on the other hand, one important result of this regulatory structure is that no environmental assessment is required for any tower construction project in which the agency or the licensee has determined that no significant environmental impacts will occur, unless an interested person petitions the agency otherwise.[58]

The ability of licensees to make environmental impact determinations independently is further enabled by another section of the FCC's internal regulations. In effect, the FCC permits licensees to become "non-federal representatives" (and thus less subject to the requirements of federal statutes such as NEPA) who are able to self-determine whether their proposed activities would threaten the environment. The FCC rarely takes any further action on any proposal for which the licensee self-declares that no adverse environmental impacts are expected.[59]

When a dispute arises, courts will typically rule against an agency like the FCC only if a particularly "arbitrary and capricious" statutory violation can be found – and that judgment tends to apply to an agency's governing statute rather than non-agency-specific statutes like NEPA.[60] This means that the FCC is more likely to be sanctioned for violating its own mission than for violating a related pan-agency statute such as NEPA. Courts have traditionally deferred to the FCC's expertise in telecommunications and its mandate to maintain a robust American communications network. Thus, courts cannot presume that the FCC possesses enough environmental expertise to comply with all the requirements of NEPA and affiliated environmental statutes.[61] Internal agency discretion also extends to the agency's view of its own agenda, allowing the agency to determine whether the environmental assessment process, and the management of the resulting information, favors its own agenda or not. This degree of deference may also tempt the agency in question to understate environmental impacts altogether.[62] Unfortunately for proponents of environmental protection, NEPA is not powerful enough to steer any federal agency away from its primary mission.

The environmental consequences of tower licensing by the FCC, and construction by licensees, transcend mere land use challenges because of the well-documented problem of bird collisions with towers. Researchers have reached a conservative estimate of four to five million avian deaths at communications towers annually in the United States, and some researchers estimate as much as forty to fifty million. All estimates are rising quickly each year, as are the towers themselves.[63] This potentially severe environmental problem causes ramifications not just for compliance with NEPA, but also the Endangered Species Act, the Migratory Bird Treaty Act, and various other wildlife protection statutes. Bird lovers and environmentalists have attempted to take the FCC to task for violating these statutes, but have been stymied by the administrative focus of federal law.

The FCC has acknowledged that bird collisions with towers are a problem, but claims that a solution is beyond its responsibilities because its statutory mandate is only to foster an efficient nationwide telecommunications network. It is not a land planning or environmental agency, and it defers environmental responsibilities to its licensees and applicants. The FCC also claims not to have the resources to actively monitor tower sites, and it also does not have an environmental review office.[64] In terms of tower siting, the agency has the mandate to determine whether the general public interest would be better served by environmental protection or by the efficiency of the communications network.[65]

The challenges of citizen oversight of environmentally-relevant agency activities, with lessons to be learned for all of American administrative jurisprudence, are exemplified in a recent district court lawsuit in which environmentalists attempted to force the FCC to take responsibility for the deaths of millions of birds at communications towers. In 2005, a consortium of citizens' groups concerned about the fate of birds in Hawai'i filed a lawsuit against the FCC, claiming that the agency could mitigate the avian mortality at its towers, especially those where significant bird deaths were known to occur, by more closely observing its own internal environmental regulations as well as the National Environmental Policy Act and the Endangered Species Act. This case came to an unceremonious close as the district court denied the citizens' request for judicial review on purely jurisdictional grounds.[66] The FCC successfully used procedural arguments to avoid courtroom discussion of the most vexing questions raised in the case, including its lackluster efforts to consider the environmental impacts of tower siting and construction, and whether it should be required to do so, based upon its own rules for complying with NEPA.

The problem of bird deaths at communications towers may appear esoteric in light of larger matters of government regulation, but the outcome of the Hawai'i case is indicative of the difficulty in applying federal environmental statutes to government agencies. Longstanding traditions in American administrative jurisprudence place greater emphasis on an agency's governing statute whenever that statute creates a conflict with a higher pan-agency statute such as NEPA that does not have its own enforcement mechanisms. In the case of the FCC, courts are likely to more closely review the requirements of the Communications Act of 1934, which defines the FCC's primary mission. This leaves outside statutes like NEPA with less authority over agency actions, regardless of the fact that all agencies are required to comply with NEPA's procedural requirements. This does not mean that the FCC and other agencies have no concern for the environment, but American law demands that these agencies fulfill their own statutory mandates first. Unless Congress decides to amend NEPA to include more self-enforcement, and unless the courts enact a long-term (and highly unlikely) shift away from traditional views of administrative procedure, the environmental policy goals of NEPA and its affiliated statutes will continue to come up short in citizen disputes over agency actions toward the natural world.

Chapter 5 Notes

---

[1] 42 U.S.C. § 4333. The next two sections of the statute did allow for coordination with existing agency rules and regulations, noting that the goals of NEPA were meant to supplement the established missions of the various government agencies rather than completely replace them. 42 U.S.C. §§ 4334-4335.

[2] Matthew J. Lindstrom, "Procedures Without Purpose: The Withering Away of the National Environmental Policy Act's Substantive Law," *Journal of Land Resources & Environmental Law* 20 (2000): 254.

[3] Richard A. Liroff, *A National Policy for the Environment: NEPA and its Aftermath* (Bloomington, Ind.: Indiana University Press, 1976), 140. Note that the Environmental Protection Agency did not exist until after the enactment of NEPA, and that agency's administrative structure and decision-making apparatus are largely based on, and inspired by, NEPA.

[4] Samuel P. Hays, *Wars in the Woods: The Rise of Ecological Forestry in America* (Pittsburgh, Pa.: University of Pittsburgh Press, 2007), 15.

[5] The establishment of the EPA was pursuant to a departmental reorganization of the federal government enacted by President Richard Nixon. Phil Wisman, "EPA History," U.S. Environmental Protection Agency, http://www.epa.gov/history/topics/epa/15b.htm, accessed 23 June 2010.

[6] U.S. Environmental Protection Agency, *About EPA*, http://www.epa.gov/epahome/aboutepa.htm, accessed 23 June 2010.

[7] Richard J. Lazarus, *The Making of Environmental Law* (Chicago: University of Chicago Press, 2004), 68-69.

[8] J. Brooks Flippen, *Nixon and the Environment* (Albuquerque, N.M.: University of New Mexico Press, 2000), 85-87.

[9] 40 C.F.R. §§ 6.200-6.210.

[10] James W. Spensley, Esq., "National Environmental Policy Act", in *Environmental Law Handbook*, vol. 14, ed. Thomas F.P. Sullivan (Rockville, Md.: Government Institutes, Inc., 1997), 407-408. These exemptions are allowed under specific provisions within other statutes, including the Clean Air Act and Clean Water Act. In one specific example of exemption from NEPA, the EPA is not required to prepare an environmental impact statement for emergency cleanup operations at toxic chemical sites, per the Comprehensive Environmental Response, Compensation, and Liability Act (CERCLA), 42 U.S.C. §§ 9601-9675 (1980).

[11] Spensley, 426-427.

[12] Robert L. Fischman, "The EPA's NEPA Duties and Ecosystem Services," *Stanford Environmental Law Journal* 20 (2001): 500-501. The responsibility to review all EISs was given to the EPA under the Clean Air Act, 42 U.S.C. § 7609(a) (1970), which states that the EPA must review "any matter relating to duties and responsibilities granted" under any federal statute that delegates some sort of authority to the EPA.

[13] Fischman, 502.

[14] Ibid., 509.

[15] 40 C.F.R. § 1501.7.

[16] Fischman, 517.

[17] Alaska v. Andrus, 580 F.2d 465 (D.C. Cir. 1978).

[18] 580 F.2d 475, 487. This strictly procedural focus toward EPA review of EISs was confirmed in a later ruling in the same court on a related matter of oil and gas leasing as managed by the Department of the Interior. Natural Resources Defense Council v. Hodel, 865 F.2d 288, 298-300 (D.C. Cir. 1988).

[19] 40 C.F.R. § 1501.3.

[20] 490 U.S. 332, 353 (1989). This case involved citizen disagreement with an EIS prepared by the U.S. Forest Service for a proposed ski resort in Washington's Okanogan National Forest.

[21] Baltimore Gas & Electric Company v. Natural Resources Defense Council, 462 U.S. 87, 100 (1983). This case stemmed from the citizens' group's objection to an esoteric rule change by the Nuclear Regulatory Commission concerning daily operations at nuclear power facilities.

[22] A variety of such statutes will be discussed in detail in Chapter 6.

[23] 26 Stat. L. 1095 (1891). This act was amended in 1897 and codified at 16 U.S.C. §§ 475-482. The U.S. Forest Service currently oversees 155 national forests and 20 national grasslands, adding up to about 193 million acres of federal lands. In 1891, the first parcel of land to be protected in this way was 2.4 million acres in Wyoming adjacent to Yellowstone National Park, and now known as Shoshone National Forest.

[24] The U.S. Forest Service was established when Congress transferred jurisdiction over the existing network of forest reserves from the Department of the Interior to the Department of Agriculture, within which the Forest Service became an agency. Transfer Act of February 1, 1905, 33 Stat. L. 628 (1905).

[25] 16 U.S.C. § 1600-1614 (1976). This statute was originally an amendment to the Forest and Rangeland Renewable Resources Act of 1974, which was not confined to national forests but initiated the modern regulatory philosophy of resource extraction and development on federal lands.

[26] Harold K. Steen, *The U.S. Forest Service: A History* (Durham, N.C.: Forest History Society, 2004), 74-78.

[27] 7 C.F.R. § 2.60. This regulation delegates responsibility to the USFS for "renewable and nonrenewable resources of forests" and the management of forest resources "including but not limited to recreation, range, timber, minerals, watershed, wildlife and fish; natural scenic, scientific, cultural and historical values of forests and related lands; and derivative values such as economic strength and social well being."

[28] The economic and development focus of the USFS was instigated by its first Chief Forester, the controversial conservationist Gifford Pinchot, who wrote that "all the resources of the forest reserves are for *use*, and this use must be brought about in a thoroughly prompt and businesslike manner, under such restrictions only as will insure the permanence of those resources." Gifford Pinchot, *Breaking New Ground* (New York: Harcourt, Brace, 1947), 261. Pinchot originally made this statement in 1905; emphasis in original.

[29] Michael J. Mortimer, "The Delegation of Law-Making Authority to the United States Forest Service: Implications in the Struggle for National Forest Management," *Administrative Law Review* 54 (2002): 909.

[30] Ibid., 910.

[31] Resources Limited, Inc. v. Robertson, 789 F.Supp 1529, 1540 (D. Mont. 1991). In this case, a consortium of citizens' groups challenged the USFS management plan and accompanying environmental impact statement for Montana's Flathead National Forest.

[32] Izaak Walton League v. Butz, 522 F.2d 945, 948 (4th Cir. 1975). The conservation group was named after British author Izaak Walton, best known for the 1653 book *The Compleat Angler*, a treatise on fishing that has become known as a very early example of literary appreciation for the outdoors.

[33] 16 U.S.C. § 1600-1614 (1976).

[34] Hays, *Wars in the Woods*, 16-17.

[35] 16 U.S.C. § 1604, 1604(d).

[36] Hays, *Wars in the Woods*, 18.

[37] Elise S. Jones and Cameron P. Taylor, "Litigating Agency Change: The Impact of the Courts and Administrative Appeals on the Forest Service," *Policy Studies Journal* 23 (1995): 322-323. One noteworthy example is the management plan for Pennsylvania's Allegheny National Forest, where the USFS has granted leases for more than ten thousand oil and gas wells while restricting public participation during each permit's EIS process, inspiring lawsuits from dozens of different conservation groups. After arguing for several years that it lacked the authority to regulate drilling in the region (due to complex subsurface ownership regulations inherited from the state), in 2008 the USFS changed course and announced a new plan to provide more regulatory oversight of drilling in Allegheny National Forest. Anne Martin, "Tell the Forest Service: Strong Oil and Gas Regulations Needed on National Forests," American Lands Alliance, 18 February 2009, http://www.americanlands.org/index.php?id=464, accessed 23 June 2010.

[38] Mortimer, 979-980.

[39] California v. Block, 690 F.2d 753, 774-776 (9th Cir. 1982).

[40] Healthy Forests Restoration Act, 16 U.S.C. § 6501 (2003).

[41] Bradley C. Karkkainen, "Whither NEPA?," *New York University Environmental Law Journal* 12 (2004). 337.

[42] Sierra Club v. Bosworth, 510 F.3d 1016 (9th Cir. 2007).

[43] 67 Fed. Reg. §§ 77038-77039 (2002). This regulatory decision was also inspired by an especially brutal forest fire season in 2000.

[44] 510 F.3d 1026. The Ninth Circuit also used the phrase "clear error of judgment" under administrative law doctrine, per Marsh v. Oregon Natural Resources Council, 490 U.S. 360, 378 (1989).

[45] 510 F.3d 1034.

[46] 36 C.F.R. § 219.6.

[47] National Research Council of the National Academies, *Public Participation in Environmental Assessment and Decision Making* (Washington, D.C.: The National Academies Press, 2008), 42.

[48] The primary statute governing the FCC is the Communications Act of 1934, 47 U.S.C. §§ 151-614 (1934). The 1934 act officially created the FCC, and still governs the agency, with the addition of amendments from the Telecommunications Act of 1996, Pub. L. 104-104, 110 Stat. 56 (1996) (codified as amended at 47 U.S.C. §§ 101-710).

[49] 47 U.S.C. § 310(d).

[50] 47 C.F.R. §§ 1.1301-1.1319 (1971).

[51] U.S. Federal Communications Commission, Wireless Telecommunications Bureau, *Compliance with Commission's Rules Implementing the National Environmental Policy Act of 1969*, http://wireless.fcc.gov/siting/npaguid.html, accessed 23 June 2010.

[52] "Agency discretion" is a general doctrine within American administrative jurisprudence in which a government agency is assumed to have the knowledge and authority to act upon its primary area of expertise first, and to deal with outside requirements later, with minimal oversight or interference from the other branches of government.

[53] 47 C.F.R. § 1.1305.

[54] The categorical exclusion is found at 47 C.F.R. § 1.1306. This section then refers to § 1.1307, which lists actions that are specifically covered.

[55] 47 C.F.R. § 1.1307.

[56] 47 C.F.R. §§ 1.1307(a)(1)-1.1307(a)(8).

[57] 47 C.F.R. § 1.1307(c).

[58] Rachael Abramson, "The Migratory Bird Treaty Act's Limited Wingspan and Alternatives to the Statute: Protecting the Ecosystem without Crippling Communication Tower Development," *Fordham Environmental Law Journal* 12 (2000): 261.

[59] 47 C.F.R. § 1.1307. This possibly improper delegation of authority was argued in American Bird Conservancy v. Federal Communications Commission, 408 F.Supp.2d 987, 989 (D.Hawai'i, 2006). In that case, the FCC had allowed a licensee to determine if its own actions would affect the habitat of an endangered species believed to reside in the area of a proposed communications tower. The case will be discussed in more detail later in this section.

[60] "Arbitrary and capricious" agency decisions can be overturned by the courts per the Administrative Procedure Act at 5 U.S.C. § 706(2)(A); while the focus on an agency's governing statute during judicial review is usually based on the *Chevron* doctrine in modern administrative law: Chevron USA, Inc. v. Natural Resources Defense Council, 467 U.S. 837 (1984).

[61] Susannah T. French, "Judicial Review of the Administrative Record in NEPA Litigation," *California Law Review* 81 (1993): 987.

[62] Daniel A. Dreyfus and Helen M. Ingram, "The National Environmental Policy Act: A View of Intent and Practice," *Natural Resources Journal* 16 (1976): 255.

[63] For a variety of estimates, and a discussion of the difficulties in formulating accurate counts, see Albert M. Manville, "The ABCs of Avoiding Bird Collisions at Communication Towers: The Next Steps," Proceedings of the Avian Interactions Workshop, December 2, 1999, http://www.fws.gov/migratorybirds/issues/towers/abcs.html, accessed 23 June 2010.

[64] Ava Holly Berland, "Licensing Concerns, NEPA Sitings, Telecommunications Act Mandates: The FCC Perspective," Proceedings of the Avian Mortality at Communications Towers Workshop, 11 August 1999, http://www.fws.gov/migratorybirds/issues/towers/berland.html, accessed 23 June 2010. At the time these comments were made, Berland represented the FCC's Office of General Counsel.

[65] 47 U.S.C. § 310(d).

[66] American Bird Conservancy v. F.C.C, 408 F.Supp.2d 987, 993-994 (D.Hawai'i, 2006). The American Bird Conservancy was the primary plaintiff, joined by the Forest Conservation Council and Conservation Council for Hawai'i. The FCC advanced a complex argument based on which level of the federal court system (district or appeals) had been granted jurisdiction by the Communications Act of 1934 and related statutes, and the course of action to be taken in the courts when the agency is suspected of violating its own governing statute, but not environmental statutes.

CHAPTER 6

The Informational Provisions of American Environmental Laws

There are two basic approaches to government regulation, environmental or otherwise. With a "hard" approach the government simply makes certain types of behaviors illegal and punishes wrongdoers after the fact. With a "soft" approach the government attempts to proactively change the behavior of regulated parties, with less threat of punishment, by encouraging them to think about the harms they are causing and by publicizing those harms. The "soft" approach requires the collection and dissemination of information, especially when legal prosecution is inappropriate or impractical. This is often the case with pollution, in which it can be difficult to determine exactly who or what caused a certain instance of pollution and is therefore to be punished retroactively. In the realm of American environmental law, many statutes have been designed for the collection and dissemination of information, and the very existence of such government-held knowledge has often discouraged pollution and other types of environmental degradation.[1]

There are a plethora of federal environmental laws, most of which are administered by the Environmental Protection Agency. As will be seen below, many of these laws have informational and/or transparency provisions, which are all influenced by the National Environmental Policy Act.[2] These laws range from the well-known and frequently enforced Clean Air Act and Clean Water Act, to obscure or industry-specific toxic substance control statutes like the Resource Conservation and Recovery Act. NEPA, from the administrative standpoint, serves as the umbrella for most of these other federal environmental statutes.

According to the Environmental Protection Agency, NEPA "establishes the broad national framework for protecting our environment."[3]

This chapter describes additional environmental statutes, beyond NEPA, that feature informational components of one type of another, from requirements for information that must be provided to the government, to special transparency provisions that aim to make the resulting government-held information available to the public. This chapter analyzes a variety of pollution control statutes, toxic substance control statutes, and statutes of special note including the Emergency Planning and Community Right-to-Know Act and the Endangered Species Act. These statutes all result in environmentally relevant information that is then collected and managed by the federal government. Whether or not this information becomes useful to citizens is the question that this chapter attempts to answer.

Government-Held Information Gathered During Environmental Activities

The environmental impact assessment process, as mandated by the National Environmental Policy Act, does not directly inform agency decision-making, as discussed in earlier chapters. But while the process may not allow citizens to predict how an agency will go forward with a particular project, there has been a more diffuse and long-term effect on agency behavior, because for every project agencies are required to fully explain the potential environmental consequences of project activities. So, while the assessment process has less of an impact on the actual and immediate implementation of agency plans, it does increase knowledge through the collection and management of information.[4] In fact, one of the major accomplishments of NEPA is its coordination of the submission and management of environmental information required by a wide variety of other environmental statutes, thus increasing transparency and access for all of the environmental information held by the government.[5]

The Environmental Protection Agency also oversees voluntary auditing and disclosure programs in the industries it regulates.[6] This process creates additional government-held information that may be of use to citizens if it is made accessible and transparent, often in the form of permits for operators in polluting industries and reports that those parties must submit upon carrying out their activities.

Furthermore, the volume of information collected under American environmental laws is essential for the enforcement of those laws, thanks to the "knowing" doctrine in American jurisprudence. Under traditional principles of criminal law (though note that most environmental law falls under civil law), there is an assumption that the lawbreaker was at some level conscious of his own wrongdoing or blameworthiness. This does not require that the perpetrator be completely familiar with the applicable law, but knows that what he is doing would be considered wrong under wider aspects of the law.[7] This makes the presence and availability of government-held environmental information all the more important.

Likewise, the courts have ruled that ignorance of the law is not an acceptable defense during an environmental prosecution.[8] The courts have relaxed this requirement slightly in environmental law, as compared to general criminal law. For example, in a prosecution under the Resource Conservation and Recovery Act (RCRA, a toxic substance statute to be discussed in detail below), the Second Circuit Court of Appeals ruled that government prosecutors do not have to prove that the defendant knew that materials are regulated by specific statutes, but only that the defendant knew the materials were hazardous. In the court's words, with a hazardous substance "the possibility of regulation is so great that anyone who is aware he is in possession of them or dealing with them must be presumed to be aware of the regulation."[9] In a similar case of a violation of RCRA, the Eleventh Circuit ruled that the defendant did not have to be familiar with specific regulations, but only that "[the] material had the potential to be harmful to others or to the environment."[10] The Fifth Circuit adopted a modified version of this doctrine in another case involving RCRA, noting that a party that dumps a hazardous substance into the environment need only know that the material is potentially hazardous, and no technical knowledge of proper or improper disposal techniques is necessary to prove a violation of the statute.[11]

Furthermore, given the public interest focus of modern American environmental law, the "knowing" doctrine has also been applied to reckless endangerment by polluting industries. In an important precedent involving dangers to the unknowing employees of a polluting industry, the Tenth Circuit Court of Appeals ruled that RCRA is equipped for the prosecution of parties that endanger citizens, especially if the defendant was aware that endangerment was likely. In the words of the court, a regulated entity can be charged with knowing endangerment if it is aware that a regulatory violation "places another person in imminent danger of death or serious bodily injury."[12]

Circumstantial evidence can also be used to demonstrate actual knowledge, including evidence that the defendant deliberately ignored or disregarded the relevant environmental regulations. This doctrine applies to the employees of regulated industries as much as it does to the industries themselves. In *United States v. Self* the Tenth Circuit ruled that the professional position and responsibility of the defendant can be used as circumstantial evidence, as can knowledge of prior activity that was found to be in violation of environmental regulations. A corporate employee's familiarity with the regulations governing his firm's regular business, thanks to the filing of environmental reports with the government and his own prior dealings with investigations of environmental wrongdoing, was deemed sufficient circumstantial evidence of the defendant's knowledge of the law.[13] Here, the informational requirements of American environmental law are crucial for finding responsibility for violations. The reports and other documents required under various environmental statutes, and their collection and management by the government, are crucial factors in whether industry personnel "know" that they are violating the law, especially when those personnel are regularly involved in filing or contributing to the required reports.[14]

On the other hand, the government's reliance on regulated parties to examine their own operations and report on how much they really know about their environmentally-relevant activities leads to another problem for transparency and citizen access to government-held information. In short, the American tendency (during certain periods in the cycle of political ideology) to allow commercial and industrial players to police themselves creates real difficulties for citizen knowledge of how their natural world is being used. During the Reagan administration and its philosophy of deregulation, reductions in staff and funding forced the EPA to introduce a voluntary compliance program while encouraging industries to comply with environmental statutes through effective auditing practices. Under a guise of voluntary self-regulation, industries were encouraged to pick up the slack by instituting their own internal auditing practices, with the results to be delivered to the EPA for further analysis.[15] In 1986 the EPA announced a new voluntary auditing policy that was developed to:

> (a) encourage regulated entities to institutionalize effective audit practices as one means of improving compliance and sound environmental management, and (b) [...] guide internal EPA actions directly related to regulated entities' environmental auditing programs.[16]

Here the EPA was asking regulated entities to establish their own auditing and inspection bureaucracies. However, the policy statement was not binding, and the EPA stated that it would not "routinely" request audit reports while ironically trying to encourage the creation of those same reports.[17] This policy was updated in 1995, in an attempt to encourage more voluntary compliance by reducing the threat of civil penalties if a violator follows up noncompliance complaints promptly and correctly.[18] However, this updated policy is still a guidance document only, and not a binding regulation. This allows the EPA to use its discretion in demanding information from regulated entities and then using that information in its own environmental decision-making processes.[19]

But there is no guarantee that the EPA, even when it demands a voluntary audit report, will use the information to hold the regulated party liable for any environmental violations mentioned in the audit. Remarkably, some courts have ruled that federal agencies (including the EPA) do not have the authority to collect the voluntary audits that they have encouraged through their own regulations. In 1996, the Seventh Circuit Court of Appeals ruled in *Logan v. Commercial Union Insurance Company* that "work product privilege" (or the right to keep internal business decisions and results confidential) could be used to withhold voluntary audit reports from regulating authorities.[20]

There is still a need for strengthened regulations that remove the disincentives for industry that are engendered by the EPA's modern lack of enforcement. This problem illustrates another weakness of the American legal system, in that a happy medium has not yet been found between purely voluntary self-regulation by industry and command-and-control intervention by the government.[21] From the citizen's point of view, transparency of environmental information is hindered by the EPA's tolerance of "voluntary" compliance (or *de facto* non-compliance) by industry. Since industrial players are private parties, the National Environmental Policy Act and the Freedom of Information Act do not provide citizen access to any documents that these parties create (voluntarily or otherwise) but then refuse to turn over to government regulators.

This discussion applies to environmental regulation in general and high-level enforcement by the Environmental Protection Agency and other relevant government agencies. Fortunately, as will be discussed below, several American statutes contain specific informational and transparency provisions that should make environmentally-relevant information more accessible to citizens. This is especially true for a family of pollution control statutes, toxic substance control statutes, and a few other statutes that regulate specific types of environmental protection.

Note that the statutes to be discussed in the upcoming sections are much larger and more complex than their respective informational and/or transparency provisions. To keep the discussion manageable, the larger goals of each statute will be introduced, but the subsequent legal analysis will focus on information and transparency. Also, the statutes discussed here have been selected for their importance in American environmental jurisprudence, but there are some other statutes not covered here that contain specific transparency provisions as well. Nonetheless, the efficacy and effectiveness of the informational and transparency provisions of the laws to be discussed below are crucial for understanding the true transparency of government-held environmental information in America.

Pollution Control Statutes

As discussed in an earlier chapter, mankind's efforts to control pollution inspired some of history's very first environmental protection efforts. Pollution (and its effects on public health) has been a concern since the beginning of agriculture and settled villages. Until relatively recent times, population densities were low and few people were concerned about the loss of pristine areas, so the traditional method of fighting pollution was to allow Mother Nature to dilute it, blow it away, or send it downstream. It was not until modern times, particular in the post-World War II era, that an increase in industrial waste and artificial chemical substances created popular and political efforts to prevent pollution before it occurs, and to clean up areas where the air, water, or land were already polluted.[22] By the early 1970s, the policy goals of the National Environmental Policy Act inspired pollution-control statutes enforced by dedicated government agencies under the oversight of the Environmental Protection Agency, rather than just locally-oriented regulations. First, the most obvious and ubiquitous vectors of pollution, air and water, were targeted for a comprehensive clean-up.

The air that Americans breathe inspired the first post-NEPA overhaul to existing pollution control regulations. In 1967 the federal government originally attempted to regulate air pollution with the Air Quality Act,[23] which was merely a set of principles to encourage states to regulate the release of pollutants from industrial and agricultural sources. But with the trend toward a comprehensive federal environmental policy embodied in NEPA, as well as public discontent with worsening air quality and new scientific knowledge of the trans-border nature of pollution and its effects, just three years later Congress decided to get much tougher with the parties that abuse the air breathed by the electorate. The Clean Air Act of 1970,[24] passed just months after NEPA, was originally designed as a series of amendments to the earlier Air Quality Act, but it soon emerged as one of America's most pervasive and complex environmental statutes.

The Clean Air Act was designed to combine the best available technology in pollution control with the regulatory efforts of states and the federal government. The act encourages government cooperation with industrial firms and private organizations in finding solutions to air pollution, and supports research and development into control technologies. The Clean Air Act also features heavily-enforced informational provisions (especially regarding permitting and reports) that provide for citizen participation in government and industry decisions affecting air quality.[25]

The Clean Air Act originally attempted to clean up American air with a three-pronged approach. First, all new and existing sources of air pollution are prohibited from emitting any particulates or other substances that would violate the act's permitted levels of air quality. The acceptable level of air quality is defined with public health and welfare in mind,[26] and must be enforced by states as they oversee their own industry, agriculture, and other sources of air pollution.[27] Second, new sources of potential air pollution are subjected to stringent oversight of control technologies and strict permitting requirements.[28] Third, the act also includes specific provisions dealing with special problems of acid rain and quality-of-life issues such as visibility.[29] In 1990 Congress amended the Clean Air Act with a fourth pollution control strategy – a comprehensive program to manage permits and the information generated as permit holders navigate through their various requirements.[30]

The Clean Air Act does not contain any provisions that deal precisely with transparency or citizen access to information, but the act does generate a great amount of potentially accessible information in the form of permits. Citizens fighting particular air pollution crises may be able to make use of the information contained in the paperwork related to permits, particularly the permit holder's understanding of how to comply with the act.

In its original text, the Clean Air Act required two different kinds of permits for new sources of pollution (typically new industrial or commercial operations, and sometimes existing operations that are expanding) depending on the air quality of the surrounding area and the levels of particular pollutants. New sources in areas that have attained acceptable air quality levels are subjected to a permit that prohibits additional pollution that could potentially place that area's air quality outside of acceptable levels. This is also known as the Prevention of Significant Deterioration permitting program.[31] New sources in areas that have not attained acceptable air quality standards are subjected to the Nonattainment permit program.[32] Both of these permitting schemes require significant amounts of information to be delivered from the operator to the government before construction can begin.

In order to receive a Prevention of Significant Deterioration permit, the operator of the pollution source must show that the source will attempt to prevent significant deterioration of the area's ambient air quality, will employ the best available technology to control each pollutant it is expected to emit in significant amounts, and will avoid adverse impacts on public lands such as national parks and wilderness areas.[33] The latter requirement became more complicated (and informational) in 1996 with the establishment of a database that cross-references all parcels of federal lands with nearby air pollution sources, and confirmation of this information is required before a permit is considered complete.[34]

In areas that have not attained acceptable ambient air quality standards for a particular pollutant, new operators are required to obtain a Nonattainment permit. This permit program is managed by the states under the guidance of the Environmental Protection Agency, and operators are required to demonstrate a commitment to achieving the "lowest achievable emission rate" under the best available technology. Operators are also required to provide information on how the economic benefits of their facility are expected to outweigh the environmental and social costs.[35] The state must manage this process among all its permit holders in order to make progress toward achieving acceptable ambient air quality standards. The EPA exercises significant guidance and influence over this process.[36]

Prior to 1990, the only operators required to applied for permits under the Clean Air Act were new sources prior to construction (with some exceptions), while pre-existing sources were regulated under state implementation plans or grandfathered under various state pollution control statutes.[37] As a result, there was not a nationally integrated permitting program for all sources of pollution. The Clean Air Act was amended in 1990 to integrate state permitting programs and to give the EPA authority to review and approve all permits for both new and existing sources of air pollution.[38] This places even more pollution-related documents in the hands of the federal government.

Under the 1990 amendments, any operator seeking a permit from any state must submit a complete application, describing how the operator plans to comply with all applicable requirements under the Clean Air Act.[39] The EPA, or a state that has been delegated authority by the EPA, can rule a permit application incomplete if the proper information has not been provided, and can request additional information. A complete permit application must describe all expected emissions of major pollutants (as defined in the act) and other regulated pollutants. The application must also identify all emission points, rates of emission, control equipment, control techniques, and the operator's current compliance with air quality standards or plans to attain compliance.[40]

When administrators grant a permit to an operator, still more information is created on the nature of the operator's pollution patterns and compliance plans. The permit must contain descriptions of how the operator can stay within compliance (including certification and testing requirements), planned inspection schedules and strategies, and provisions for regular compliance reports to be submitted to administrators.[41] Under the act, permits are valid for five years, with a fairly straightforward renewal process if the operator has not made any significant changes in emissions levels. However, in the event of "environmentally significant" changes a complex permit renewal and revision process is required, including full reporting to the government of all new relevant information.[42]

Overall, the Clean Air Act generates huge amounts of information about polluting industries, and this information is collected and managed by the government. Vast quantities of permit information and reports are thus available to any citizen with an interest in local pollution incidents or the air quality of the nation. While perfectly clean air is still a dream, information about why this dream remains unfulfilled is plentiful. The informational requirements of the Clean Air Act have inspired similar provisions in its sister pollution control statute, the Clean Water Act.

America has battled water pollution for as long as it has battled air pollution. Federal protection of water sources dates back to the Refuse Act of 1899,[43] which prohibited unauthorized dumping in waterways, though this statute was more concerned with keeping waterways navigable for commerce. A patchwork of similar federal and state laws had been created by the 1960s.[44] The first comprehensive nationwide water pollution statute was passed as the Federal Water Pollution

Control Act in 1972,[45] and was later renamed the Clean Water Act upon the passage of significant amendments in 1977.[46]

The ultimate goals of the Clean Water Act are to provide for the protection of fish and other waterborne wildlife, the protection of recreation in and on the water, and the elimination of discharges of pollutants into waterways.[47] The 1977 amendments placed special emphasis on the use of the best available technology to control pollutants and improve water quality standards. In particular, the 1977 amendments recognized that, like air pollution, water pollution could best be controlled not by cleaning up already fouled waterways (though this was also a concern at the time), but by managing pollutants at the point of discharge – usually industrial or municipal sources.[48]

Most importantly for the present discussion, the Clean Water Act instituted a permitting program that is administered by states on an industry-by-industry basis. Permitting is contingent upon the operator's use of the best available pollution control technology, but the act also allows more stringent controls on particular sources if the available technology is insufficient in achieving acceptable water quality levels in the area.[49] But unlike the Clean Air Act, which sets ambient air quality standards and works backwards to try to control sources of pollution that endanger those standards, the Clean Water Act deliberately sets acceptable levels of effluent discharge and makes all violations of those levels immediately illegal. Furthermore, states are not allowed to adjust permitting requirements, must always encourage regulated parties to use the latest available control technology, and must not tolerate the degradation of high-quality waterways.[50]

Under the Clean Water Act, permits are required for any new source of effluent or discharge, as well as modifications to any existing source. A great amount of information must be provided by the operator about the facility (municipal, industrial, or otherwise) and the nature of the discharges. The act also requires that all forms associated with the permit be signed by a "responsible corporate officer" for private companies, or either a "principal executive officer" or "ranking elected official" for municipalities.[51] The importance of the information contained in these documents can be seen in the following mandatory certification for the person signing the permit:

I certify under penalty of law that this document and all
attachments were prepared under my direction or supervision
in accordance with a system designed to assure that qualified
personnel properly gather and evaluate the information
submitted. Based on my inquiry of the person or persons who
manage the system, or those persons directly responsible for
gathering the information, the information submitted is, to the
best of my knowledge and belief, true, accurate, and complete.
I am aware that there are significant penalties for submitting
false information, including the possibility of fine and
imprisonment for knowing violations.[52]

Permit forms and the information therein must be disclosed to the
public per the Clean Water Act's public participation requirements.
EPA regulations allow any person to contest or appeal a permit within
thirty days of its issuance. Until administrative review of this appeal is
complete, the permit will not take effect, and the permit could be
revoked as a result of the appeal.[53]

The permitting process also includes numerous reporting and
monitoring requirements. Permit holders must regularly monitor their
compliance with the requirements of their permit and of the Clean
Water Act in general. Periodic information must be provided (usually
once per year) on the nature of the operator's effluents and discharge,
and whenever practical, the water quality levels of the body of water
that receives the discharge.[54] Special reports and notifications must be
delivered to the EPA immediately in the event of an accidental
discharge of a hazardous substance into navigable waters and their
adjacent shorelines, where people and wildlife are most likely to be
affected.[55] Failure to submit this report, which can be crucial to both
immediate government cleanup efforts and to citizens fighting future
complications, is punishable by up to five years in prison for the
responsible corporate officer or elected official.[56]

In addition to the reporting and information requirements of the
Clean Water Act, the federal government has enacted public
participation requirements in matters of water pollution control. For
example, the Environmental Protection Agency requires public

participation in any government decision made under the Clean Water Act:

> Public participation is that part of the decision-making process through which responsible officials become aware of public attitudes by providing ample opportunity for interested and affected parties to communicate their views. Public participation includes providing access to the decision-making process, seeking input from and conducting dialogue with the public, assimilating public viewpoints and preferences, and demonstrating that those viewpoints and preferences have been considered by the decision-making official. Disagreement on significant issues is to be expected among government agencies and the diverse groups interested in and affected by public policy decisions. Public agencies should encourage full presentation of issues at an early stage so that they can be resolved and timely decisions can be made. In the course of this process, responsible officials should make special efforts to encourage and assist participation by citizens representing themselves and by others whose resources and access to decision-making may be relatively limited.[57]

The EPA's regulations not only require the public to be involved in the decision-making process, but also demand that no government decisions be made without acknowledging public opinion and that government employees exercise all means necessary to maximize participation by interested members of the public.[58]

Like with the Clean Air Act, the permitting requirements of the Clean Water Act have inspired literally thousands of lawsuits in the federal courts, and once again the vast majority of these concern disputes over permitting decisions or efforts to enforce standards for wayward operators. As will be discussed below, the public participation and transparency provisions of the Clean Water Act have a much shorter legal history, though the matter has been argued once before the Supreme Court.

The informational requirements of the Clean Air Act and Clean Water Act have not been tested extensively in the courts, so potentially crucial matters of access to government-held pollution information do not enjoy definitive precedents. Instead, such matters are subjected to the winds of administrative law and agency discretion, neither of which allow for easy oversight by citizen watchdogs. For both of these statutes, the lion's share of litigation involves administrative disputes over standards, such as acceptable ambient air quality standards or the structure of state implementation plans. The two acts have also inspired hundreds of suits in the federal courts regarding disagreements over permitting decisions or efforts by citizens to force operators to observe the requirements of their permits.[59]

For instance, the Clean Air Act is among the most litigation-intensive of America's environmental statutes, with most cases dealing with penalties imposed on private companies (and sometimes cities and states) that violate clean air standards.[60] However, the informational requirements of the act, particularly the data to be collected during the permitting process and made available to citizens, have much less of a case history. And while some cases regarding air quality violations and the ensuing government penalties have reached the U.S. Supreme Court, disputes over the informational provisions of the Clean Air Act have not made it beyond the circuit court level. The cases discussed herein are certainly illustrative, but the transparency of the information engendered by the Clean Air Act, like that of the other environmental statutes discussed in this chapter, have not yet been significantly tested in the courts.

After more than two decades of federal attempts to clean up the nation's air by penalizing polluters, the definition of a "major source" of pollution, and the usefulness of that piece of information to the American public, was not reviewed at the circuit court level until 1995. The dispute regarded a 1990 amendment to the Clean Air Act, in which the previous public health-based regulation of air pollutants was replaced with a technology-based regulatory scheme in which hazardous materials were determined via testing at the source rather than via investigation of later public health crises.[61] Accordingly, in 1992-93 the EPA categorized air pollution sources by physical plant location rather than by industrial category, thereby increasing the usefulness of the official list of hazardous airborne substances for local residents near particular industrial sites.[62]

In *National Mining Association v. EPA*, a group of industrial permit holders objected to this new categorization method, and asked for judicial review to find if the new classification method was outside of the EPA's authority. The Court of Appeals for the D.C. Circuit found the agency's new method of classifying sources by physical location to be reasonable and within the agency's authority.[63] This brought the EPA's list of actionable hazardous air pollutants up to par with recent scientific testing, and also made that list more meaningful for citizens by categorizing the information by location. In 2006, the Eleventh Circuit ruled that the 1990 amendments also required that all relevant emissions and compliance information be consolidated into a single document based on the source facility in question, for ease of use by regulators and citizens.[64]

In 2008, the true usefulness of the Clean Air Act's informational requirements became an issue in an unconventional circuit court dispute over a permitting decision for a Texas power plant. Regardless of the source-specific classification of hazardous pollutants under the 1990 amendments, the information therein still may not benefit citizens until after pollutants are emitted. Reflecting the primacy of administrative procedure rather than substantive policy in American jurisprudence, according to the Fifth Circuit in *CleanCOALition v. TXU Power*,[65] citizens cannot make use of information regarding pollutants, even if the EPA knows about it, *before* a facility is constructed.

In the *CleanCOALition* case, citizens attempted a suit to block the construction of a coal-fired power plant after learning that the proposed plant, upon commencing operations, would emit air pollutants listed as hazardous by the EPA under the Clean Air Act. The court ruled that other provisions in the Clean Air Act either prohibited citizen lawsuits for air quality violations during the pre-construction permitting process, or disallowed prevention requirements (from the EPA and state authorities) during this phase of the process.[66] The supposed inappropriateness of pre-construction citizen lawsuits was not rationalized by the court not via the substantive pollution-control goals of the Clean Air Act. Instead, the court interpreted the administrative procedures relevant to the case indirectly, through the lens of the equal protection clause of the Fourteenth Amendment, and ruled that federal review of pre-construction for any development project would disrupt state policymaking decisions.[67] An appeal of this Fifth Circuit decision was denied by the Supreme Court,[68] and the circuit court ruling is a potentially troubling precedent that makes citizen-obtained information on hazardous air pollutants useless at the time it matters most – before sources are constructed.

Another recent decision from the Eleventh Circuit may also damage the usefulness of air pollution-related information that is collected by the EPA and state authorities and made available to citizens. While the Clean Air Act ensures the transparency and access of this information, its delivery to interested citizens may still be ineffective in preventing or reducing pollution at the source. Once again, the culprit is longstanding tradition in administrative jurisprudence. In *Sierra Club v. Johnson* in 2008, citizens objected to the issuance by the EPA of a permit renewal for two Georgia power plants that were already known to emit large amounts of air pollution. In 1999, the EPA had found the two plants to be in violation of clean air requirements after building unauthorized additions to their facilities, and upon learning of this development, citizens demanded that the EPA instigate a civil suit for these unpermitted modifications.[69] The EPA had issued a violation notice to the parent company, which became a matter of the public record, but decided to take no further action. Upon reviewing the citizen claim against this decision by the agency not to act, the circuit court noted that the EPA's decision was curious but within a reasonable interpretation of the Clean Air Act.[70] While this ruling was based on principles of administrative jurisprudence, the circuit court may not have realized the implications of making agency-held information that had been dutifully provided to the public – permit data and violation notices – useless in citizen efforts to act upon that very same information.

A similar trend can be seen in the case history surrounding the informational and public participation requirements of the Clean Water Act. Similarly to Clean Air Act, the vast majority of litigation surrounding the Clean Water Act involves suits brought by the EPA or by citizens against permit holders who have violated water quality standards.[71] Also in league with the Clean Air Act, some cases involving Clean Water Act permits and violations have made it to the Supreme Court, but with one exception, the informational and public participation provisions of the act have not been argued beyond the circuit courts.

Soon after the Clean Water Act went into effect, a seminal circuit court case helped to define the federal government's powers under the act, as well as the usefulness of the information engendered by the act. In 1974, an oil company brought suit against the federal government, with the case originating in Kentucky followed by an appeal to the Sixth Circuit. The Ashland Oil Company was charged with discharging thousands of gallons of oil into a Kentucky creek, and then failing to report the incident, both of which are violations of the Clean Water Act. The ensuing penalty (just $500) inspired the company to question federal authority under the act, with an argument based on the Commerce Clause of the Constitution. The circuit court rejected the Commerce Clause argument and found no constitutional or statutory difficulties with the federal government's ability to regulate and prevent water pollution.[72] This ruling also upheld the constitutionality of the Clean Water Act's provision requiring immediate reporting (to the government, and by extension to citizens) of unpermitted discharges and accidental spills.[73]

Shortly thereafter, the Clean Water Act's public reporting requirement survived a void-for-vagueness argument at the Ninth Circuit, which ruled that the requirement to "immediately" notify the "appropriate government agency" of "harmful quantities" consisted of adequately defined terms and was precise enough to satisfy due process.[74] A few years later, in the only case regarding the reporting or informational requirements of the Clean Water Act to make it to the Supreme Court, the reporting provision and its ensuing penalties were subjected to a Fifth Amendment argument, with an oil and gas company claiming that the act's requirement to report an act of violation against it required self-incrimination.[75] The circuit court agreed with this argument, but the high court reversed, turning to statutory construction and ruling that Congress intended for the reporting provision to lead to a civil penalty (usually in the form of a fine), while the Fifth Amendment applies to criminal prosecutions. Similarly, the high court found that per Congressional intent, the Clean Water Act sought to clean up the nation's waterways in the public interest, and not necessarily through the punishment of wrongdoers.[76]

So in regards to self-incrimination, the Supreme Court has ruled that polluters must report their unpermitted acts of water pollution to the authorities and to the public, and cannot refrain from doing so by claiming rights under the Fifth Amendment.

The application of the Clean Water Act's reporting requirement has also been upheld for even the lowest levels of pollution. For instance, in 1990 the Fifth Circuit ruled in *Chevron v. Yost* that the federal government can fine violators for small discharges with no requirement of proof of direct harm to the environment. In this case, the defendant company found penalties under the reporting requirement to be unwarranted because it had been charged with a dozen miniscule and accidental discharges, and even though it dutifully reported each incident, each one supposedly did not result in any real harm to the environment. But the circuit court rejected this argument via a straight reading of the relevant provisions of the Clean Water Act, which give the federal government authority over any unpermitted discharges that "*may* be harmful to the public health or welfare of the United States."[77]

Thus, the Fifth Circuit ruled that when a violator abides by the reporting provision of the act, it is not in a position to determine how the resulting information is used in the charging of fines or other penalties. And in the most recent circuit court case involving the public information requirements of the Clean Water Act, the Ninth Circuit ruled that the reporting requirement can apply both to a company and to an employee responsible for a discharge incident.[78]

Toxic Substance Control Statutes

The Clean Air Act and Clean Water Act, and other statutes like them, focus on "conventional" pollutants, which are usually recognizable as industrial or agricultural by-products that are discharged in large quantities and carry the threat of known health problems. These conventional pollutants have been understood, if not necessarily opposed by the populace, since ancient times. But with the advent of modern industry and the environmental movement of the second half of the 20th Century, less well-known toxic substances have entered the public consciousness. These are either natural or synthetic chemicals that can present a health risk even at low levels of exposure.[79]

Conventional pollutants, like those regulated by the Clean Air Act and Clean Water Act, are unwelcome wastes from otherwise useful processes that municipalities and industries would like to put out of sight and out of mind, such as coal smoke or residential sewage. On the other hand, toxic substances can be valuable products in themselves and can be not only the outputs of industrial or agricultural processes, but also the inputs for those processes or even free-standing consumer items. An exemplary category of such substances is pesticides, which are important products for legitimate use by farmers or residential consumers, but which also pose health risks if used incorrectly or in excessive amounts.[80]

Regulating toxic substances is very difficult because unlike smoke or sewage they usually have legitimate uses. Furthermore, each individual substance carries its own particular health risks, which may affect individual people differently. The level of usage between legitimate application and health risk is also unique for each substance and often unknown or difficult to quantify. For some toxic substances, there is no acceptable level of human exposure before health problems set in, but since the substances are used in industrial or commercial processes that may lessen or neutralize the dangers, economic questions often arise when the government attempts to regulate those substances. These issues can be profound because the chemical industry is responsible for more than 10% of the gross domestic product of the United States, and is one of the few industrial sectors in which the country still enjoys a trade surplus.[81]

For these reasons and others, conventional pollution control statutes like the Clean Air Act and Clean Water Act are inappropriate for the regulation of toxic substances, necessitating a series of specific statutes with their own substance control as well as informational requirements. Given the scientific uncertainty in determining acceptable exposure levels and the concomitant health risks, toxic substance control statutes feature a particular focus on collecting and managing all the information that is available on such substances, in the event of a public or personal health crisis.[82]

The first major federal law to regulate toxic substances was passed slightly after the era of public interest environmental statutes, when environmentalists and regulators began to learn that the omnibus policy goals of the National Environmental Policy Act and the conventional pollution controls of the Clean Air Act and Clean Water Act were insufficient for dealing with the peculiarities of toxic substances. In 1976, Congress passed the Toxic Substances Control Act (TSCA).[83] This act lays down ground rules for the regulation of toxic substances in general, and also includes specific regulations focused on asbestos, indoor radon, and lead-based paint. More generally, unlike other statutes that regulate particular toxic substances after they are released into the environment, the major objective of TSCA is to identify the possible risks posed by any toxic substance before it enters commerce. Given the economic questions posed by toxic substances that are also valuable consumer or industrial products, TSCA does not regulate all chemicals that pose risks to humans or to the environment, but only those that pose "unreasonable" risks.[84]

TSCA is a reporting-based statute, and places the responsibility on manufacturers of potentially harmful substances to provide information on the health and environmental risks posed by their products. The act's reporting requirements are extensive and can be quite burdensome for manufacturers, which did not deter Congress from enacting such requirements in the public interest.[85] Reports are submitted to and managed by the EPA, and they must be updated regularly and made available to EPA personnel on demand. Any new information brought about by scientific research, product modifications, or review by regulators must also be included in regular reports.[86]

The act includes provisions for pre-manufacture testing of new substances planned by manufacturers, meaning that testing is required even before the first batch of a new substance is produced. This also applies to significant new applications or uses of existing chemicals that are expected to add to levels of human exposure. TSCA also requires manufacturers to report to the EPA on any health problems suffered by workers at sites where the regulated chemicals are manufactured or processed, or the health and environmental effects noted by citizens who have contacted the company directly. The EPA may also require manufacturers of certain substances to provide information on any relevant health or public safety studies of which they are aware, conducted by themselves or by independent experts.[87]

The EPA uses all of this information to keep industry and citizens posted on the potential risks posed by new and existing chemical substances, and to assess the viability of its own enforcement mechanisms.[88] TSCA also places informational and reporting requirements on the EPA itself. The agency is required to disseminate information through public notices, which must include the reasons for all licensing or non-licensing decisions and the data behind those decisions. The agency is also required to compile and publish a regularly-updated list of all regulated chemical substances that are manufactured or processed for commercial purposes in the United States. This list, known as the TSCA Chemical Substance Inventory, must also distinguish between existing chemicals that are already regulated under TSCA and new chemicals that have been suggested for pre-manufacture review by the EPA.[89] In 1986 the EPA added a requirement for manufacturers to report on current production volume and the size of manufacturing facilities.[90] The resulting inventory is made available to the public by the EPA. All of this information, as supplied by both the EPA and the manufacturers it regulates, allows an informed public to take legal action against toxic threats and to exercise market pressure by refusing to purchase chemicals that are known to be unsafe.[91]

While TSCA regulates the manufacture of toxic substances, the act says little about their disposal and the steps to be taken if they continue to pose a threat while sitting in landfills or other disposal sites. A variety of federal and state statutes address the problems of waste disposal. Thanks to the American quality of life, more than 40 million tons of refuse is dumped at more than 20,000 disposal facilities every year, including nearly five pounds of toxic waste per American per day.[92] All waste presents potential health hazards, particularly the phenomenon of "leachate," the liquid by-product of the decomposition of landfill waste that can leak into nearby groundwater and surface water, thus contaminating drinking water sources with poorly-understood toxins. About one percent of incoming landfill waste is toxic, while an unknown quantity becomes toxic later through intermingling and decomposition. In either case, even small quantities of toxic waste in landfills can have serious effects on the health of local citizens and the quality of nearby ecosystems.[93]

The primary federal statute dealing with the problem of hazardous waste is the Resource Conservation and Recovery Act (RCRA) of 1976.[94] This act gives the EPA authority to regulate hazardous solid waste "from cradle to grave," all the way through generation, transportation, treatment, storage, and disposal.[95] RCRA declares a national policy for the reduction or elimination of hazardous waste as expediently as possible, with a prohibition of open dumping in landfills and the precise management of such waste to minimize threats to human health and the environment.[96] The act authorized the EPA to identify all hazardous substances, leading to three different regularly-updated lists that categorize substances from non-specific (ambient) sources, those from specific (usually industrial) sources, and commercial chemical products.[97] The list of hazardous substances as identified by the EPA is now available in an extensive online database. This database is so extensive that a complete report or basic list of substances is impractical, necessitating the need for search engines and a long list of pointers for the interested citizen who seeks information on a particular substance.[98] This is not a technical weakness in the database, but an indication of how many toxic substances are extant in the American waste stream.

RCRA instituted a permit system for the operators of treatment, storage, and disposal facilities, who are required to report a great amount of information about their facilities in permit documents. Especially important under the act is information concerning hazardous (not merely toxic) substances, with operators required to report on the exact location of hazardous waste storage; plus the composition, quantities, concentrations, mixtures, transport patterns, and disposal methods of any substance named as hazardous by the EPA.[99] In return for receiving a permit, operators are required to take corrective action toward, and report on, all releases of hazardous waste from their facilities. Permit holders, when relevant, are also required under RCRA to obtain special (and even more information-intensive) permits for underground storage tanks and to report in great detail on accidental releases or discharges from such tanks, which pose special threats to groundwater.[100]

Permits can be revoked by the EPA, an act that requires a public hearing and the recording (under established rules of administrative procedure) of all arguments that take place during the hearing and all information that is discussed. Most importantly for the present discussion, RCRA has its own transparency provision, requiring that all records and reports submitted by operators or compiled by government agencies (usually the EPA) must be made available to the public.[101]

RCRA authorizes the Environmental Protection Agency to clean up pollutants that pose an immediate and substantial danger to public health or welfare, thus giving birth to a separate statute to handle the management of especially serious cleanup efforts. The Comprehensive Environmental Response, Compensation and Liability Act of 1980 (CERCLA),[102] commonly called the "Superfund" act, is unique in American environmental law in that it imposes a retroactive liability for the payment of all cleanup costs on responsible parties without regard to the proportion of their fault. Firms that have contributed to especially dangerous pollution incidents can be required to perform and/or pay for the cleanup.[103] Government cleanup efforts are funded by a large pool of money (the "Superfund") that is authorized by CERCLA and collected via taxes imposed on the petroleum and chemical industries and a general environmental tax collected from all corporations.[104]

The Superfund act was inspired by several highly controversial and dangerous toxic waste dumps left behind by industry. The most influential for lawmakers was the Love Canal disaster in Niagara Falls, New York, surrounding a former industrial toxic waste site upon which houses were built in the 1950s, and where toxic leakage began to cause severe health problems for residents by the late 1970s.[105] Also in the late 1970s, another controversy was ongoing at the Valley of the Drums near Louisville, Kentucky, where a locally approved (and much less concealed) 23-acre dumping ground for toxic waste containers made the adjacent areas nearly uninhabitable.[106] Another infamous Superfund site was the entire town of Times Beach, Missouri, now uninhabited and unincorporated, where a 1971 effort to control dust on dirt roads via the spraying of contaminated oil caused an epidemic of health problems that drove away all residents by 1985.[107]

As of mid-2010, the Environmental Protection Agency reported 1,279 identified Superfund cleanup sites and 61 proposed sites. Throughout the history of the Superfund program through mid-2010, only 341 Superfund sites have been delisted (that is, deemed to no longer violate the acceptable levels of toxicity under CERCLA).[108] The Center for Public Integrity, a government watchdog group specializing in transparency and access to information, reports that New Jersey, Pennsylvania, New York, and California have more than a hundred Superfund sites each, and that half of all Americans live within ten miles of a Superfund site.[109]

The parties facing liability during Superfund cleanups may include current and former owners as well as those who treated or transported hazardous substances. These parties may face significant financial responsibility, at amounts that they are not always able to pay (even when the responsible parties are located by government investigators). A 2008 study found that the average Superfund site costs $55 million and more than a decade to clean up, and the entire Superfund program costs companies (or taxpayers, if the companies cannot be found or compelled to pay their share) as much as $30 billion per year.[110]

Given environmental and statutory realities, the process of discovering and cleaning up Superfund sites is slow and complicated. After a preliminary assessment process, if the EPA determines that further action is necessary, the agency formulates a comprehensive cleanup program. The process in which the EPA becomes aware of a site and the site is deemed worthy of a comprehensive cleanup plan averages more than four years in length. Initial site investigation and an official EPA decision on how to ultimately remediate the pollution problem (known as the "record of decision" under the CERCLA statute) take as much as five more years on average, after which actual cleanup finally begins.[111]

Like the other toxic substance control statutes discussed above, CERCLA makes great use of reporting to bring the attention of the Environmental Protection Agency (and the public) to sites that are in need of extensive cleanup. Under the act, information on toxic sites can be reported to the EPA in a variety of ways. First, the EPA must become aware of the site's existence, which usually happens as the result of citizen complaints, actions by a state or local government, or investigations by other government agencies.[112] The EPA then places the site in the CERCLA Information System, a computerized database that contains approximately 35,000 potential cleanup sites. A regularly updated version of the database has been made available to the public via the EPA website.[113] Like the RCRA online database, the CERCLA online database is so extensive that a complete report or basic list of Superfund sites is impractical, necessitating the need for search engines for the interested citizen who seeks information on a particular site. This apparent technical limitation is actually an illustration of how much severe toxic pollution has taken place in America. The much smaller number of sites earmarked for actual federal cleanup efforts are placed in the National Priorities List, also available online.[114]

CERCLA also requires a considerable amount of record-keeping and reporting, resulting in the creation of voluminous government-held documentation that can be of great use to citizens who are concerned about particular toxic sites. All EPA decisions on the listing or delisting of a Superfund site and any cleanup plans must be entered into the administrative record, including the public health and environmental factors behind such decisions.[115] All records are subjected to public comment, and the EPA must record all such comments and its own responses to them.[116] There are also special reporting requirements for all known releases of federally-defined hazardous substances at a Superfund site, as discovered by either the operator or by government agency personnel. Failure to report a known release of hazardous substances from a Superfund site can result in punishment as severe as five years in prison and $25,000 in fines per day.[117]

CERCLA has provided the impetus for thousands of court disputes, usually concerning cleanup costs imposed on owners and efforts to find out who the owners of long-abandoned sites actually were. For purposes of the present discussion, the act of listing a site as eligible for Superfund cleanup, and the reporting requirements of owners and administrators once cleanup efforts have commenced, have inspired a series of court disputes that are limited in quantity but high in significance.

The informational and reporting requirements of the all these toxic substance control statutes have been argued in court much less often, with no argument rising above the circuit court level. But the case history at that level does indicate that manufacturers of toxic chemicals have found ways to prevent their commercial products and industrial sites from appearing in official government lists, making those lists less useful for regulators and for citizens who may suffer direct impacts from toxic pollution.

For example, early in the career of the Toxic Substances Control Act (TSCA), a prominent manufacturer attempted to use statutory language to exclude some of its research programs from toxic substance regulation. In 1979, Dow Chemical argued in the Court of Appeals for the Third Circuit that the public reporting requirements of TSCA should only apply to substances that are produced for commercial sale.[118] According to the statute, "the Administrator [of the EPA] shall require any person who manufactures, processes, or distributes in commerce or who proposes to manufacture, process, or distribute in commerce any chemical substance or mixture... to submit [scientific studies] to the Administrator."[119]

Dow Chemical believed that the language of this provision, particularly the term "commerce," precluded substances it did not plan to sell, but manufactured only for research purposes. The circuit court agreed with the company in spirit but turned to statutory construction, finding that Congress intended for TSCA to give the EPA the authority to obtain information in the public interest. The court also found a synonymous relationship between the terms "commerce" and "manufacture" in the statutory text, which inspired it to give deference to the EPA in its procedural dispute with Dow. This circuit court ruling ultimately became a discussion of proper agency deference and statutory construction, with the court lamenting how TSCA and other statutes were disincentives to technological innovation.[120] But the circuit court missed the larger theme behind the reporting and informational provision of TSCA that was really at issue, in that the presence of hazardous chemicals at a physical location can have a real impact on local citizens and ecosystems, regardless of the ultimate use of those substances.

A similar challenge to government definitions, this time brought by an environmental group that suspected politicking in the categorization of substances, occurred fairly early in the history of the Resource Conservation and Recovery Act (RCRA). That statute classifies wastes into two types of pollutants, with solid wastes receiving less regulation under Subtitle D, and hazardous wastes receiving more regulation under Subtitle C.[121] In *Environmental Defense Fund v. EPA*, the public interest group argued that the agency's relatively lenient Subtitle D classification of mining wastes was in contravention of the informational requirements of RCRA.[122]

The Court of Appeals for the D.C. Circuit found evidence in the legislative history of RCRA that Congress was concerned about the toxicity of by-products from the mining industry.[123] Environmental Defense Fund argued that the scientific evidence showed that the substances in question should be regulated more closely as hazardous materials under RCRA, and that the EPA's Subtitle D classification was arbitrary and capricious. However, the circuit court turned to longstanding administrative jurisprudence and adopted a strategy of agency deference, ruling that despite the Congressional intent toward strict regulation of mining wastes, there was not enough evidence in the legislative history to find that Congress demanded Subtitle C regulation for those substances under RCRA.[124] This case illustrates a recurring theme in American environmental jurisprudence, in that administrative traditions of procedural deference to federal agencies can regularly trump the substantive goals of environmental law, even when evidence of harm to the natural world (and to citizens) is plentiful.

Two years later, the distinction between Subtitle C and Subtitle D regulation under RCRA came up again in the same circuit court. In *American Mining Congress v. EPA*, the industry group objected to the agency's reclassification of several substances (by-products of mining and smelting operations) from "solid" under Subtitle D to "hazardous" under Subtitle C.[125] This time the manufacturers argued that the agency action was arbitrary and capricious. Here the D.C. Circuit used the same strategy as in the previous case, turning to an analysis of statutory language and agency deference in order to find if proper procedures were followed by the EPA. In this case, the circuit court found that the EPA did not violate the procedural requirements of administrative law, and that the decision about the substances in question was not arbitrary and capricious.[126]

The problem is that in neither of these cases, regardless of their opposite outcomes from the procedural point of view, did the D.C. Circuit Court consider the public interest ramifications of the classification of hazardous substances under RCRA and whether the resulting public information is truly effective for citizens. Also, all federal appeals court cases involving the official listing and categorization of solid waste and hazardous substances under RCRA have been heard in the D.C. Circuit, resulting in a case history in which the precedent is to rule only on agency observance of strict procedural requirements. As the above cases show, at least for RCRA, consistent procedures have resulted in inconsistent listing of hazardous substances and, most importantly for the present discussion, inconsistent informational benefits for citizens who need to know the exact nature of toxic chemicals in the event of environmental or public health crises.

The federal circuit courts of appeals are also the highest courts that have reviewed the reporting requirements of the final toxic substance control statute discussed here, CERCLA (the "Superfund" act). That act requires reporting, to the relevant federal agency, of any unpermitted spill or discharge of any hazardous substance that might require federal cleanup efforts later.[127] These reports then become part of the public record, for use by regulators and citizens when toxic dump sites raise issues of public and environmental health. In an early case at the Second Circuit, the court ruled that CERCLA (and in particular, its reporting requirements) does not just target companies but also employees who may have been acting without their employers' permission.[128]

Regardless, the ultimate reporting requirements of CERCLA involve the National Priorities List (NPL), which includes all sites across the country that have been targeted for an investigation of toxicity, after which a Superfund cleanup may be instigated by the federal government. The NPL provides the most information to citizens, regulators, and public health advocates on the risks of living near a possibly deadly toxic dump. Proprietors of toxic sites have found ways to resist having their sites included on the NPL, damaging the potential usefulness of that list. The Court of Appeals for the D.C. Circuit has issued some important rulings on the statutory language of CERCLA, in which site operators have attempted to find semantic loopholes in order to avoid the ultimate embarrassment (and liability) of being named a Superfund site.

In *Linemaster Switch Corporation v. EPA*, the proprietor of a troublesome site tried to use a statutory deadline to avoid being added to the NPL,[129] exploiting a potentially catastrophic loophole that would allow polluters to escape liability regardless of the public health and environmental damage done by their facilities. A 1986 amendment to CERCLA required a new classification system for certain hazardous substances, utilizing a ranking system based on direct effects on human health, to be developed within 18 months; sites at which such materials have been found would be added to the NPL accordingly.[130] Linemaster Switch Corporation, finding some of its facilities on the NPL due to this new classification system, argued that the listing was beyond the EPA's authority due to a missed deadline. Here the circuit court relied on established administrative procedure and looked to Congressional intent, finding no evidence that Congress would want the EPA to exclude sites from the NPL only because of a missed deadline.[131]

The Linemaster sites remained on the NPL, but the circuit court came extremely close to allowing the deadline issue to trump the public interest and environmental goals of CERCLA by once again turning to procedural and administrative jurisprudence. The public information benefit of the NPL, at least for the Linemaster sites, was saved by the court's inability to find that Congress believed its own deadline to be inflexible. A slightly different interpretation of legislative intent may have formed a dangerous precedent in which citizens could be kept in the dark about nearby toxic dumps due to procedural technicalities.

Fortunately, the D.C. Circuit has ruled positively on the effectiveness of the Superfund NPL in a case involving public participation and the attendant administrative procedure requirements. In *Honeywell International, Inc. v. EPA*, site operators attempted to utilize the public notice and comment requirements of the Administrative Procedure Act[132] to support their own disagreement with having their sites included in the NPL.[133] While the EPA followed the appropriate public comment procedures upon its ruling that the sites in question should be listed, the proprietors argued that their own "public comments" demanding scientific proof of toxicity and the need for cleanup, and the agency's lack of a specific response, made the agency's listing decision arbitrary and capricious. The court did not find this argument persuasive because inclusion in the NPL is just one step of a much larger investigation and cleanup process under CERCLA. In the court's words, "the NPL is not in itself remedial action – inclusion on the NPL requires no cleanup nor any other action by site owners." In other words, the EPA was not required to discuss all potential cleanup strategies and their necessity upon adding a site to the NPL, and scientific evidence would not become an issue until future disputes over penalties.[134] This ruling is a useful precedent in that toxic site proprietors must face the public embarrassment of being added to the Superfund NPL and cannot avoid this fate by abusing the public participation process. Here the public interest in knowing the location and danger of toxic sites survived a challenge based on administrative procedure.

The Emergency Planning and Community Right-to-Know Act

One major environmental statute that has unique proactive transparency provisions is the Emergency Planning and Community Right-to-Know Act (EPCRA) of 1986.[135] From the legislative standpoint, this statute was made possible by the aforementioned Superfund Amendments and Reauthorization Act of 1986, one title of which focused on increased information requirements and became a standalone statute to be called EPCRA.[136] More fundamentally, EPCRA was inspired by the Bhopal disaster in India two years earlier, during which a toxic leak from a Union Carbide plant killed or injured several thousand people.[137]

EPCRA requires proactive reporting by American factories of their emissions of toxic substances. In rather unassuming language, the statute merely requires manufacturers to disclose "by telecommunications and other means" the quantities of toxic substances they have released into the air, onto the land, or into the water, by chemical and by facility.[138] Unlike pollution control laws, EPCRA does not limit emissions, but simply requires companies to compile and disclose information about those emissions. EPCRA has been successful in not only increasing the transparency of the information it regulates, but in indirectly reducing emissions themselves. This effect has been dubbed "regulation by revelation."[139]

The power of this information was eye-opening not just to the public but often to the companies themselves. For example, Monsanto (manufacturer of chemical products ranging from the food item NutraSweet to the potent herbicide Roundup), in its first year of reporting under EPCRA, was shocked to find that it had released 374 million pounds of toxic waste into the environment the previous year. Monsanto and other large American industrial companies like AT&T, Dow Chemical, and Texaco were surprised by the extent of their emissions and embarked on community public relations efforts to handle the adverse publicity caused by the new EPCRA reporting requirements. The first annual reports under EPCRA revealed that nationwide, 328 different toxic chemicals, adding up to seven billion pounds of emissions, had been released into the environment in 1987.[140]

As opposed to the toxic substance control statutes discussed in the last section, EPCRA does not rely just on reports that are then subjected to established administrative law provisions for distribution and public comment. Any of this industry information would theoretically be available to citizens under the Freedom of Information Act, but like most American informational statutes, that act only works for information that is already in the hands of government agencies. EPCRA proactively puts the burden on the chemical industry, rather than the citizen, and focuses on self-reporting of information that would not be collected by the government otherwise.[141]

Soon after the act went into effect, government watchdogs and industry officials were surprised by the magnitude of the reports. Regulators learned more about the extent of accidental toxic leaks by industry, while companies gained more knowledge of problems with their own chemical storage and management processes.[142] Another indicator of the power of EPCRA's information requirements is that toxic chemical releases by American industry have been cut nearly in half since the effective date of the act's reporting requirements in 1988.[143] Apparently, the potentially embarrassing or controversial public information required under EPCRA inspired some of the regulated companies to make that information more palatable by reducing the actual emissions on which the reports are based. For example, under pressure from environmentalists emboldened by EPCRA reports, by the end of the 1980s the management of an Ohio B.F. Goodrich plant pledged to reduce toxic emissions by 70 percent, and an Amoco Steel plant in the same state vowed to spend millions of dollars to all but eliminate benzene emissions.[144]

Under EPCRA, any operator of a facility involved in the production, storage, or use of toxic substances must notify community representatives and government administrators of leaks and emissions that pose a threat to persons outside of the facility. The act requires a great amount of detail in this notice: including the name of the substance, the quantity released, the time and duration of the accident, any anticipated effects on public health and the surrounding environment, suggested precautions for local residents, and contact information for a responsible official at the company.[145]

Each company's standing inventory of hazardous chemicals (known formally as the TRI, or Toxics Release Inventory), whether or not they have been accidentally released into the community, is also subjected to intensive reporting requirements under EPCRA. These reports must include the maximum and average daily amounts of each substance present in the facility, their locations, and storage techniques. Any piece of this information must be made available to members of the public upon request, and entire reports must be released to the public at the request of state or local emergency planning officials.[146]

EPCRA embodies a unique informational approach to environmental law in which the public is provided with information, and the unpopularity of that information can inspire public pressure which in turn influences market forces that inspire the polluter to change its ways.[147] Thus, a direct requirement for information has indirectly reduced pollution. While EPCRA only deals with private companies and not government officials, the "regulation by revelation" effect illustrates the basic philosophy behind the Freedom of Information Act and transparency theory in general: parties will act more in the public interest if enough information exists for those parties to be held accountable for their actions. In fact, EPCRA and its associated EPA regulations allow the agency to take legal action against any company that does not comply with the act. Failure to adequately report chemical emissions emergencies to the public, or to provide information on hazardous substance inventories, can cost a company up to $75,000 per day per violation, with responsible officials facing up to five years in prison.[148]

The Emergency Planning and Community Right-to-Know Act features some of the most robust and specific reporting and public participation requirements of any environmental statute in America. These provisions have not yet inspired very much case law, either because they are so well delineated or because the act hasn't yet had time to build an extensive case history. In any event, the informational requirements of EPCRA have only been argued at the district court level and no useful precedents have yet been created. But the existing case law does indicate that Congress tailored EPCRA in such a way that polluting industries have very little chance of evading their responsibilities via loopholes or creative interpretations of the statute.

Of special interest is the ability of citizens to bring suit against private companies for violations of the act's reporting and public information requirements. The first such case arose in New York State just a few years after EPCRA went into effect. In *Atlantic States Legal Foundation v. Whiting Roll-Up Door Manufacturing Corporation*, the citizens' legal support group argued that the company should be cited by the EPA and the state authorities for past violations of EPCRA reporting requirements.[149] Unlike many other American environmental statutes, EPCRA authorizes citizen suits against any party that fails to comply with the act's reporting requirements.[150] Of note in the *Whiting Roll-Up Door* case is the fact that the manufacturer had actually complied fully with the act by the date of the suit, but for previous years the required reports on toxic substances in the facility were not delivered to government administrators on time. The defendant moved to dismiss the suit because the violations were not ongoing and were eventually resolved. The district court conducted a thorough reading of the statute and found that the provision authorizing citizen suits was directed at any party that failed to comply, with no further discussion of deadlines or eventual resolutions. In the words of the court, "the plain language of EPCRA's reporting, enforcement and civil penalty provisions, when logically viewed together, compel a conclusion that EPCRA confers federal jurisdiction over citizen lawsuits for past violations."[151]

The same district court, in a very similar case brought two years later by the same citizens' legal foundation, applied this ruling to another dispute over timely EPCRA reporting. In this later case, the defendant claimed that the citizen suit violated constitutional due process. After a statutory analysis similar to that in the case above, the district court ruled that EPCRA is indeed constitutional.[152] Citizen suits based on the same issue of timely EPCRA reporting have also been allowed to proceed in the district courts of Arizona and Colorado.[153]

In all of these cases, the citizen suits were allowed to go forward, and each district court's procedural ruling confirmed the great powers of enforcement that EPCRA allows not just for government regulators but also for concerned citizens. Based on these precedents, there is little doubt that EPCRA requires immediate and detailed reporting of any unpermitted or accidental release of toxic substances at any commercial facility, plus periodic reports on toxic substance inventory levels. However, this is the extent of the case law surrounding EPCRA's public reporting requirements, and without higher court precedents, the true usefulness to citizens of the information engendered by EPCRA could be placed in jeopardy if operators concoct new creative interpretations of the statutory text.

The Endangered Species Act

The Endangered Species Act (ESA)[154] can be considered an informational and procedural statute not unlike the National Environmental Policy Act, which directly inspired it. ESA was the first substantial wildlife protection statute in America, adding a new philosophy (for federal law) that considered plants and animals to be natural resources that were worthy of protection.[155] In turn, not unlike the aforementioned CERCLA, the Endangered Species Act requires the creation and upkeep of an official government list, this one a list of threatened and endangered plants and animals, which can be especially useful for environmentally concerned citizens. However, also like CERCLA, the exact pieces of information on that list and how they got there, and the absence of other pieces of information and why they're not there, is a politicized phenomenon in which accuracy and usefulness can be trumped by political trickery and administrative procedure.

The need to protect rare species and the resulting benefits to humanity (as well as commerce) first came up in the U.S. Senate during the environmental policy debates of 1969. In the opinion of the Senate, rare species should be preserved to "permit the regeneration of species to a level where controlled exploitation of that species can be resumed" because "with each species we eliminate, we reduce the [gene] pool... which may subsequently prove invaluable to mankind in improving domestic animals or increasing resistance to disease or environmental contaminants."[156] While debating the Endangered Species Act a few years later, the House of Representatives was inspired by the latest scientific knowledge indicating that the preservation of habitat was essential for a creature's survival, and for many creatures their habitats were falling to unchecked construction and development. "As we homogenize the habitats in which these plants and animals evolved... we threaten their – and our own – genetic heritage."[157] It should be noted that Congressional debates during the passage of the Endangered Species Act were often based on commerce and the profitability of natural resources. In fact, the Congressional record indicates a rationale for protecting rare species that can be quite different from that of environmentalists who are concerned about ecosystem health or the philosophical and ethical issues surrounding human-caused extinctions. For example, the House of Representatives noted the need to ensure the survival of rare plants and animals for the "continuing availability of a wide variety of species to interstate commerce."[158]

ESA includes precise definitions of "endangered" and "threatened" species, followed by the requirement that all federal agencies must insure that any regulated development is not likely to jeopardize the continued existence of an endangered or threatened species, under the rationale that it is in the public interest to save such species from extinction. The key method of protecting endangered species from extinction, according to the philosophy of ESA, is to prohibit habitat destruction.[159]

The Endangered Species Act generated little political opposition at the time of its enactment in 1973. The lawmakers who passed ESA also had no idea how controversial the act would become, with no member of the Senate and only four members of the House of Representatives voting against its passage, after a relatively tame debate focused on the need to save glamorous animals like grizzly bears. There was also little media coverage of the act's passage.[160] However, within a few years the philosophy of habitat protection would generate intense controversy toward not just ESA but toward all of environmental law.[161]

The act was placed under the administration of the U.S. Fish and Wildlife Service (FWS), which has been granted expert authority over wildlife management issues.[162] ESA applies to all federal agencies and mandates FWS investigation into any action by those agencies that may damage the habitat of any animal or plant that has been placed on an official government-managed list of "endangered" or "threatened" species, terms that are precisely defined in the act.[163] The first version of this list was published by the FWS in 1967, six years before the enactment of ESA, illustrating the rising public and political concern over extinctions during that period.[164]

Whenever warranted, federal agencies are also required by ESA to call upon the FWS for expert guidance on species population levels and the necessity of habitat protection prior to taking action. These requirements for inter-agency cooperation are a particular point of controversy.[165] Another source of opposition to ESA is the use of independent scientists in the formulation of the official list of endangered and threatened species, information on those species' crucial habitats, and how and to what extent to protect those habitats in the planning of development projects. The use of independent scientists often inspires ESA opponents and those disadvantaged by project alterations or cancellations to accuse scientists of poor methodology or, ironically for the present discussion, a lack of transparency.[166]

But the greatest source of contention for ESA is its power to derail the actions of any government agency or regulated party in order to protect the habitat of even the smallest endangered or threatened species, with little room for debate over how to balance the benefits of species preservation and the costs of restricting development.[167] The act requires all federal agencies to ensure that any regulated action is not likely to jeopardize the continued existence of an endangered or threatened species, and most importantly, the type of action most likely to jeopardize a species' existence is damage or alteration to its habitat. Consequently, the most controversial aspect of ESA is its power to restrict residential, commercial, and industrial development if an endangered species is found to reside in a given location. This has inspired development interests to lobby federal officials to ease or eliminate enforcement of the act for particular projects. Public controversy over derailed developments has politicized the process in which species are listed as "endangered" or "threatened," and has encouraged disputes in court and in Congress over whether the act violates the Commerce Clause of the U.S. Constitution.[168]

It was not long before the Endangered Species Act inspired a highly contentious and controversial Supreme Court case, *Tennessee Valley Authority v. Hill*[169] (discussed in detail in Chapter 3). That case confirmed the ability of ESA to derail a major government development project in the interests of protecting the habitat of a small fish (the snail darter) that had no economic or cultural value, though it was believed to be near extinction at the time. Recall that in the political aftermath of the Supreme Court decision, Congress amended ESA to allow the formation of a special committee that could exempt any government project from the requirements of ESA, essentially by fiat.[170] This is what happened in the *Tennessee Valley Authority* case, with the dam in question eventually being built thanks to the intervention of this special committee, known colloquially as the "God Squad."

In the ensuing history of ESA, the only other noteworthy exemption granted by the God Squad involved the northern spotted owl in the forests of the American northwest during the early 1990s. This inspired an illustrative court challenge concerning the transparency of this committee and the public participation requirements of the Endangered Species Act. An Oregon chapter of the Audubon Society, the well-known bird lover's organization, took the God Squad to task for the opaqueness of its decision about the northern spotted owl. At issue were *ex parte* contacts between the committee and the White House, which had become involved in the political controversy over protecting the northern spotted owl and the effects on logging interests.[171] The citizens' group found this to be a violation of the spirit of ESA, which requires that the God Squad's meetings and the records thereof be open to citizens.[172]

Judge Stephen Reinhardt of the Ninth Circuit Court of Appeals found the matter to be "a most important and controversial case."[173] The court found the undisclosed *ex parte* communications to be violations of both ESA and the Administrative Procedure Act, and "prohibited by law." Under both statutes, full public participation in committee meetings and disclosure of records were required.[174]

However, this was a pyrrhic victory for the environmentalists, because as is usual in administrative law, the remedy for the violation was framed as a matter of judicial review. Per the Administrative Procedure Act, the God Squad was required to supplement the official record to include the disputed *ex parte* communications, and to conduct another hearing in which the public was invited.[175] After this was done, the procedural requirements were satisfied but the God Squad's substantive decision did not change. Ironically, a minor victory for transparency under the Endangered Species Act resulted in absolutely no protection for the threatened creature at the heart of the dispute.

The majority of case law surrounding the Endangered Species Act concerns restrictions on development plans, in scenarios similar to that found in the *Tennessee Valley Authority* case. For present purposes, it is useful to look at a less prominent aspect of ESA case law – that surrounding the accuracy of the official list of endangered and threatened species, which illustrates the importance of information and the processes of its creation. This list is imminently useful in government oversight efforts by citizens who wish to preserve species from extinction and those who wish to raise legal challenges against unwanted development projects. As mentioned above, vociferous opposition from conservative economic interests and property rights activists has turned the listing of species as officially endangered or threatened into a highly contentious and politicized process with its own history of court disputes, with potentially damaging consequences for the informational integrity of the act.

ESA does attempt to remove economic or political considerations from the official listing of a species as worthy of protection. Via an agency petition and response process supported by the Administrative Procedure Act,[176] any citizen can make a request to the U.S. Fish & Wildlife Service for protection of a particular species, and the FWS is required to determine the merit of the petition and respond within ninety days. The FWS then has one year to conduct scientific studies, and is required to officially list the species if it finds that "natural or manmade" factors threaten the species with extinction.[177]

There is no requirement for the FWS to consider political factors in this decision, and given the use of scientific expertise during the listing process, courts have traditionally been reluctant to overturn FWS species listings simply because of political controversy.[178] The *Tennessee Valley Authority* case was the only noteworthy example of a dispute over the protection of endangered species habitat reaching the Supreme Court, but the species in question was already officially listed by the FWS via proper procedures under ESA. As for the listings themselves, judicial deference to agency expertise, notwithstanding political controversy, was the ultimate question in a case argued in a district court in Washington State. Once again, the unlucky northern spotted owl, which merely chooses to live in ancient hollow trees, was at the source of the dispute.

In the late 1980s, the northern spotted owl instigated a nationwide debate over the conflict between species preservation and economic development, with particularly nasty rhetoric being exchanged between progressive proponents of environmental protection and conservative proponents of development and property rights. This controversy was the instigator of a widespread and contentious political debate over the Endangered Species Act itself.[179] Logging companies wished to extract timber from the old growth forests of the region, which aroused the opposition of environmentalists, who then attempted a legal challenge based on the existence in the area of the northern spotted owl – at the time a *potentially* endangered species. If this bird were to be officially listed as endangered or threatened, destruction of its habitat would then be illegal per the Endangered Species Act. Thus, ESA could restrict economically lucrative logging over a large region of the American northwest.

A large coalition of environmental groups petitioned the U.S. Fish & Wildlife Service to add the northern spotted owl to the official list of endangered and threatened species. After its legally mandated investigation process, the FWS declined to list the bird. As opposed to the much more frequent pressure from economic interests to *not* list a species as endangered,[180] here there was great political pressure from environmentalists to list the bird as endangered in order to strengthen their opposition to logging. The environmental coalition subsequently sued the FWS under both the Endangered Species Act and the Administrative Procedure Act, claiming an error in the decision not to list the northern spotted owl.[181] The district court found that the FWS had indeed erred in its decision and ordered the agency to perform a more robust scientific examination and then issue another decision on whether to list the species. In addition, the court concocted a useful precedent in declaring that decisions of endangered species listings should be overturned by the courts only when the FWS fails to articulate a satisfactory explanation for its actions.[182] The result of the second decision-making process was the listing of the northern spotted owl as a "threatened" species, leading to a 1991 court-ordered stoppage of logging in certain forested areas in Washington and Oregon. Due to continuing disputes over the alleged economic viability of logging and the jobs generated by it, the listing of the northern spotted owl has continued to be controversial up to the present day.[183]

Political pressure for or against (usually against) the listing of endangered species is a continual problem for the credibility of the Endangered Species Act and the viability of its mandates for useful and transparent information for the concerned citizen. In 1995, the Republican-controlled Congress forced a one-year moratorium on the listing of any new species under ESA, at the behest of property rights and economic development interests. The continual political pressure has forced the FWS to create a new category called "candidate species," through which it can defer official decisions on listing certain creatures until the political winds change. This category has contained as many as 250 species waiting for official protection against extinction. The FWS has even been known to avoid politically contentious species listings by encouraging states and municipalities to enact land use restrictions pertaining to the habitats of the species in question.[184] Few of these political efforts make the transition to legal challenges in court, but the political pressure has still been effective in influencing protection decisions by the FWS and perhaps damaging the integrity of the official endangered species list as an accurate piece of information to be used by citizens.

The political controversy surrounding the Endangered Species Act, brought most vociferously by property rights activists and federal politicians with deregulatory interests, has made the act one of the most manipulated and tweaked federal statutes in history, going through several rounds of weakening, strengthening, and attempted reforms. To start, Congress has never provided nearly enough funding to the U.S. Fish & Wildlife Service to fully protect listed species through habitat preservation.[185] During a period of especially vehement Congressional opposition to ESA, in 1998 the Clinton Administration enacted some regulatory reforms including a "no surprises" policy to reduce uncertainty for landowners by restraining government action on their property until all scientific questions have been fully studied.[186] During the administration of George W. Bush, the deregulatory and property rights ideologies of the time resulted in several efforts to weaken the Endangered Species Act, including an attempt to remove habitat loss and population level as the defining factors in what makes a species endangered, which would have made the informational requirements of the act, not to mention the very meaning of "endangered," essentially meaningless.[187] Bush also instituted a round of eleventh-hour regulations just before leaving office, including the elimination of the ESA requirement that government agencies consult with the U.S. Fish & Wildlife Service when overseeing any project with a potential impact on the habitat of a listed species.[188] In March 2009, new president Barack Obama announced a roll-back of Bush's eleventh-hour efforts.[189]

The informational focus of the Endangered Species Act is both a blessing and a curse to its public interest goals, not to mention the threatened creatures that the act strives to save from extinction. With the official list of endangered species acting as the catalyst for government action, any species and its habitat can be abused until the political process of adding that creature to the official list is complete. And once that happens, landowners who possess areas sufficiently similar to those named as habitat for a listed species might be inspired to willfully damage that habitat before government investigators discover it on their lands, thus avoiding future government action against what they deem to be their property rights. Landowners have also been known to directly exterminate listed species residing on their lands for the same reason, before government investigators become aware of their local presence. Here the Endangered Species Act ironically encourages the destruction of the habitat that is crucial to the creatures it is trying to protect, with landowners (the regulated parties under ESA) making use of the informational focus of the act in ways that directly contradict its environmental spirit.[190]

Of course, the ultimate goal of the Endangered Species Act is not to turn threatened creatures into pieces of information by adding them to the official list, but to later remove them from the list. Listing and delisting are ostensibly indicators of a creature's endangerment and later recovery, which itself should be inspired by the creature's presence on the list. But as discussed above, listing and delisting are heavily politicized and controversial processes, and a creature's initial listing is wholly dependent on scientific knowledge about that creature. Scientists believe the official endangered species list to be woefully inadequate, with only about 15% of the world's plant and animal species having been studied enough to know if their populations and habitats are threatened; while in the United States alone, the official endangered species list may only include (and therefore attempt to protect) 10% of species that are actually endangered.[191]

Meanwhile, in the first three decades of ESA, of the more than one thousand officially listed species, only 33 have been delisted, and seven of those were delisted because they had become extinct. Twelve species were delisted because of taxonomic revisions or changes in regulatory requirements. Only fourteen endangered species, including some general success stories like the peregrine falcon and the American alligator, were delisted because their populations had actually recovered enough to make them no longer endangered.[192] Another supposed Endangered Species Act success story, the bald eagle, has moved in and out of the official list several times, and not always for scientific reasons, but because of the bird's cultural and political value.[193] Therefore, the crucial information made possible by the Endangered Species Act – the official list of protected species – does not adequately reflect the severity of the environmental problems it purportedly informs the public about, while delisting is not an adequate indicator of the act's ability to actually bring threatened species back from the brink of extinction.[194]

Chapter 6 Notes

[1] James Salzman and Barton H. Thompson, Jr., *Environmental Law and Policy* (New York: Foundation Press, 2003), 45-46.

[2] Richard J. Lazarus, *The Making of Environmental Law* (Chicago: University of Chicago Press, 2004), 86-87.

[3] U.S. Environmental Protection Agency, *Summary of the National Environmental Policy Act*, http://www.epa.gov/lawsregs/laws/nepa.html, accessed 23 June 2010.

[4] Samuel P. Hays, *Wars in the Woods: The Rise of Ecological Forestry in America* (Pittsburgh, Pa.: University of Pittsburgh Press, 2007), 25.

[5] James W. Spensley, Esq., "National Environmental Policy Act", in *Environmental Law Handbook*, vol. 14, ed. Thomas F.P. Sullivan (Rockville, Md.: Government Institutes, Inc., 1997), 411.

[6] Thomas L. Adams, Esq., "Enforcement and Liability", in *Environmental Law Handbook*, vol. 14, ed. Thomas F.P. Sullivan (Rockville, Md.: Government Institutes, Inc., 1997), 64-66.

[7] Ruth Ann Weidel, John R. Mayo, and F. Michael Zachara, "The Erosion of *Mens Rea* in Environmental Criminal Prosecutions," *Seton Hall Law Review* 21 (1991): 1100. The Clean Water Act and the Clean Air Act, to be covered in detail below, contain precise "knowing" provisions. See 33 U.S.C. §§ 1319(c)(2)-1319(c)(3) and 42 U.S.C. § 7413(c)(5), respectively.

[8] United States v. Hopkins, 53 F.3d 533, 536 (2nd Cir. 1995). The defendant in this case was charged with violating the well-known Clean Water Act, but claimed ignorance of that act's specific requirements.

[9] United States v. Laughlin, 10 F.3d 961, 965 (2nd Cir. 1993). Here the defendant was charged with illegally dumping creosote, but claimed not to know that the substance was regulated under RCRA.

[10] United States v. Goldsmith, 978 F.2d 643, 645 (11th Cir. 1992). This case involved the transport of a variety of substances regulated under RCRA, and whether the defendant knew that certain transport permits and methods were required per the statute.

[11] United States v. Sellers, 926 F.2d 410 (5th Cir. 1991). The substance at issue in this case was waste paint.

[12] United States v. Protex Industries, Inc., 874 F.2d 740, 743 (10th Cir. 1989). At issue in this case were several violations of RCRA by the company, which

knew that its activities could endanger employees but did not inform them of the imminent risks or provide them with proper protection.
[13] 2 F.3d 1071, 1088-1089 (10th Cir. 1993). The first of these two provisions is based on the responsible corporate officer doctrine from corporate law, in which an executive officer is presumed to understand his/her company's regular operations and cannot claim ignorance in the event of a major regulatory violation. In this case, the corporate officer was charged with violating RCRA by attempting to evade requirements for the storage and transport of natural gas condensate (a by-product of extraction processes) by blending it with automotive gasoline and selling it at a gas station.
[14] Wendy E. Wagner, "Commons Ignorance: The Failure of Environmental Law to Produce Needed Information on Health and the Environment," *Duke Law Journal* 53 (2004): 1694.
[15] Voluntary self-regulation is often promoted under a politically conservative philosophy of deregulation and limited government. At the practical level, voluntary self-regulation becomes necessary when that same conservative philosophy leads to staff and funding reductions at federal agencies. Arguing the effectiveness of self-regulation is beyond the scope of the present discussion, but the argument is a perennial one in political circles. Natasha Rossell Jaffe and Jordan D. Weiss, "The Self-Regulating Corporation: How Corporate Codes Can Save Our Children," *Fordham Journal of Corporate and Financial Law* 11 (2006): 909-917.
[16] 51 Fed. Reg. §§ 25,004, 25,006 (1986).
[17] Adams, "Enforcement and Liability," 64.
[18] 60 Fed. Reg. § 66,706 (1995).
[19] James T. Banks, "EPA's New Enforcement Policy: At Last, a Reliable Roadmap to Civil Penalty Mitigation for Self-Disclosed Violations," *Environmental Law Reporter* 26 (1996): 10227.
[20] 96 F.3d 971, 976-977 (7th Cir. 1996). This case did not originate with the EPA or an environmental dispute, but with a company's self-reporting of compliance with workers' compensation insurance regulations. In a similar case, a district court ruled that attorney-client privilege could be used for the same purpose, per a balancing test between the privilege and the public interest. Postal Service v. Phelps Dodge Refining Corp., 852 F.Supp. 156, 159-166 (E.D.N.Y. 1994).
[21] Adams, "Enforcement and Liability," 65-66, n.147.

[22] Salzman and Thompson, 8-9.

[23] 42 U.S.C. § 7401 (1967).

[24] 42 U.S.C . §§ 7401-7671 (1970).

[25] Doyle J. Borchers, "The Practice of Regional Regulation Under the Clean Air Act," *Natural Resources Lawyer* 3 (1970): 63.

[26] 42 U.S.C . §§ 7408-7409. The acceptable level of air quality is known formally as the National Ambient Air Quality Standard (NAAQS).

[27] 42 U.S.C. § 7410. Efforts by states to regulate their own sources of air pollution are defined as state implementation plans (SIPs), the variety and inconsistencies of which (among different states) are the primary catalyst of government and citizen litigation surrounding the Clean Air Act. Still, the Clean Air Act has been deemed a successful embodiment of "cooperative federalism," as both the federal government and the states are involved in its enforcement. Salzman and Thompson, 81. It is also important to note that scientists have since found that cars and trucks are the source of as much (or more) air pollution as industry and agriculture, but the effective regulation of these vehicles via the Clean Air Act has been elusive due to various social and economic issues.

[28] This endeavor is known formally as "new source review," which is codified at 42 U.S.C. § 7411. Permitting requirements are discussed in more detail below.

[29] 42 U.S.C. §§ 7472, 7475.

[30] 42 U.S.C. § 7661.

[31] 42 U.S.C. §§ 7470-7479, 7491-7492.

[32] 42 U.S.C. §§ 7501-7515.

[33] 40 C.F.R. § 52.21 (1978).

[34] 61 Fed. Reg. §§ 38285-38286 (1996). The most easily accessible database for citizens collects Clean Air Act permit requests and the EPA's responses to them. This database can be searched for facilities that are near public lands. U.S. Environmental Protection Agency, *Title V Petition Database*, http://www.epa.gov/region07/programs/artd/air/title5/petitiondb/petitiondb.htm , accessed 23 June 2010.

[35] 42 U.S.C. § 7503

[36] 51 Fed. Reg. § 43814 (1986). Statewide management efforts are usually achieved via emissions trading schemes, overseen by the EPA, though states

vary widely in attainment levels. Emissions trading is permitted under the Clean Air Act at 42 U.S.C. § 7661a(b)(10).

[37] Salzman and Thompson, 86-87.

[38] 42 U.S.C. §§ 7661b(a)-7661(b).

[39] 42 U.S.C. §§ 7661b(a); 40 C.F.R. § 70.5(a)(1).

[40] 40 C.F.R. §§ 70.7(a)(4), 40 C.F.R. § 70.5(c).

[41] 40 C.F.R. § 70.6(c). Note that possession of a permit makes the operator legally compliant with the terms of the Clean Air Act, but not necessarily ambient air quality standards. 42 U.S.C. § 7661(c)(f).

[42] 59 Fed. Reg. § 44460; 60 Fed. Reg. § 45530.

[43] 33 U.S.C. § 407 (1899).

[44] Prior to 1972, the most recent federal effort was the Water Quality Act, Pub. L. No. 89-234, 79 Stat. 903 (1965).

[45] Pub. L. No. 92-500, 86 Stat. 816 (1972).

[46] 33 U.S.C. §§ 1251-1387 (1972). The 1977 amendments are codified at Pub. L. No. 95-217, 91 Stat. 1582-1586 (1977).

[47] Salzman and Thompson, 127.

[48] Ridgway M. Hall, Jr. "The Clean Water Act of 1977," *Natural Resources Lawyer* 11 (1978): 343. The 1977 amendments to the Federal Water Pollution Control Act were made necessary by complex implementation requirements and some cases of vague statutory language in the 1972 statute. Ibid., 372.

[49] This permitting regime under the Clean Water Act is called the National Pollutant Discharge Elimination System (NPDES). 33 U.S.C. §§ 1311(a), 1362(12). The NPDES program combines the enforcement of precise effluent discharge levels at the sources of pollution with goals toward achieving precise water quality levels. Regulated pollutants were originally suspended solids only, with toxic chemicals being added in 1976 after a suit by environmental activists. Natural Resources Defense Council v. Train, 1976 U.S. Dist. LEXIS 14700 (D.D.C. 1976).

[50] Salzman and Thompson, 128-130, 145-146. This regulatory strategy reflects the aspirational nature of the Clean Water Act, though after more than three decades the act's goals of perfectly clean water sources throughout America are nowhere near fruition.

[51] 40 C.F.R. §§ 122.21, 40 C.F.R. § 122.22(a).

[52] 40 C.F.R. § 122.22(d).

[53] 40 C.F.R. §§ 124.74, 124.15(b), 124.16(a). This process is overseen by an administrative law judge at the EPA, though evidentiary requirements and matters of timing and standing are subject to state law. Either party in a dispute can also appeal the administrative law judge's decision to the federal circuit courts. 33 U.S.C. § 1369(b)(1)(F).

[54] 40 C.F.R. §§ 122.44(i)(2), 122.45(b), 122.48. These ongoing reports are called Discharge Monitoring Reports.

[55] 33 U.S.C. § 1321(a)(2). An accidental discharge is defined as including, but not limited to, "any spilling, leaking, pumping, pouring, emitting, emptying or dumping."

[56] 33 U.S.C. § 1321(b)(5).

[57] 40 C.F.R. § 25.2(b).

[58] 40 C.F.R. §§ 25.2(c)(1)-25.2(c)(7).

[59] A simple search of online legal services indicates the large quantity of lawsuits inspired by the Clean Air Act and Clean Water Act. For instance, in 2008, 172 cases involving Clean Air Act permits and 286 involving Clean Water Act permits were decided in the federal court system. The majority of these cases were disputes over EPA (or state authority) permitting decisions brought by either local citizens, environmental public interest groups, or the parties seeking the permits.

[60] Ivan Lieben, "Catch Me if You Can – The Misapplication of the Federal Statute of Limitations to Clean Air Act PSD Permit Program Violations," *Environmental Law* 38 (2008): 676-680.

[61] Pub. L. No. 101-549, 104 Stat. 2399 (1990), codified as amended at 42 U.S.C. § 7412.

[62] 57 Fed. Reg. § 31,576.

[63] 59 F.3d 1351, 1354, 1365 (D.C. Cir. 1995). The precise statutory definition of "major stationary source" under the Clean Air Act was also disputed at the circuit court level in Sierra Club v. Leavitt, 368 F.3d 1300 (11th Cir. 2004). Here the Eleventh Circuit ruled on a particular permit dispute in Georgia in which the EPA added uncertainty by defining "major stationary source" two different ways in the same sentence. The EPA's actions in this particular permit dispute were found to be "arbitrary and capricious" under the terms of the Clean Air Act and the Administrative Procedure Act.

[64] Sierra Club v. Georgia Power Company, 443 F.3d 1346, 1348-49 (11th Cir. 2006).

[65] 536 F.3d 469 (5th Cir. 2008).

[66] 536 F.3d 471. The relevant provisions of the Clean Air Act are at §§ 7604(a)(1), 7604(a)(3), 7604(f)(3), 7604(f)(4).

[67] 536 F.3d 471. The court supported this argument with a 1943 administrative law precedent that predated not only most modern American environmental jurisprudence, but the Administrative Procedure Act as well: *Burford v. Sun Oil Co.*, 319 U.S. 315 (1943).

[68] CleanCOALition v. TXU Power, *cert. denied*, 129 S. Ct. 648 (2008).

[69] 541 F.3d 1257, 1262 (11th Cir. 2008). The Clean Air Act authorizes the EPA to take action upon major modifications by a permit holder. 42 U.S.C. § 7413(a)(1).

[70] 541 F.3d 1266-1267. The Clean Air Act at 42 U.S.C. § 7661d(b)(2) allows discretion by the EPA in such matters, which then provided courts with a reason to exercise deference toward agency decisions.

[71] William L. Andreen, "Motivating Enforcement: Institutional Culture and the Clean Water Act," *Pace Environmental Law Review*, 24 (2007): 81-85.

[72] United States v. Ashland Oil and Transportation Company, 504 F.2d 1317, 1320-1329 (6th Cir. 1974).

[73] 33 U.S.C. § 1321(b)(5). Some of the argument surrounding this provision had to do with the term "navigable waters" and whether the creek in question qualified for that designation. The circuit court noted that the creek did qualify, and then went on to rule that the entire reporting provision was within Congress's constitutional powers. 504 F.2d 1324-1325.

[74] United States v. Kennecott Copper Corporation, 523 F.2d 821, 823-824 (9th Cir. 1975). This dispute stemmed from a leak in a pipeline carrying diesel fuel, with thousands of gallons spilling into a nearby pond and river.

[75] United States v. Ward, 448 U.S. 242 (1980). Here an Oklahoma oil company was charged with failing to report a leak into a tributary of the Arkansas River.

[76] 448 U.S. 248-251. In a noteworthy dissent, Justice John Paul Stevens found that the fines imposed under the Clean Water Act could be considered criminal penalties, per procedural precedent, because they entail punishment of lawbreakers who are then compelled to pay for the cleanup of their transgressions. Ibid. 257-260. It is also important to note that other sections of the Clean Water Act do denote criminal penalties for specific violations of water quality standards. For instance, a violator who has acted with negligence can be charged criminally under the act at 33 U.S.C. § 1319(c)(1)(a).

[77] Chevron USA, Inc. v. Yost, 919 F.2d 27, 28 (5th Cir. 1990). Emphasis in the ruling. The relevant provisions of the Clean Water Act are found at 33 U.S.C. §§ 1321(b)(3). 1321(b)(4).

[78] United States v. Knopfle, 2004 U.S. App. LEXIS 4384 (9th Cir. 2004). This case mostly dealt with evidentiary matters in finding whether the employee or his company was ultimately responsible for the discharge incident, and the ensuing imposition of penalties.

[79] Salzman and Thompson, 148. Rachel Carson's *Silent Spring* is often acknowledged as the first work to alert the general public of the dangers of toxic substances – the pesticide DDT in particular and synthetic industrial chemicals in general. Rachel Carson, *Silent Spring*, 40th Anniversary ed. (Boston: Houghton Mifflin, 2002).

[80] Salzman and Thompson, 148.

[81] Ibid., 148-149.

[82] Ibid., 156-158.

[83] 15 U.S.C. §§ 2601-2692 (1976). Note that a few more specific toxic substance control statutes were already in place, such as the Federal Insecticide, Fungicide, and Rodenticide Act, 7 U.S.C. § 136 (1972). That statute and some others dealt with the specific characteristics and risks of their particular substances, but did not attempt policy goals toward toxic substances in general, as did TSCA.

[84] Stanley W. Landfair, "Toxic Substances Control Act," in *Environmental Law Handbook*, vol. 14, ed. Thomas F.P. Sullivan (Rockville, Md.: Government Institutes, Inc., 1997), 226-227.

[85] Kevin Gaynor, "The Toxic Substances Control Act: A Regulatory Morass," *Vanderbilt Law Review* 30 (1977): 1161-1163.

[86] 15 U.S.C. § 2607(a).

[87] 15 U.S.C. §§ 2604(a)(2), § 2607(c), 2607(d).

[88] Landfair, 260.

[89] 15 U.S.C. §§ 2603-2604, 2607(b).

[90] 51 Fed. Reg. § 21,438.

[91] Gaynor, 1183-1184. The TSCA Chemical Substance Inventory is sold by the National Technical Information Service in a variety of hard copy or soft copy options, though the most recent hard copy version was compiled in 1990. The up-to-date version is often only available in the form of a very pricey CD-ROM. U.S. Environmental Protection Agency, New Chemical Program. *What*

is the TSCA Chemical Substance Inventory?, http://www.epa.gov/opptintr/newchems/pubs/invntory.htm, accessed 23 June 2010.

[92] Salzman and Thompson, 170.

[93] Ibid., 170-171.

[94] 42 U.S.C. §§ 6901-6992 (1976). This act is sometimes referred to as the Solid Waste Disposal Act, the original 1965 act that was amended by RCRA in 1976. In turn, RCRA was significantly amended by the Hazardous and Solid Waste Amendments of 1984, Pub. L. No. 98-616, 98 Stat. 3221 (1984).

[95] U.S. Environmental Protection Agency, *Summary of the Resource Conservation and Recovery Act*, http://www.epa.gov/lawsregs/laws/rcra.html, accessed 23 June 2010. Note that the vagaries of the text of RCRA allow "solid waste" to also include liquid and gas, which has caused a great amount of legal difficulty. The term "hazardous" is also poorly defined throughout the text of the act. See also Salzman and Thompson, 171-172.

[96] 42 U.S.C. § 6902(b).

[97] 40 C.F.R. §§ 261.31-261.33.

[98] U.S. Environmental Protection Agency, *RCRA Online*, http://www.epa.gov/epawaste/inforesources/online/index.htm, accessed 23 June 2010.

[99] 42 U.S.C. §§ 6925(a), 6925(b).

[100] 40 C.F.R. §§ 264.90, 264.101, 270.60, 280 (various subsections). The required information on a leak from an underground storage tank must include the regulated substance in question, areas that have been contaminated, any known equipment failures that contributed to the leak, actual or suspected effects on groundwater and soil, a corrective action plan, and the results of any cleanup efforts by the operator.

[101] 42 U.S.C. §§ 6928(b), 6991d(b). Confidential information, such as company trade secrets in the design and manufacture of commercial chemicals, may be exempted under the Freedom of Information Act.

[102] 42 U.S.C. §§ 9601-9675 (1980).

[103] David P. Franz and William H. Hefter, "Providing Reliable Information to Clients: The Case of Environmental Remediation," *International Journal of Applied Quality Management* 2 (1999): 213.

[104] This financial structure was authorized under the1986 Superfund Amendments and Reauthorization Act, Pub. L. No. 99-499 (1986). Some general tax funds are also used in the Superfund.

[105] Sam Howe Verhovek, "After 10 Years, the Trauma of Love Canal Continues," *New York Times*, 5 August 1988, B1. Health problems in the Love Canal neighborhood ranged from skin rashes and respiratory difficulties to unnaturally high rates of cancer and birth defects. In 1979, 900 residents were relocated at government expense. In 2004, the EPA announced that the Love Canal site no longer presented a threat to human health, and the site was removed from the Superfund list.

[106] James Bruggers, "Toxic Legacy Revisited: Valley of the Drums, 30 Years Later," *Louisville Courier-Journal*, 14 December 2008, http://www.courier-journal.com/article/20081214/NEWS01/81214001, accessed 23 June 2010. At the time of writing, the Valley of the Drums is still being cleaned up by EPA personnel.

[107] "Contaminated Town is Relegated to History," *New York Times*, 14 Apr. 1985, A26. The former location of Times Beach, just west of St. Louis, is now the site of a park commemorating historic U.S. Route 66. The site was deemed rehabilitated enough for removal from the Superfund list in 2001.

[108] U.S. Environmental Protection Agency, *National Priorities List*, http://www.epa.gov/superfund/sites/query/queryhtm/npltotal.htm, accessed 23 June 2010. A Superfund site is delisted if the EPA and other government entities involved in the cleanup determine that the requirements of CERCLA have been satisfied. Potential sites are sometimes delisted before Superfund cleanup begins, if the EPA finds that no further action is required. U.S. Environmental Protection Agency, *How Sites are Deleted from the NPL*, http://www.epa.gov/superfund/sites/query/queryhtm/npltotal.htm, accessed 23 June 2010. In either case, delisting is based on the statutory requirements of CERCLA and not necessarily on whether the site has been returned to pristine health and cleanliness.

[109] The Center for Public integrity, *Wasting Away: Superfund's Toxic Legacy*, http://projects.publicintegrity.org/superfund/?gclid=COyGraCF3ZgCFQu-GgoduVWOeA, accessed 23 June 2010.

[110] Jeff Hirsch, "Superfund May Not Be So Super." *Massachusetts Institute of Technology News*, 5 August 2008,

http://web.mit.edu/newsoffice/2008/superfund-0805.html, accessed 23 June 2010.

[111] Franz and Hefter, 213.

[112] 42 U.S.C. § 9603(a), 40 C.F.R. § 300.405. See also Franz and Hefter, 213.

[113] U.S. Environmental Protection Agency, *Superfund Information Systems*, http://www.epa.gov/superfund/sites/cursites/, accessed 23 June 2010.

[114] U.S. Environmental Protection Agency, *National Priorities List*, http://www.epa.gov/superfund/sites/npl/npl.htm, accessed 23 June 2010. Unlike some of the aforementioned EPA databases, this site provides both an overview of the concentration of NPL sites across the country and a great amount of interlinked documentation on each individual site.

[115] 40 C.F.R. § 300.430(f)(5).

[116] 42 U.S.C. §§ 9613(k), 9617(b).

[117] 42 U.S.C. §§ 9602, 9603, 9603(b), 9603(c). Hazardous substances are preliminarily defined under the Resource Conservation and Recovery Act (RCRA). In the event of contamination of water supplies, reporting requirements under the Clean Water Act are also pertinent to investigations at Superfund sites.

[118] Dow Chemical Company. v. EPA, 605 F.2d 673 (3rd Cir. 1979).

[119] 15 U.S.C. § 2607(d).

[120] 605 F.2d 681-682, 689.

[121] 42 U.S.C. §§ 6941- 6949a , 6921- 6939b.

[122] 852 F.2d 1309 (D.C. Cir. 1988).

[123] 852 F.2d 1310-1311. Here the court quoted U.S. House of Representatives Report No. 1491-15 (1976), in which Congress directed the EPA to study the issue.

[124] 852 F.2d 1313-1316.

[125] 907 F.2d 1179 (D.C. Cir. 1990). RCRA directs the EPA to regulate substances that are both solid *and* hazardous under the more stringent requirements of Subtitle C. 42 U.S.C. §§ 6903(5), 6921(b).

[126] 907 F.2d 1190-1192. The D.C. Circuit confirmed this interpretation of RCRA and its legislative history, with a victory for the accuracy of the EPA's official list of hazardous substances, in a very similar case four years later, Natural Resources Defense Council v. Environmental Protection Agency, 25 F.3d 1063 (D.C. Cir. 1994).

[127] 42 U.S.C. § 9603(a).

[128] United States v. Carr, 880 F.2d 1550 (2nd Cir. 1989). Here the defendant, a supervisor at a military facility from which hazardous materials had to be removed, was charged with violating CERCLA but attempted to argue that he was merely following orders.

[129] 938 F.2d 1299 (D.C. Cir. 1991).

[130] 42 U.S.C. § 9605(c)(1).

[131] 938 F.2d 1302-1304. Interestingly, the court found that an investigation of agency deference requirements was not relevant after analyzing Congressional intent.

[132] 5 U.S.C. § 553(b).

[133] 372 F.3d 441 (D.C. Cir. 2004).

[134] 372 F.3d 445.

[135] 42 U.S.C. §§ 11001-11050 (1986).

[136] Pub. L. No. 99-499 (1986).

[137] Vivek Ramkumar and Elena Petkova, "Transparency and Environmental Governance," in *The Right to Know: Transparency in an Open World*, ed. Ann Florini (New York: Columbia University Press, 2007), 279-280.

[138] 42 U.S.C. § 11023(j).

[139] Ann Florini, "The End of Secrecy," *Foreign Policy* 111 (1998): 50-51. This concept will be discussed in more detail in Chapter 7.

[140] Mary Graham, *Democracy by Disclosure: The Rise of Technopopulism* (Washington, D.C.: Brookings Institution Press, 2002), 22-23.

[141] Ramkumar and Petkova, 280-281.

[142] Lazarus, 112.

[143] Ramkumar and Petkova, 279-280. More data on reductions in toxic chemical emissions from 1988 to 2001 can be found in Graham, 51-53.

[144] Graham, 42.

[145] 42 U.S.C. §§ 11004(b)(1), 11004(b)(2).

[146] 42 U.S.C. §§ 11022(d), 11022(e)(3).

[147] Salzman and Thompson, 166.

[148] 42 U.S.C. § 11045. Penalties are assessed at the discretion of the EPA administrator.

[149] 772 F. Supp. 745 (W.D.N.Y. 1991).

[150] 42 U.S.C. § 11046(a)(1).

[151] 772 F. Supp. 750. Some reporting deadlines are mentioned in the act, particularly at 42 U.S.C. § 11021(d)(1). The statutory language elsewhere in

EPCRA does not exclude missed deadlines from the violations that can be grounds for government action or a citizen suit.
[152] Atlantic States Legal Foundation v. Buffalo Envelope, 823 F. Supp. 1065 (W.D.N.Y. 1993).
[153] Don't Waste Arizona v. McLane Foods Inc., 950 F. Supp. 972 (D.Ariz. 1996); Neighbors for a Toxic Free Community v. Vulcan Materials Company, 964 F. Supp. 1448 (D.Colo. 1997).
[154] 16 U.S.C. §§ 1531-1544 (1973).
[155] George Cameron Coggins, "Conserving Wildlife Resources: An Overview of the Endangered Species Act of 1973," *North Dakota Law Review* 51 (1974): 320.
[156] U.S. Senate Report No. 91-526 (1969), 3.
[157] U.S. House of Representatives Report No. 93-412 (1973), 4-5.
[158] Ibid.
[159] 16 U.S.C. § 1533.
[160] Salzman and Thompson, 255.
[161] Rudy R. Lachenmeier, "The Endangered Species Act of 1973: Preservation or Pandemonium?" *Environmental Law* 5 (1974): 29-30.
[162] The U.S. Fish & Wildlife Service is a unit of the Department of the Interior that is assigned to manage and preserve wildlife. The FWS manages the endangered species protection program as well as national wildlife refuges and national fish hatcheries, among other responsibilities. The FWS has law enforcement authority. U.S. Fish & Wildlife Service, *Conserving the Nature of America*, http://www.fws.gov/index.html, accessed 23 June 2010.
[163] 16 U.S.C. § 1533. The official list of endangered and threatened species in America is maintained by the FWS and includes species deemed worthy of protection by teams of scientists that work for and with that agency. Citizens may also petition for the inclusion of a particular species on the list. 16 U.S.C. § 1537(a).
[164] Bill McKibben, ed. *American Earth: Environmental Writing Since Thoreau* (New York: The Library of America, 2008), 993.
[165] Hays, *Wars in the Woods*, 7.
[166] Ibid., 25.
[167] Salzman and Thompson, 256.
[168] Philip Weinberg, "Endangered Statute? The Current Assault on the Endangered Species Act," *Villanova Environmental Law Journal* 17 (2006):

394-398. See also the Constitution of the United States of America, art. I, § 8, cl. 3, giving Congress the power to regulate interstate commerce. Many states have also attempted to regulate the protection of endangered or threatened species, with a preponderance of state regulations that add confusion and politicization (fueled by both developers and conservationists) to the entire species protection process, regardless of whether federal or state statutes are in question. Jean O. Melious, "Enforcing the Endangered Species Act Against the States," *William & Mary Environmental Law & Policy Journal* 25 (2001): 609-612.

[169] 437 U.S. 153 (1978).

[170] Pub. L. 93-632, 92 Stat. 3751 (1978). This 1978 amendment authorized the special cabinet-level committee and added that authorization to ESA at 16 U.S.C. § 1536(a)(2), with the procedures for finding an exemption codified at § 1536(h).

[171] Portland Audubon Society v. Endangered Species Committee, 984 F.2d 1534 (9th Cir. 1993). Introduced into this case was the declaration of a government employee who claimed that the God Squad faced political pressure from the George H.W. Bush Administration to exempt the northern spotted owl from the Endangered Species Act, thus allowing logging and development projects in the region to proceed. 984 F.2d 1550-1551.

[172] 16 U.S.C. § 1536(e).

[173] 984 F.2d 1536.

[174] 984 F.2d 1538-1541.

[175] 984 F.2d 1548-1549.

[176] 5 U.S.C. § 553.

[177] 16 U.S.C. §§ 1533(b)(3)(A), 1533(b)(1)(A).

[178] Salzman and Thompson, 259-260. Note that ESA includes a requirement for the consideration of economic and national security impacts upon listing a species, but this pertains to the effects of losing the species in question or its habitat, not the effects of restricting planned development projects. 16 U.S.C. § 1533(b)(2).

[179] Mark Bennett and Kurt Zimmerman, "Politics and Preservation: The Endangered Species Act and the Northern Spotted Owl," *Ecology Law Quarterly* 18 (1991): 124-129.

[180] Salzman and Thompson, 260.

[181] Northern Spotted Owl v. Hodel, 716 F. Supp. 479 (W.D. Wash. 1988). The bird was listed as the primary plaintiff on its own behalf, supported by a wide variety of environmental and conservation groups as secondary plaintiffs.

[182] 716 F. Supp. 481-483. The initial decision was ruled to be "arbitrary and capricious" under the Administrative Procedure Act, 5 U.S.C. § 706(2)(A).

[183] Brad Knickerbocker, "Northern Spotted Owl's Decline Revives Old Concerns," *Christian Science Monitor*, 27 June 2007, http://www.csmonitor.com/2007/0627/p02s01-sten.html, accessed 23 June 2010.

[184] Salzman and Thompson, 260.

[185] Ibid., 255.

[186] 63 Fed. Reg. § 9958.

[187] Hays, *Wars in the Woods*, 161-163.

[188] 73 Fed. Reg. § 76272. This and other similar regulations were enacted by Bush in December 2008, just prior to leaving the White House. Endangered Species Coalition, "President Obama Restores Endangered Species Protections," press release, 3 March 2009, http://www.stopextinction.org/cgi-bin/giga.cgi?cmd=cause_dir_news_item&news_id=61841&cause_id=1704, accessed 23 June 2010.

[189] U.S. White House, Office of the Press Secretary, *Memorandum for the Heads of Executive Departments and Agencies, Subject: The Endangered Species Act*, 3 March 2009, http://www.whitehouse.gov/the_press_office/Memorandum-for-the-Heads-of-Executive-Departments-and-Agencies/, accessed 23 June 2010.

[190] Salzman and Thompson, 270. This phenomenon of willful habitat destruction or species extermination by landowners is common enough to have earned its own nickname: "shoot, shovel, and shut up."

[191] Davis S. Wilcove and Lawrence L. Master, "How Many Endangered Species are There in the United States?," *Frontiers in Ecology and the Environment* 3 (October 2005): 414.

[192] Salzman and Thompson, 272.

[193] Saralaine Millet, "Birds Make Comeback," *Atlanta Journal-Constitution*, 2 August 2007, A19.

[194] Jeffrey J. Rachliniski, "Noah by the Numbers: An Empirical Evaluation of the Endangered Species Act," *Cornell Law Review* 82 (1997): 363-364. This article builds upon a review of the book *Noah's Choice: The Future of*

Endangered Species, in which authors Charles C. Mann and Mark L. Plummer proposed a moratorium on the Endangered Species Act due to scientific uncertainty, inaccurate reporting, and lack of success in actually protecting threatened species.

CHAPTER 7

The Impact of Environmental Information on Government Transparency

The transparency of environmental information in America was defined in the goals of the National Environmental Policy Act, which has influenced most environmental statutes enacted in the years since. In an ambitious policy statement, NEPA attempted to overhaul institutional decision-making across the entire federal government, with agencies being held accountable for their own actions affecting the environment.[1]

The National Environmental Policy Act and many of the subsequent statutes it influenced are largely built upon information disclosure, in the form of environmental impact statements, permit forms, and inventory reports; and the distribution of those documents to the public. NEPA forced government agencies to strive for better understanding of their own internal environmental practices, and perhaps more importantly, to adjust those processes to allow for greater procedural transparency.[2] NEPA has become one of the cornerstones of the modern American administrative state, and its requirement that every government agency prepare a detailed environmental impact statement for every proposed action restructured agency behavior almost as fundamentally as the Administrative Procedure Act.[3]

The scientific uncertainty of environmental protection had previously reduced the effectiveness of the documents managed by government agencies, and those that happened to find their way into the hands of citizens. The transparency and public participation provisions of NEPA were originally intended to reduce the effects of scientific uncertainty, and the act has had some important benefits for government transparency in general.[4] Environmental protection through information disclosure, while indirect, can lead to greater overall results for the natural world. For example, a pollution control statute like the Clean Air Act is criticized by industrial interests for its burdensome permit requirements, and is also criticized by environmentalists for its failure to truly clean up America's air quickly enough or comprehensively enough. On the other hand, informational and transparency requirements are easier to administer, and often more politically acceptable because they are procedural rather than substantive. It is easier to determine if an agency has followed procedural requirements during environmentally relevant activities than to determine if water is truly clean or if endangered species have been truly saved from the brink of extinction. Instead of unlikely substantive results, information disclosure requirements promote comprehensive planning and decision-making by government.[5]

However, the ambitious policy goals of NEPA quickly ran afoul of the established procedural focus of American administrative law, which has enabled government agencies to evade forward-looking decisions in favor of procedural minutiae that may have little positive effect on the natural world – or on the transparency of government-held environmental information.

Environmental Transparency and Modern Administrative Jurisprudence

The convergence of government transparency and environmental protection represents improvements in both realms, because each has been enhanced through the enactment of laws that require the observance of both.[6] In particular, the National Environmental Policy Act, in its precise requirements for the submission of environmental impact statements and the level of detail therein, has greatly increased the transparency of the federal government's environmental activities. Evidence also indicates that NEPA, coming as it did in an era of ambitious procedural statutes, has positively influenced the transparency of government agencies in general.[7]

A requirement for everyone to follow the same procedures is less likely to generate political opposition than a statute that punishes one polluter while doing nothing to other polluters who are doing the same thing. Political opposition is also less likely for statutes that focus on information disclosure, because disclosure can be framed as an enabler of economic freedom and free market principles. A fundamental premise of free market ideology is perfect information, which theoretically allows both buyers and sellers to make rational choices. With environmental statutes, this is particularly relevant for consumers who may reject companies that release toxic chemicals into the environment, so those companies will then be inspired to alter their processes.[8]

Another example of this phenomenon is the rapid growth of consumer safety and food testing regulations, complete with policies for reviewable labeling, that have been passed since the 1980s.[9] Another encouraging trend is the increase in transparency requirements by the Securities and Exchange Commission (SEC) for the fair buying and selling of company equities. The SEC has ruled that disclosure of company financial information should extend to the company's environmental activities and compliance with applicable statutes, further illustrating the convergence of environmental information disclosure and other forms of transparency at government agencies and the parties they regulate.[10]

The public participation provisions of the National Environmental Policy Act, and subsequent federal environmental statutes, have also been highly influential for American administrative policy in general. For statutes addressing pollution and other environmental problems, the resulting rules are better received by all parties if the public is included in the drafting of those laws. Given the complexity of nature and the scientific uncertainty of environmental problems, no politician, regulator, or scientist can possess the required breadth of knowledge and expertise, and government bureaucrats have a well-known tendency to resort to economic and/or technological risk analysis while forgetting to consider the effects of environmental problems on citizens and communities. Therefore, the unique perspective of citizens can be crucial to truly effective environmental regulation.[11]

More fundamentally, environmental law is inherently controversial, especially those statutes that give government regulators significant police powers over private property or private industrial interests, like the Endangered Species Act or the Superfund Act (CERCLA). Many critics also bemoan the seemingly impossible substantive goals of other statutes, like the pristine water quality philosophy of the Clean Water Act. But there is a value to public participation that transcends the question of whether the substantive goals of any law are realistic.[12] Public participation has been known to reduce the polarizing effects of controversial laws, because citizens from all sides of a controversy place value in being involved. The greater the participation in the drafting and enforcement of a statute or regulation, the more likely will be the acceptance of the resulting decisions even by those parties who must face the consequences of those decisions. A feeling of involvement in lawmaking can make the effects of those laws seem less involuntary, even to those who come out on the losing end of government regulatory actions.[13]

In this regard, environmental law after NEPA has had a profound impact on American administrative jurisprudence. Federal agencies previously behaved with a mechanical efficiency in transforming broadly-conceived statutes into mind-numbingly complex technical regulations. But agencies like the Environmental Protection Agency and the U.S. Department of the Interior, under the requirements of NEPA and affiliated statutes, were responsible for a significant transformation of government regulation into a more inclusive political process in which a wide variety of interests are (in theory) equally represented, from regulators to industrial interests to citizens. The transparency and public participation requirements of modern American environmental law have been instrumental in sparking this general trend across the entire federal government.[14]

Since the 1970s, the specific information disclosure practices that were defined by NEPA have influenced federal administrative practices at the fundamental level. Under the Freedom of Information Act (FOIA), the citizen has to request information through a fairly laborious codified process, so even though government-held information is accessible in theory it may might be difficult to obtain in practice. Documents in the hands of government agencies are restricted to those that are collected during their normal operations, regardless of whether such documents are likely to have any relevance to citizens. Also, citizens must know beforehand that a desired document exists before embarking on the request process, so obscure documents remain secret and opaque by default.[15]

But thanks to the procedural innovations of NEPA and the subsequent statutes (not just in environmental law) that it inspired, information disclosure has become more proactive. Under basic FOIA procedural requirements, government-held documents would have to be tracked down by citizens long after crucial agency decisions were made, and citizen action is often restricted to after-the-fact oversight of activities by government or by regulated parties. On the other hand, under NEPA and its affiliated statutes, information is collected primarily for the benefit of public participation and ongoing citizen oversight of government decisions and industry activities. The collection and disclosure of government-held documentation under these statutes can also be seen as a regulatory tool for proactively altering agency behavior, with greater accountability for the regulators whose decisions are recorded on those documents.[16]

Procedurally speaking, public participation and transparency can force regulators to determine acceptable levels of risk (of pollution or any other social problem worth regulating) through public pressure rather than bureaucratic analysis. Consequently, the determination of risk is subjected to a wide variety of influences, including the opinions of consumers, investors, and community residents (also known as voters), and not just the interests of regulators and industry players. More fundamentally, information itself becomes a regulatory tool. Unlike taxes and fees, which only affect behavior through the lens of financial decisions, information disclosure strategies force regulated parties to alter their behavior based on public perceptions and the resulting success or failure in the marketplace – both the marketplace of ideas and the economic marketplace.[17]

Regulation by Revelation

A useful new strategy for regulating environmental damage before it happens was instituted with the Emergency Planning and Community

Right-to-Know Act (EPCRA) in 1986. The potentially embarrassing or controversial public information required under EPCRA inspired some of the regulated companies to make that information more palatable by reducing the actual toxic emissions on which the reports are based. This effect has been termed "regulation by revelation."[18] In other words, a direct requirement for information has indirectly reduced pollution. While EPCRA only deals with private companies and not government officials, the "regulation by revelation" effect illustrates the basic philosophy behind transparency theory in general – that parties will act more equitably if enough information exists for those parties to be held accountable for their actions.[19] This regulatory strategy is becoming fairly common in American jurisprudence, though its true effectiveness across the board is open to dispute.[20]

The convergence of government transparency and environmental protection reflects the American public's desire for laws that better serve the public interest and allow citizens to check the activities of the government through access to government-held information. Most American environmental laws, building upon the National Environmental Policy Act, aspire to ensure that the information needed by citizens is fully developed and disclosed, and some laws (particularly toxic substance control statutes) assign full responsibility for the accuracy and delivery of that information to industry players, who in turn are required to fully cooperate with the government agencies that regulate them.[21] Thanks to the influence of environmental transparency on administrative practices across the federal government, citizens are armed with more and more information that they can use to do what has traditionally been done only by regulators: encouraging manufacturers, organizations, and authorities to work for the improvement of public health and safety.[22] Studies indicate that industrial firms are likely to alter their decisions on pollution and emissions if they face pressure from public watchdogs and community activists, and this pressure is enabled by greater information disclosure by those same firms.[23]

While American lawmakers have often allowed self-regulation by industry, the public has displayed an aversion to allowing polluters (and other industry players with an impact on the public interest) to regulate their own behavior with no information being provided to the government or to citizens.[24] When manufacturers are required by law to disclose information on their patterns of pollution or any other activity that has an impact on the public interest, their decisions are invested with the accountability and legitimacy that would be missing if they only provided information to the public voluntarily (or refused to do so), with no oversight of the accuracy or usefulness of the information provided.[25]

Surprisingly, statutes that enforce "regulation by revelation" are often supported by the parties regulated under them. These information disclosure requirements place great amounts of company information in the hands of the public, with corporate reputations at stake. Such requirements give industry a glimpse of not just the power of regulation, but the power of citizens – and not only their consumption choices but their political power as well. For instance, the chemical industry was generally accepting of the information disclosure requirements of the Emergency Planning and Community Right-to-Know Act because they believed that disclosure, no matter how burdensome, could reduce the chances of stricter regulations and penalties for violations after environmental damage had been done.[26]

The public information that has been made available under the "regulation by revelation" strategy has enhanced citizen knowledge on a wide variety of social problems – a task that has also been made easier by advances in information technology and Internet access. For example, the reports required under the various toxic substance control statutes have been compiled by the group Environmental Defense Fund onto the popular *Scorecard* website, on which citizens can find nearby sources of pollution by zip code. The site provides links to full scientific descriptions of the chemicals reported to the government, a wide variety of user-defined report options, and automatic transmission of e-mails to the user's government representatives.[27] Soon after *Scorecard* was launched in 1998, Frederick Webber, president of the Chemical Manufacturers Association (an industry lobbying group), warned his members that *Scorecard* would create immediate and lasting public pressure to cut toxic emissions, thus illustrating the political power of the site, and of public information disclosure.[28] By 2002 a network of environmental groups had put together an even more detailed site on toxic pollutants by geographic location and by industry called *RTK Net* (*RTK* stands for "right to know"). This site makes use of information made available by the Emergency Planning and Community Right-to-Know Act.[29]

Environmental and public heath activists have made efforts to alter the behavior of companies based on the information provided to, and by, these and similar websites. For example, *Scorecard* has posted not just what is known about regulated toxic chemicals and their effects on public health, but what is *not* known, and its easily configured reports have highlighted the gaps in government knowledge and industrial disclosure. Activists have also learned via *Scorecard* that industries frequently introduce chemical substances into wide use (usually in internal manufacturing processes but sometimes in consumer markets) before their health effects are fully known.[30] The political ramifications of this information (or lack thereof) became a reality in 1998 when Environmental Defense Fund collaborated with Vice President Al Gore on an initiative to increase the speed of collection and distribution of industrial toxicity information. The chemical industry agreed to an extensive and enhanced testing program at a cost of more than $20 million dollars per year, thanks to statutory requirements for information disclosure.[31]

Disclosure of information is often more effective as a regulatory tool than traditional command and control strategies, which are built on ordering specific types of behavior and then punishing transgressions. Proactively encouraging industry to disclose information can reduce the risk of future citizen lawsuits or government penalties for those industrial players, and can also reduce the likelihood of environmental damage that will have to be cleaned up later by parties other than the company that did the damage. Meanwhile, industry players can be encouraged to alter their behavior voluntarily before releasing potentially troublesome information to the public.[32]

However, effective implementation and enforcement are essential to achieving the goals of such statutes.[33] A university study of "regulation by revelation" statutes, ranging from nutritional labeling requirements to the Toxic Release Inventory under the Emergency Planning and Community Right-to-Know Act, found that these types of statutes do not always achieve their substantive goals because of a lack of two-way communication. While the mandatory disclosure of information is directly informative to citizens, there is usually no codified method of returning information about public reactions to the industry players regulated by the statutes. So it is possible to affect industry behavior through "regulation by revelation," but the public's knowledge returns to industry via a route that is indirect at best. This perpetuates the need for punitive government measures and can even defeat the purpose of requiring disclosure in the first place.[34]

A related problem is the organization of the information that changes hands between government and citizens. Most of the documentation mandated by American environmental statutes moves from the government agency to the citizen in unfiltered and unorganized form, often resulting in severe data overload. The average citizen is unlikely to be able to sift through imposing piles of technical documents. So even though agencies and the parties they regulate may very well deliver the required information, true "regulation by revelation" is held back by procedural quantity over substantive quality. Much of the time, American environmental regulation is rich in paperwork but poor in truly useful information.[35]

The final problem with "regulation by revelation" is that it is inherently dependent on self-reporting by industry. Some commentators find agency encouragement of self-reporting to be more desirable than heavy-handed command and control regulation. However, given the immense regulatory demands brought about by modern American industrial and economic patterns, with agency personnel and enforcement budgets that are limited and frequently manipulated by Congress for political gain, agencies can become dependent on self-reporting by their regulated parties – and industry knows it.[36] Thus, the overload of mind-numbing documents engendered by environmental statutes and the government's dependence on industry self-reporting are the Achilles heels of environmental transparency in the modern American administrative state.

The Viability of Environmental Transparency Statutes

The National Environmental Policy Act has achieved mythic status as a regulator of government agency behavior and as a statement of America's concern for the natural world. But where the rubber meets the road, NEPA is simply another statute subjected to the whims of Congress and the courts, vulnerable to the type of administrative interpretation that has significantly weakened or marginalized the act's substantive environmental goals.[37] The act's ambitious policy mandate and vague procedural requirements have left it prone to patterns of judicial review and laborious litigation that have sapped both its principles and its procedures.[38]

Also, the act's central provisions are framed in lofty generalities that leave a great amount of discretion to the entities that execute its requirements, including any federal agency that regulates a development project with environmental consequences, and the act gives those entities little detailed instruction on how to comply with it.[39] So while NEPA attempted to institute a far-reaching policy of environmental protection across the American government, an absence of *a priori* compliance mechanisms have given federal agencies plenty of leverage in finding ways to ignore or discredit the act's substantive goals of natural protection.[40]

The act's vagueness was critiqued by the Court of Appeals for the D.C. Circuit just one year after it went into effect. In one of the earliest cases involving a dispute over an environmental impact statement, the seminal *Calvert Cliffs* case, the D.C. Circuit noted with disdain that "NEPA, like so much other reform legislation of the last 40 years, is cast in terms of a general mandate and broad delegation of authority."[41] The policy goals of NEPA fared little better a few years later at the Supreme Court. In the *Vermont Yankee* case,[42] a crucial precedent for both environmental law and administrative law, Justice William Rehnquist laid down this restrictive and limited view of NEPA:

NEPA does set forth significant substantive goals for the Nation, but its mandate to the agencies is essentially procedural. It is to insure a fully informed and well-considered decision, not necessarily a decision the judges of the Court of Appeals or this Court would have reached had they been members of the decisionmaking unit of the agency. Administrative decisions should be set aside in this context, as in every other, only for substantial procedural or substantive reasons as mandated by statute, not simply because the court is unhappy with the result reached.[43]

Significantly, during its procedural discussion the high court added that the outcome of any agency action in which procedures were properly followed would be enough to satisfy the agency's obligations under both NEPA and the Administrative Procedure Act, and only a procedural flaw could possibly render the resulting decision moot during judicial review.[44] Two years later in the *Strycker's Bay* case,[45] the Supreme Court essentially killed once and for all any judicial enforcement of NEPA's substantive policy goals. Using *Vermont Yankee* as a procedural precedent in the present dispute over an agency decision based on a properly-compiled environmental impact statement, the high court stated that:

...once an agency has made a decision subject to NEPA's procedural requirements, the only role for a court is to insure that the agency has considered the environmental consequences; it cannot interject itself within the area of discretion of the executive as to the choice of action to be taken.[46]

In other words, the only role for the courts in a dispute over an environmental impact statement is to enforce a poorly-defined "consideration" of environmental values and to ensure that agencies reach their decisions in accord with established administrative procedures.[47] This narrow procedural focus, as defined by the Supreme Court in *Vermont Yankee* and *Strycker's Bay*, placed NEPA and most subsequent environmental jurisprudence squarely within the realm of administrative law. This does not bode well for citizens who attempt to use NEPA and its affiliated environmental statutes to compel the American government to observe the act's substantive goals of natural protection, because the courts have ruled that an environmental impact statement (and by extension, many other kinds of government-held environmental documents) are only exercises in the procedural compilation of information. Little can be done about poor agency decisions that are made with that information, other than cleaning up environmental damage later.

Meanwhile, environmental information requirements are laborious by definition and often unrealistic at the practical level, inspiring government agencies to find procedural workarounds or legal strategies to avoid those requirements altogether. Most notably, NEPA demands that a government agency supply a huge amount of information all at once in the form of an environmental impact statement. The EIS is a one-time project built upon mostly *ex ante* information and is expected to predict and forecast all possible environmental consequences as well as reasonably foreseeable methods of mitigation. In short, NEPA requires an agency to predict, in detail, everything that's going to happen.[48] These predictive requirements can have tragic and unintended consequences for the environment, by forcing the analysis of *possible* protection rather than the enactment of *actual* protection. Also, while American environmental law is focused on *ex ante* prediction, there is usually no requirement for agencies to subsequently verify that their predictions were accurate, and no penalties for inaccurate predictions.[49] NEPA also contains no distinct guidelines for the level of accuracy within documents associated with the environmental impact statement, as long as proper procedures were followed when that possibly false information was drawn up.[50]

The emphasis on information and analysis inspires critiques of environmental law from all quarters. Economic and industrial players are known to be frequent critics of American environmental statutes, but environmentalists are often critical of the basic structure of those statutes as well. For example, the analysis required by the Toxic Substances Control Act (TSCA) and similar statutes, in which government agencies are required to perform various types of risk assessment, can lead to a phenomenon derided by environmentalists as "paralysis by analysis." With the Environmental Protection Agency required to compare the risks and benefits of each new toxic chemical, the agency may get bogged down in analysis and run through its budget before embarking on its true mission of controlling or restricting the chemical in the public interest.[51]

This problem became an issue in a court dispute concerning TSCA, *Corrosion Proof Fittings v. EPA*.[52] The case dealt with the

EPA's process of deciding to ban asbestos in the late 1970s. At the time, asbestos was one of the most widely-studied toxic substances in the world, and scientists possessed voluminous and extensively-reviewed data on its dangers to people and the environment. Regardless, the EPA followed the analysis-intensive procedures dictated by TSCA and took nearly ten years reviewing information and building its case, creating tens of thousands of pages of administrative records in the process.[53] The agency finally announced in 1988 that it had decided on a total ban of asbestos, based on a cost-benefit analysis involving the value of jobs lost and lives saved. Upon an industry request for review of this decision, the Fifth Circuit Court of Appeals reversed the EPA's decision with disdain for its narrow yet time-consuming analytical method. The court pointed out the irony of paralysis by analysis: "of most concern to us is that the EPA has failed to implement the dictates of TSCA."[54] The EPA was following the requirements of TSCA as it understood them, but in its drive for administrative comprehensiveness the agency failed to see that at some point its lengthy analysis created cost overruns and bureaucratic inaction that damaged its mission of regulation in the public interest. And all the while, people were still being exposed to asbestos.[55]

This type of laborious cost/benefit analysis also suffers from a paradoxical lack of transparency despite the enormous amount of documentation. An overload of statistical minutiae can allow government regulators to cook the books and cover up the scientific uncertainty that is natural in any analysis of environmental risks and rewards. The obscurity of the investigative process and the uncertainty of the resulting data can allow agencies to reach wide varieties of conclusions without proper public oversight. Indeed, the ultimate agency decision might be based more on policy than science, and information overload reduces the ability of the public to detect possible inequities in such decision-making processes.[56]

The basic scientific uncertainty behind environmental problems and proposed solutions is another serious problem in itself. The character and magnitude of environmental risks is almost always a matter of speculation, and there is no guarantee that proposed mitigation measures will be successful. These uncertainties are especially onerous in the regulation of toxic substances. Statutes like the Toxic Substances Control Act and the Resource Conservation and Recovery Act contain many provisions for the collection and management of information for use by the public, but with so much scientific uncertainty, more information may not necessarily be better. Knowing more about risks does not guarantee the development of effective solutions, and being misinformed about risks can lead to much wasted effort by regulators and interested citizens.[57]

The true viability of environmental transparency statutes has also run afoul of the more practical issue of trade secrets and confidential company information. The result of this phenomenon, once again, is incomplete information of dubious usefulness to regulators or citizens. Toxic substance control statutes feature many bail-out provisions that allow regulated parties, even though they created the need for toxic substance information disclosure in the first place, to avoid providing any more than rudimentary data on their toxic inventories. And notwithstanding the philosophical benefits of full disclosure of information with public health ramifications, the toxic substance control laws provide no incentives for industry to provide information with the level of detail that will be most useful to citizens but will lead to fines or other punishment for the company in question. Thus, industrial producers of toxic chemicals are unlikely to see any benefit in proactively disclosing their information, particularly under the reporting requirements of the Toxic Substances Control Act (TSCA). On the other hand, they might be willing to take their chances with future penalties or even to obfuscate the information that is released, leading to public ignorance rather than knowledge of the true details of toxic dangers.[58]

A variety of statutes, environmental and otherwise, also allow private companies to maintain their trade secrets and to avoid disclosing that information to the government, if disclosure is likely to damage the company's profits when the released information falls into the hands of competitors. This conflict over the protection of trade secrets in the face of the substantive goals of environmental and other public interest statutes remains unresolved, and the focus on intellectual property may have subsumed true protection of public health. Industry is likely to overstate the need for trade secrets protection for information that might not be so sensitive in reality, while transparency advocates are just as likely to overstate the need for more information on anything related to public health.[59]

The Toxic Substances Control Act, which features requirements for the transparency of chemical information from industry, is especially vulnerable to the non-disclosure of trade secrets. In light of the trade secrets exemption to the Freedom of Information Act (FOIA),[60] TSCA allows the EPA to treat as "confidential" any industry information that has been affirmatively earmarked by a company as a trade secret.[61] This information must not be disclosed to the public, under TSCA or FOIA, unless the EPA determines that disclosure is necessary "to protect health or the environment against an unreasonable risk of injury."[62] The problem here is that the company can declare the information in question to be a trade secret, which then inflicts the EPA with the burden of proof in determining if it is *not* a trade secret under FOIA. Here, TSCA creates an incorrect burden of proof that forces a regulatory inconsistency with FOIA, which then requires the EPA to justify the withholding of industrial toxic substance information upon citizen request.[63]

This discrepancy has allowed chemical manufacturers to overstate which pieces of their information supposedly deserve confidential trade secrets protection, from the basic ingredients used in manufacturing their toxic substances to the location of manufacturing plants. The burden is then on the EPA to determine if the claim of confidentiality is valid and if non-disclosure is in the public interest – a determination that requires review of the very same information that the company claims is confidential and therefore refuses to disclose.[64] TSCA makes it quite easy to make inappropriate claims of this magnitude, reducing the usefulness of the government's official list of toxic substances and requiring agencies and citizens to fight for information in the event of damage to the environment or to public health. This adds some doubt as to whether the Toxic Substances Control Act is truly effective in informing the public about toxic dangers,[65] with lessons to be learned from competing philosophies of transparency and confidentiality in American administrative jurisprudence.

In addition to the protection of trade secrets, the informational requirements of American environmental laws have also been subjected to the winds of political change and the prevailing interpretation of the spirit of the Freedom of Information Act. While FOIA endorses full disclosure of government-held documents at citizen request, the act includes nine exemptions for types of documents in which the costs of disclosure to certain parties may outweigh the benefits to public knowledge. These exemptions are prone to political interpretation, particularly the national security exemption,[66] which became a matter of great contention during the George W. Bush Administration. The administration's definition of "national security" expanded greatly after the September 11, 2001 terrorist attacks and the subsequent military operations in Afghanistan and Iraq,[67] and environmental information was swept along with the tide.

In 2003, Bush convened a NEPA Task Force to determine the types of environmental information that could be considered "sensitive" in the new political and military arena. The resulting report shows how environmental protection had entered the age of political diligence against terrorism, making use of a Department of Defense definition of "sensitive" information that includes any knowledge "that could be used by someone to harm the health and safety of the public or otherwise undermine U.S. security interests."[68] This could include information on major infrastructure like dams, bridges, airports, and public drinking water systems; as well as information on toxic chemical research and production.[69]

The Task Force report did not recommend blanket exemptions of these types of information from disclosure requirements under NEPA (via environmental impact statements) or FOIA, but it did state that the transparency and public participation objectives of those acts must be balanced against the protection of "sensitive" information for security purposes.[70] The security-related restriction of government transparency, particularly in regards to environmental information, sharply contradicts both the substantive policy goals and administrative procedure requirements of NEPA. While the federal government's perceived need for greater information security eventually cooled, it is worth noting that environmental transparency can be subjected to increases in government-mandated secrecy inspired by security crises.[71] As noted above, the lofty goals of NEPA make it prone to political manipulation.

Exemptions for trade secrets and national security tend to occur in cycles, based on the economic ideologies and political developments of the time. But the information disclosure requirements of American environmental laws also suffer from more timeless handicaps. At the fundamental level, the sheer volume of data and reports required under NEPA and affiliated environmental statutes is a drawback for both protection and transparency. While NEPA requires a great amount of information and investigation during the environmental impact statement process, the resulting document is often quite uninformative. Many EISs are literally thousands of pages long and few people read all the way through, not even those involved in their creation. An environmental impact statement is usually cumbersome and boring, and hundreds are complied every year across the federal government.[72]

More information is not always better, and over-inclusiveness can make it difficult to separate the bad (or useless) information from the good. The EIS itself is rarely a good device for informing anyone interested in a government environmental decision – not agency personnel and certainly not the public layperson. Due to the time and expense, an EIS is also typically submitted for public comment after the environmental decision has already been made, and only for those decisions that were deemed to be so potentially destructive that the agency could not avoid compiling the EIS in the first place.[73]

It is also important to note that a far greater number of preliminary environmental assessments find no significant environmental impact,[74] in the form of tens of thousands of government documents indicating how NEPA-mandated environmental analysis was avoided. Despite the enormous complexity of the modern American administrative state, the number of full environmental impact statements submitted across the entire federal government per year is surprisingly small, averaging approximately 500 per year since the early 1980s. However, from the enactment of NEPA in 1970 to the early 1980s, the number of EISs per year was considerably higher, peaking at approximately 2000 per year in the early 1970s but then declining rapidly each year.[75]

The difference is a change in procedure, namely the advent of the preliminary environmental assessment (EA), The number of environmental assessments (the investigations in which agency regulators determine if an EIS is necessary) that predict no significant environmental impacts number in the tens of thousands each year, indicating another issue with the procedural focus of NEPA, in which reporting procedures are given precedence over substantive environmental protection. When the EA announces that a full EIS will not be necessary, NEPA allows an unceremonious end to environmentally enlightened government decision-making. This allows the agency to conclude during the EA phase that no more environmental investigation is needed, thus making a decision that circumvents the core requirements of NEPA and requiring citizens to challenge the process after the fact.[76]

Depending on one's views of lawmaking, litigation, and bureaucracy, there are different ways to assess NEPA's effectiveness in promoting environmental decision-making. A transparency activist would conclude that forcing government agencies to confront information they otherwise would not consider, via the environmental impact statement process, leads directly to more informed and rational agency decisions,[77] while also increasing the democratic goals of public participation.[78] An active environmental activist may find little use for the tedious information found in an EIS, but will make use of NEPA's procedural requirements to legally challenge the EIS process in order to delay or kill unwanted development projects. This activist knows that preparing an EIS is a time-consuming and expensive endeavor for any government agency, and litigation around a faulty EIS is even more time-consuming and expensive – giving environmentalists the weapon of bureaucracy. This transforms NEPA into a negative weapon for legal obstruction, rather than a positive tool for enlightened environmental protection.[79]

Government officials and watchdogs also have their own views of NEPA. Skeptics see the act as allowing obstructionism from special interest groups (environmentalists and other foes of development projects), forcing budgetary overruns and bureaucratic minutiae, and hindering economic development.[80] A broader version of this viewpoint would find a perhaps unconstitutional burden on government processes, with the legislative branch trying to micro-manage executive branch activities.[81]

And finally, some legal thinkers would find NEPA not too burdensome, but too anemic.[82] The act's mandate for proper procedures and reports forces a focus on the information collection process but not the decisions made with that information. In other words, NEPA should be less procedural and more substantive in order to be truly effective in promoting actual environmental protection.[83] In either case, NEPA and its affiliated environmental statutes place a rather naïve trust in the ability of government actors and regulated parties to supply information that may reflect badly upon them. This leads inevitably to incomplete and contested information about the true causes of government-caused environmental harm, which in turn damages research into possible solutions.[84]

The procedural focus of NEPA has also weakened the very same information that the act mandates. NEPA indeed requires an environmental impact statement for all government regulatory decisions that are expected to significantly impact the environment. But administrative procedure has allowed government agencies, in all but the most extreme cases of possible damage, to avoid the EIS and its laborious reporting and public participation requirements altogether.

This is accomplished via a regulatory tool that was not envisioned in the original text of NEPA, the finding of no significant impact (FONSI). A "mitigated FONSI" allows an agency to avoid triggering a full-scale EIS by redefining the proposed project to include structured mitigation efforts, which would purportedly repair the very same environmental damages that would have been described in the full EIS.[85] The mitigated FONSI was legitimized by the Court of Appeals for the D.C. Circuit, which ruled in 1982:

> An EIS must be prepared only when significant environmental impacts will occur as a result of the proposed action. If, however, the proposal is modified prior to implementation by adding specific mitigation measures which completely compensate for any possible adverse environmental impacts stemming from the original proposal, the statutory threshold of significant environmental effects is not crossed and an EIS is not required.[86]

This interpretation of administrative procedure does not comply with the statutory text of NEPA, which requires agencies to "include in every recommendation or report on proposals for legislation and other major Federal actions significantly affecting the quality of the human environment, a detailed statement by the responsible official."[87] Nevertheless, the use of mitigated FONSIs has become overwhelmingly popular with federal agencies, who have found that the proposed physical mitigation efforts might cost less than the research requirements and bureaucratic demands of a full EIS, not to mention future lawsuits over environmental damages.[88]

But the problem with this process is that even though courts have found that a FONSI is procedurally acceptable under NEPA, the FONSI process has somehow escaped the NEPA transparency requirements which, in an absurd quirk of procedural interpretation, still only apply to the full EISs. Detailed information on the exact number of FONSIs produced across the federal government, and their contents, has traditionally been unavailable because agencies are not required to report FONSIs to the EPA and sometimes not even to their own agency headquarters.[89]

And with FONSIs becoming the chosen method of environmental investigation for agencies, another administrative quirk has appeared that damages the substantive goals of NEPA. In short, even though courts have validated the FONSI process through a creative reading of NEPA, they have avoided interpreting the requirements of the act any further in terms of enforcement, in which the plain statutory language still holds sway. NEPA does not clearly require that the proposed mitigation efforts of a FONSI actually be implemented, and the Supreme Court has found such documents to be nonbinding, ruling in 1989 that NEPA requires "mitigation [to] be discussed in sufficient detail to ensure that environmental consequences have been fairly evaluated," but also noted that the act does not require "a complete mitigation plan [to] be actually formulated and adopted."[90] Thus, the courts have allowed government agencies to avoid full research of environmental impacts by bypassing the EIS process with a FONSI that merely proposes mitigation efforts, but have ruled that those efforts need not be implemented at all.[91] This weakens both the transparency requirements and the substantive goals of NEPA.

NEPA has some other critical shortcomings, but not simply because it demands too much information from federal agencies.

Instead, NEPA falls short because it demands the wrong types of information at the wrong times. The major drawback of the environmental impact statement process is that it is entirely predictive, requiring government agencies to report on what is expected to happen. But if those predictions turn out to be inaccurate, especially if the environmental degradation becomes worse than expected, there is no subsequent requirement in NEPA for review or mitigation of poor prognostication.[92] Thus, inaccuracy in an EIS can be engendered by bureaucratic incompetence or malfeasance at the agency, and then blamed on scientific uncertainty, with NEPA offering no assistance in cleaning up the ensuing environmental destruction.

And finally, the substantive policy goals of NEPA are restricted by the very structure of the American economic system. The act regulates the informational transparency of federal government agencies, but those agencies are dependent on information that is ultimately handled by parties that are not subjected to the act's requirements – private parties in commerce and industry. In a capitalist economy, these parties ultimately control environmental information, and have the most influence over its accuracy and availability.[93]

NEPA's requirements for disclosure of information apply only to the interactions between government entities and private parties, and not the activities conducted by private parties before they meet with regulators. The government does not come into the possession of information until after these interactions take place, while NEPA only mandates the disclosure of information that the government actually possesses. A heavily criticized flaw in NEPA and similar statues is that there are no requirements for private actors (typically industry in this context) to furnish information to the government about their pollution and environmental degradation *before* they occur. Consequently, government (and by extension, citizens) will only become aware of industry malfeasance after environmental damage has already happened, at which point the primarily reactive American environmental statutes require the government to become involved in mitigation and cleanup efforts. This is precisely the scenario that NEPA and other American environmental laws, in spirit, try to prevent.[94]

The culprit here is the fact that the parties that are expected to disclose this information to the public are also the parties that could be penalized for the details therein. Regulated industrial parties obviously possess the most useful information about the environmental consequences of their activities, since they have probably performed robust testing and research for their own commercial purposes. But environmental statutes that "force" (from industry's point of view) the disclosure of this information are likely to inspire industry to conceal it. In their role as the users of substances or perpetrators of activities that can damage the environment, industrial parties are in the unique position of both creating and controlling the information that can be used later by regulators and citizens. This informational power encourages obfuscation and withholding.[95]

A subsequent problem with industry control of environmental information is that it becomes difficult for the EPA and other government agencies to justify their regulatory decisions. In effect, a company can challenge a regulatory decision in court, which then necessitates a burden of proof for the agency in justifying its decision. Unfortunately, that proof is often dependent on the very same information that the company refused to disclose earlier in the process. When the information that the agency does manage to obtain is incomplete or lacking in sufficient detail, agency regulatory decisions become very difficult to uphold under the requirements of administrative jurisprudence. Essentially, courts have required agencies to support decisions with unobtainable evidence.[96] This is another reason why the holders of most pollution- and public health-related information in America, industrial operators, have little incentive to disclose their own information showing that their products or processes might be dangerous to the environment.[97]

Information is power, and this is especially true for environmental protection. The National Environmental Policy Act and its affiliated statutes seek to improve the government's environmental performance by compelling the compilation and disclosure of environmental information. However, given the longstanding procedural requirements of American administrative jurisprudence and the vague substantive goals of these environmental statutes, they have proven to be awkward and inefficient vehicles for true freedom of environmental information. While these statutes mandate the creation of huge amounts of information that can increase public knowledge, that very same mandate increases the likelihood of manipulation and concealment of that information by government and industrial players who have lesser opinions on the merits of true transparency.[98]

The success of disclosure-based environmental statutes and regulations ultimately depends on the performance of citizens. Government can compel industry to provide at least some pertinent information to agencies. But that information will sit unused unless citizens actively demand information via statutory transparency provisions and transform that knowledge into political action, citizen lawsuits, or administrative redress against parties who commit damage to the environment or to public health. Without citizen action, information disclosure regulations of any kind are likely to be ignored by regulated parties and unenforced by regulators.[99] The lack of public participation might also make these laws manipulable by the only parties who still think about them – industry and regulators – and who will be tempted to restrict or alter the laws so they no longer work in the public interest.[100]

Unfortunately, the American statutes that strive for substantive progress in the transparency of government-held information, environmental protection, and the transparency of government held information *about* environmental protection, have been handicapped by the administrative and procedural focus of American jurisprudence. The statute that embodies all of these substantive goals – the National Environmental Policy Act – has suffered through an evolutionary process in which agency procedure and judicial review have drained it of the substance envisioned by its framers.[101]

Chapter 7 Notes

[1] Matthew J. Lindstrom, "Procedures Without Purpose: The Withering Away of the National Environmental Policy Act's Substantive Law," *Journal of Land Resources & Environmental Law* 20 (2000): 250.

[2] Richard J. Lazarus, *The Making of Environmental Law* (Chicago: University of Chicago Press, 2004), 185.

[3] Bradley C. Karkkainen, "Whither NEPA?," *New York University Environmental Law Journal* 12 (2004): 333-334.

[4] Lazarus, 185-186.

[5] Ibid., 186.

[6] Ibid., xiv.

[7] James Salzman and Barton H. Thompson, Jr., *Environmental Law and Policy* (New York: Foundation Press, 2003), 285.

[8] Lazarus, 186-187.

[9] Mary Graham, *Democracy by Disclosure: The Rise of Technopopulism* (Washington, D.C.: Brookings Institution Press, 2002), 77-90. The key federal statute requiring transparency in food labeling is the Nutrition Labeling and Education Act, Pub. L. No. 101-535 (1990), which was a significant amendment to the Federal Food, Drug, and Cosmetic Act, 21 U.S.C. §§ 301-910 (1938). Another crucial federal statute that is indirectly influenced by environmental transparency is the Occupational Safety and Health Act (OSHA), 29 U.S.C. §§ 651-678 (1970), which includes requirements to shield employees from workplace exposure to the toxic chemicals that are regulated by various environmental statutes. OSHA also includes some reporting and transparency provisions similar to those in the toxic substance control statutes.

[10] Cynthia A. Williams, "The Securities and Exchange Commission and Corporate Transparency," *Harvard Law Review* 112 (1999): 1246-1263. It should be noted that enforcement of SEC transparency regulations has been highly inconsistent due to the shifting political ideologies of its appointed commissioners, and its environmental information requirements have rarely been enforced as strongly as those for profit and loss information.

[11] Donald T. Hornstein, "Reclaiming Environmental Law: A Normative Critique of Comparative Risk Analysis," *Columbia Law Review* 92 (1992): 614-615.

[12] Lazarus, 190.

[13] Ibid.

[14] Richard B. Stewart, "The Reformation of American Administrative Law," *Harvard Law Review* 88 (1975): 1670.

[15] Graham, 15.

[16] Ibid.

[17] Ibid., 10.

[18] This term was coined by environmental attorney Karen Florini and first appeared in print in Ann Florini, "The End of Secrecy," *Foreign Policy* 111 (1998): 50-51.

[19] Glen O. Robinson, "Access to Government Information: The American Experience," *Federal Law Review* 14 (1983): 37-41.

[20] David Weil, Archon Fung, Mary Graham, and Elena Fagotto, "The Effectiveness of Regulatory Disclosure Policies," *Journal of Policy Analysis and Management* 25 (2006): 155-181.

[21] Wendy E. Wagner, "Commons Ignorance: The Failure of Environmental Law to Produce Needed Information on Health and the Environment," *Duke Law Journal* 53 (2004): 1663-1664.

[22] Graham, 137.

[23] Seema Arora and Timothy N. Cason, "An Experiment in Voluntary Environmental Regulation; Perception in EPA's 33/50 Program," *Journal of Environmental Economics and Management* 28 (1995): 271-286; Marianne Lavelle, "Environmental Vise: Law, Compliance," *National Law Journal* 15 (30 August 1993): S1-S9.

[24] Lazarus, 232.

[25] Graham, 139.

[26] Ibid., 140.

[27] Scorecard: The Pollution Information Site, http://www.scorecard.org, accessed 23 June 2010.

[28] Graham, 59.

[29] RTK Net: The Right-to-Know Network, http://www.rtknet.org, accessed 23 June 2010.

[30] Graham, 60.

[31] John H. Cushman, Jr., "Gore Asks Chemical Industry to Test for Any Toxic Effects," *New York Times*, 22 April 1998, A24. Testing and reporting standards for toxic chemicals were weakened significantly during the George W. Bush Administration, largely because of reductions in funding for the EPA and a

prevailing philosophy of industry deregulation. Marla Cone, "EPA is Faulted as Failing to Shield Public from Toxins," *Los Angeles Times* 13 July 2005, A18.

[32] Bradley C. Karkkainen, "Information-Forcing Environmental Regulation," *Florida State University Law Review* 33 (2006): 869, 902.

[33] Ann Florini, "Whither Transparency?," in *The Right to Know: Transparency in an Open World*, ed. Ann Florini (New York: Columbia University Press, 2007), 339.

[34] Weil, et al., 175.

[35] Bradley C. Karkkainen, "Toward a Smarter NEPA: Monitoring and Managing Government's Environmental Performance," *Columbia Law Review* 102 (2002): 916-917.

[36] Wagner, 1689-1690.

[37] Karkkainen, "Whither NEPA?," 334.

[38] Lindstrom, 255.

[39] Robert L. Fischman, "The EPA's Duties and Ecosystem Services," *Stanford Environmental Law Journal* 20 (2001): 510.

[40] Lindstrom, 255.

[41] Calvert Cliffs Coordinating Committee v. Atomic Energy Commission, 449 F.2d 1109, 1111 (D.C. Cir. 1971). This case is discussed in detail in Chapter 4.

[42] Vermont Yankee Nuclear Power Corp. v. Natural Resources Defense Council, 435 U.S. 519 (1978). This seminal ruling stemmed from several cases concerning citizen objections to a license granted by the Atomic Energy Commission for a nuclear power facility. Citizens originally disputed the agency's conduct when soliciting public comments during the licensing process, including comments about environmental risks. By the time the disputes reached the Supreme Court, the high court embarked on a lengthy analysis of not just environmental law but larger questions of administrative jurisprudence.

[43] 435 U.S. 558. Rehnquist referenced the Court of Appeals because here the high court (in a consolidated ruling) was overturning two previous decisions by the D.C. Circuit in which that court invalidated agency environmental decisions on substantive rather than procedural grounds. Natural Resources Defense Council v. Nuclear Regulatory Commission, 547 F.2d 633 (D.C. Cir. 1976); Nelson Aeschliman v. Nuclear Regulatory Commission, 547 F.2d 622 (D.C. Cir. 1976).

[44] 435 U.S. 548. An agency decision is most likely to be found moot or unenforceable under the "arbitrary and capricious" doctrine of the Administrative Procedure Act, 5 U.S.C. § 706(2)(A).

[45] Strycker's Bay Neighborhood Council, Inc. v. Karlen, 444 U.S. 223, 227-228 (1980). This case involved an EIS submitted for a housing project, and was fully introduced in Chapter 4.

[46] 444 U.S. 227-228. This statement was also inspired by another NEPA-related precedent at the high court, Kleppe v. Sierra Club, 427 U.S. 390, 410 (1976).

[47] Lindstrom, 261.

[48] Karkkainen, "Whither NEPA"," 344.

[49] Ibid.

[50] Daniel A. Dreyfus and Helen M. Ingram, "The National Environmental Policy Act: A View of Intent and Practice," *Natural Resources Journal* 16 (1976): 255-256.

[51] Salzman and Thompson, 163.

[52] 947 F.2d 1201 (5th Cir. 1991).

[53] Salzman and Thompson, 164.

[54] 947 F.2d 1229.

[55] Salzman and Thompson, 165. In another noteworthy example of paralysis by analysis, the EPA took seventeen years to do a regulatory cost/benefit analysis of the plant growth enhancer Alar (daminozide), getting bogged down in the administrative requirements of the Federal Insecticide, Fungicide, and Rodenticide Act. Ibid.

[56] Ibid., 166.

[57] Graham, 138.

[58] Wagner, 1624-1625, 1631-1632.

[59] Graham, 147.

[60] Under the Freedom of Information Act, trade secrets information that is held by government agencies can be withheld from disclosure to the public, in the event of a request from a citizen. 5 U.S.C. § 552(b)(4). The information disclosure requirements of the Emergency Planning and Community Right-to-Know Act are also tempered by a provision allowing for the protection of trade secrets. 42 U.S.C. § 11042.

[61] 15 U.S.C. §§ 2613(a), 2613(c)(1).

[62] 15 U.S.C. § 2613(a)(4).

[63] Kevin Gaynor, "The Toxic Substances Control Act: A Regulatory Morass," *Vanderbilt Law Review* 30 (1977): 1166-1167.

[64] Wagner, 1645.

[65] Julie Yang, "Confidential Business Information Reform Under the Toxic Substances Control Act," *The Environmental Lawyer* 2 (1995): 222-223, 226-227. In the mid-1990s the EPA announced substantially reduced penalties for failure to disclose required information under TSCA. Chemical companies then immediately offered 11,000 product studies and reports to the EPA voluntarily – four times the number delivered in the previous fifteen years combined. Wagner, 1648.

[66] 5 U.S.C. § 552(b)(1).

[67] Christina E. Wells, "'National Security' Information and the Freedom of Information Act," *Administrative Law Review* 56 (2004): 1209-1213.

[68] U.S. Government, NEPA Task Force. *Report to the Council on Environmental Quality: Modernizing NEPA Implementation*, September 2003, 17, http://ceq.hss.doe.gov/ntf/report/finalreport.pdf, accessed 23 June 2010. This report discussed many different aspects of NEPA enforcement and procedure, largely reflecting the current view of the act's administrative and regulatory requirements. The opening chapter was dedicated to information security.

[69] Karkkainen, "Whither NEPA?," 359.

[70] NEPA Task Force, 17.

[71] Karkkainen, "Whither NEPA?," 359.

[72] Ibid., 346-347.

[73] Ibid., 346. Recall that NEPA requires an EIS for any major regulated action with a potentially significant impact on the environment. 42 U.S.C. § 4332(2)(C). As seen in a previous chapter, an EIS can be avoided if the agency determines that the action in question is not "major," or will not have an impact on the environment. Decisions of this nature can only be challenged by citizens in court after the development project has already commenced or after the environmental degradation has already occurred, while the courts have traditionally deferred to agency expertise on such matters.

[74] Karkkainen, "Whither NEPA?," 348.

[75] U.S. Environmental Protection Agency, EPA Office of Federal Activities, *EISs Filed by Year, 1973-2006,*

http://epa.gov/enforcement/resources/publications/nepa/number_eis_1973_200
6.pdf, accessed 23 June 2010.

[76] Eric Glitzenstein, "Project Modification: Illegitimate Circumvention of the
EIS Requirement or Desirable Means to Reduce Environment Impacts?"
Ecology Law Quarterly 10 (1982): 271-272.

[77] Karkkainen, "Whither NEPA?," 338-339.

[78] Michael Herz, "Parallel Universes: NEPA Lessons for the New Property,"
Columbia Law Review 93 (1993): 1709.

[79] Karkkainen, "Whither NEPA?," 339-341.

[80] Ibid., 341-342.

[81] Frank B. Cross, "The Judiciary and Public Choice," *Hastings Law Journal*
50 (1999): 375.

[82] Karkkainen, "Whither NEPA?," 342-343.

[83] Joseph L. Sax, "The (Unhappy) Truth About NEPA," *Oklahoma Law Review*
26 (1973), 239.

[84] Wagner, 1622-1623

[85] Karkkainen, "Information-Forcing Environmental Regulation," 879-880.

[86] Cabinet Mountains Wilderness v. Peterson, 685 F.2d 678, 682 (D.C. Cir.
1982).

[87] 42 U.S.C. § 4332(C).

[88] Albert I. Herson, "Project Mitigation Revisited: Most Courts Approve
Findings of No Significant Impact Justified by Mitigation," *Ecology Law
Quarterly* 13 (1986): 69.

[89] Karkkainen, "Information-Forcing Environmental Regulation," 880.

[90] Robertson v. Methow Valley Citizens Council, 490 U.S. 332, 352 (1989).

[91] Karkkainen, "Information-Forcing Environmental Regulation," 882.

[92] Karkkainen, "Whither NEPA?," 338, 344.

[93] Wagner, 1717-1726.

[94] Ibid. The Emergency Planning and Community Right-to-Know Act is a rare
exception to this pattern.

[95] Ibid., 1641-1642.

[96] Richard J. Pierce, "Two Problems in Administrative Law: Political Polarity
on the District of Columbia Circuit and Judicial Deference to Agency
Rulemaking," *Duke Law Journal* 1988 (1988): 311.

[97] Wagner, 1680-1681.

[98] Karkkainen, "Whither NEPA?," 362-363.

[99] Vivek Ramkumar and Elena Petkova, "Transparency and Environmental Governance," in *The Right to Know: Transparency in an Open World*, ed. Ann Florini, (New York: Columbia University Press, 2007), 292.
[100] World Resources Institute, *Decisions for the Earth: Balance, Voice, and Power 2002-2004* (Washington: World Resources Institute, 2003), 57.
[101] Nicholas C. Yost, "NEPA's Promise – Partially Fulfilled," *Environmental Law Journal* 20 (1990): 533-534.

CHAPTER 8

Conclusion

Environmental information certainly exists in America, but true freedom of environmental information has only been partially achieved. Administrative procedure allows government agencies to manipulate the availability and transparency of relevant documents, and information overload can reduce the true usefulness of documents that are actually obtained by citizens. Longstanding patterns of government secrecy in all areas of public policy also have a negative impact on environmental transparency, and the structure of the American economy gives the most informational power to industrial interests who have little motive to disclose documents that may reflect badly upon them. Government regulators are largely dependent on self-reporting by industry, with no guarantee of the accuracy or usefulness of the disclosed information. And most importantly, the procedural focus of administrative law gives citizens little recourse when challenging bad government decisions that were made by following the proper procedures.

Secrecy and the Environment

Environmental information is not immune to the patterns of government secrecy that have affected American governance throughout the nation's history, and it has often been a matter of principle for American politicians to oppose government transparency.[1] The persistent political hostility derives from a practical desire to protect the confidentiality of government communications. Fortunately, the farther down the executive chain of command one goes, the less obstinate is the opposition to disclosure. Among the individuals who process the requests and authorize the disclosure of documents at government agencies, there is usually a genuine respect for transparency and the public's right to know, even if agency employees merely view disclosure as an administrative requirement under the law.[2]

Right-to-know scholar Daniel Hoffman notes that federal government secrecy in America shifts with political and social trends,[3] and the rise of popular environmentalism in the 1960s and 1970s is just one example of how the legislative branch of the federal government promoted greater transparency as a social policy, only to have that transparency run afoul of established administrative patterns in the executive branch (where regulatory agencies are housed). According to Hoffman, government secrecy is most likely to become a bone of contention during times of rapid social change – when the public demands greater political engagement and participation, and policy issues are salient and divisive.[4] This was certainly the case during the civil rights era and its aftermath, when America passed most of its more powerful environmental statutes and their transparency provisions.

Even so, the legislative battle against secrecy in the executive branch requires a climate of respect for the law, structural mechanisms for authoritative rulemaking, and a clear sense of mission and values in the formation of policy.[5] Given the increasing complexity of the modern administrative state, including the activities and structures of government agencies, the management and availability of government-held information plays a more and more important role in the ability of citizens to review how well the government protects their interests – including their interests in natural protection.[6]

Modern administrative complexity requires the government to make more use of often arcane regulatory schemes and to hire unelected scientists and industry experts, all of which are allowable under the Constitution. This makes transparency and public participation all the more crucial for the American system of checks and balances, and citizens need legislation that enables them to oversee the often mysterious and impenetrable procedures and activities of executive branch agencies. Increasingly complex inter-agency relations and conflicts also make the collection and management of accurate and useful environmental information all the more important for the lawmaking process.[7]

In the words of Supreme Court Justice and legal scholar Louis Brandeis, statutes that require disclosure of information are not momentary reactionary measures, but a means for creating continuous economic and political pressure for change. Rules and penalties are inevitably of limited effect, and Brandeis saw government-mandated publicity and disclosure as a "continuous remedial measure," and that "publicity offers a more promising remedy... which would apply automatically."[8] Thus, there is true merit to statutory requirements for the disclosure and transparency of government-held information, environmental or otherwise. But as discussed throughout this book, high-level transparency policies in the public interest tend to become less equitable for citizens when issues of control and procedure are considered.

The State of Freedom of Environmental Information in America

We live in an age of information, and information is power. In modern times, the sheer volume of information and the technological means to manage and distribute it are unprecedented. For citizens concerned about the environment, government-held information is more robust and obtainable than ever before. But as with all types of government-held information, the same technology that has made that information more accessible has also made it easier for gatekeepers to manipulate and conceal it.[9]

In recent years the use of government authority to force the disclosure of information has taken a legitimate place beside the authority to set standards and redistribute resources. Both of these are legitimate strategies for reducing risks to the public. Congress has approved a variety of environmental regulations that require systematic disclosure by corporations and other large organizations of the dangers to public health and the environmental posed by their products or activities. These statutes aim to prevent deaths and injuries from toxic chemicals, drinking water contaminants, and other environmental hazards by mandating that companies reveal detailed information about their contribution to those risks.[10] The resulting information is then managed by agencies like the EPA and provided to the public, either proactively or by request.

However, giving citizens systematic access to factual information about risks to public health and the environment has never been a dominant theme of American policy. Traditionally, rules and regulations are the products of debate among politicians and experts, and the information generated during the enactment or enforcement of those regulations usually remains in the hands of those same politicians and experts. Much of this information makes a one-way trip to federal or state government offices, where it remains in obscure files or databases until particular documents are requested by citizens.[11]

Despite the increase in recent decades of environmental statutes that mandate the disclosure of information, at the practical level transparency collides with established bureaucratic and administrative behavior. Disclosure is almost always achieved through political compromise, and regardless of the law, disclosure is dependent on the whims of powerful political interests who may have less concern about transparency and more concern about trade secrets, national security, bad publicity, or avoidance of controversy.[12] Policymaking, including the development of environmental transparency requirements, is always a power struggle among competing interests – government, corporations, and citizens.[13]

Statutory disclosure requirements, in environmental or any other type of law, offer a certain level of flexibility but also some very serious costs. In particular, a dependence on disclosure by agencies requires after-the-fact oversight by citizens who will not realize that those parties are withholding information until after the occurrence of the type of problem, such as environmental damage, that the statute in question tries to prevent. This phenomenon allows unilateral decision-making by agencies that can contradict the wishes of Congress or citizens, a breakdown of disclosure practices at agencies, a loss of respect for transparency, and a pattern of ignoring statutory mandates for purposes of political expediency.[14] This problem is compounded even further when those agencies are themselves dependent on voluntary disclosure of information by the parties they regulate.

The trend toward greater transparency and public participation in American environmental regulation has made real progress, as can be seen in the number of statutes containing provisions on those matters. But greater transparency presents both citizens and regulators with difficult choices regarding the trade-offs between competing goals, and transparency highlights the complexity of these issues but does not necessarily resolve them.[15]

While the Environmental Protection Agency administers most of the federal statutes discussed herein, the disclosure and transparency provisions of those laws are based on those in the National Environmental Policy Act. Recall that there is no higher body that oversees or enforces that act's provisions, so agency non-compliance with those provisions does not become a matter of public knowledge until interested citizens draw attention to that non-compliance – often after the occurrence of the environmental damage that the act strives to prevent.[16] In effect, NEPA has been rendered toothless by its own lack of enforcement and oversight provisions.

Federal agencies have a great amount of discretion toward which portions of the National Environmental Policy Act, the Endangered Species Act, toxic substance and pollution control laws, and other federal environmental statutes that they should observe, and to what extent. Agencies interact with the natural world in many different ways, and the resulting damage should be ameliorated by NEPA and its affiliated statutes. Unfortunately, the inadequate language of these statutes has prevented complete enforcement of their requirements for natural protection and the transparency of government-held environmental information.[17]

In the short term, particular laws could conceivably be amended to resolve damaging loopholes. Most importantly, the National Environmental Policy Act should be amended to close its major gaps in enforcement and independent oversight of its provisions. For instance, the Achilles heel of environmental information is that government agencies depend upon regulated parties in industry to furnish information voluntarily, and on their own terms, before the question of the usefulness (to citizens) of the disclosed information is raised. Agencies like the EPA have long taken a laissez-faire attitude in assuming that their regulated parties will observe environmental laws with minimal agency oversight. This process encourages disregard for those laws until after they are broken and citizens are forced to bring suit to ameliorate damage.[18]

The Council on Environmental Quality (CEQ), the executive branch office established by NEPA for *post-hoc* data collection and advisement to the President, could be elevated to an oversight body that reviews agency compliance with federal environmental statutes (including their transparency provisions) while major agency actions are in progress, with the goal of encouraging all parties to observe environmental regulations and to try to avoid damage to the natural world beforehand. In their current forms NEPA and most other federal environmental statutes offer some limited options for after-the-fact punishment of environmental transgressors (and government agencies who don't follow the proper procedures), but unfortunately these statutes are largely powerless in directly preventing environmental degradation before it occurs, and this severely damages the very spirit of American environmental policy. With more preemptive enforcement of NEPA's provisions, government agencies may be encouraged to modify their own environmental impacts rather than face the relatively small risk of citizen lawsuits after the damage is done.[19] A greater focus on transparency and disclosure of information would facilitate this process.

Longstanding trends of American jurisprudence, particularly judicial deference to agency expertise and an agency's statutory mandates, are unlikely to change without a major evolutionary shift in the nation's regulatory arena – toward agency accountability and away from procedural regularity.[20] Over the long term, the doctrine of agency deference should be modified to include not only deference to decisions directly related to the agency's primary mission, but also outside matters that might be indirectly affected by that primary mission, like environmental protection. Courts should not assume that agencies possess expertise in environmental matters, especially if the agency mission is unrelated to that subject area.[21]

Therefore, the doctrine of agency deference in the courts should be modified to reflect that agencies that are not directly mandated to protect the environment should not receive automatic deference toward their decisions and actions that cause environmental damage. Unfortunately, in the *Vermont Yankee* case, a crucial Supreme Court precedent in both environmental and administrative law, the high court ruled in the opposite fashion, placing the substantive goals of environmental law squarely within the requirements of the Administrative Procedure Act. In the words of the unanimous court, the judiciary must not "impose upon the agency [its] own notion of which procedures are 'best' or most likely to further some vague, undefined public good."[22] This statement by the Supreme Court belittles policy mandates, such as the call for a federal environmental policy in the National Environmental Policy Act,[23] as "vague" and "undefined," indicating a rhetorical triumph of procedure over substance in the eyes of American jurisprudence. *Vermont Yankee* has remained the definitive precedent on the intersection of environmental and administrative law. The latter is usually the automatic victor in court, severely reducing the judiciary's flexibility in reviewing whether agency decision-making is truly in the public interest and whether affiliated statutes (including environmental statutes) have been properly observed.[24]

It is important to remember that federal agencies, regardless of defects in their environmental records, do not necessarily ignore NEPA and other federal environmental statutes out of spite for the natural world or out of a wanton disregard for the concerns of citizens. Because of longstanding trends in administrative jurisprudence, tough decisions must be made when a pan-agency statute conflicts with an agency's statutory mandate regarding its primary mission.[25] The statutes that define an agency's mandate, and jurisprudential practices that defer to that mandate in the event of conflicting regulatory requirements, make NEPA and other federal environmental statutes weaker in comparison. Thus, American governance is bound to a regulatory and jurisprudential status quo that cannot fully discourage or prevent environmental non-compliance in the first place.[26]

Proposals for Increasing Environmental Transparency

To achieve true freedom of environmental information in America, massive reforms are necessary not just in administrative jurisprudence but in the established bureaucratic behavior patterns of federal agencies. In the short term, such radical reforms are unlikely if not impossible. However, some minor adjustments in agency administration might get the ball rolling toward substantial improvements in the transparency of government-held information.

Asking insightful questions and understanding bureaucratic behavior can be helpful to the citizen who is requesting documents. One must avoid the policy sentimentality that makes far-reaching statutes like the National Environmental Policy Act attractive to environmentalists and government watchdogs, but disdained or dismissed by career government employees. Likewise, the legal remedies available to citizens who run afoul of bureaucratic non-disclosure should be focused less on the substantive policy goals of the statute in question and more on behavioral realities.[27]

For example, citizens (during the document request process) and courts (during judicial review of non-disclosure disputes) should take a realistic view of the behavioral mechanisms behind the dispute. For instance, when disclosure of scientific information is mandated by statutes like the Toxic Substances Control Act, citizens and judges should not expect "independent" scientists to undermine the agencies that sign their paychecks, should not assume that agency employees believe or are even aware of vast statutory policy goals, should not expect agencies to turn against their employees or bureaucratic allies, and should not expect agencies to willingly deviate from their mandated missions.[28] All of these assumptions create a misunderstanding of why non-transparency happens in government agencies, and working around these assumptions can increase the likelihood of useful disclosure.

Meanwhile, one of the great substantive weaknesses of NEPA and its affiliated environmental statutes is that they mandate no follow-up to their significant informational requirements. Thanks to the vague language of the statutes and the subsequent case law, a bad decision by an agency becomes acceptable if the proper administrative procedures were followed before that decision was made. A possible solution to this fundamental conundrum would be post-decision monitoring, in which agencies are required to follow-up their own environmental impact statements and report on the accuracy of their predictions and the resulting environmental consequences.[29]

This process would engender the creation of even more government-held information (which is already one of the most prevalent criticisms of NEPA), but the resulting data could be used to improve future environmental impact statements by the same agency or involving similar natural phenomena. More importantly, this process would improve true transparency under NEPA by making agencies more accountable for their inaccurate predictions and poorly-considered decisions, and would improve government performance in environmental protection overall.[30] But as matters stand now, an agency could make a disastrous environmental decision, but as long as the EIS is procedurally adequate, the agency will suffer no sanctions and will probably escape accountability.

Processes of information collection also need to be reformed before that information becomes truly transparent and useful for citizens. Presently, under toxic substance control laws government regulators assume that industrial players will collect and manage the required information appropriately. This leads to gaps in information, as the regulated parties are unlikely to be motivated to disclose information that will reflect badly upon them. In turn, the resulting information is incomplete and slanted toward corporate interests.[31] Policymakers must drop the assumption of full voluntary compliance by regulated parties and stop expecting the information to be fully accurate and useful, and should switch to proactive efforts to encourage the disclosure of crucial information. This could be accomplished with standardized information collection and production requirements, proactive incentives, and even publicity efforts by regulators to stigmatize biased information and industry-funded research on toxic chemicals.[32]

Due to the complexities of the natural world and all its problems, the management and disclosure of government-held environmental information has turned out to be far more complicated than envisioned by the drafters of the National Environmental Policy Act and its affiliated statutes. It might be time to dispense with the assumption that environmental problems can be easily understood and ameliorated if the government simply makes enormous amounts of industrial and agency information available to citizens. The informational provisions of American environmental law are almost entirely predictive, requiring one-time documentation and analysis of complex environmental damages that have not yet occurred, for government development projects that have not yet commenced. So environmental information requirements under these statutes create two problems that are contrary to the fundamental goals of those statutes – they impose burdensome bureaucratic demands on agencies to provide potentially unrealistic information, but then do nothing to prevent those same agencies from manipulating that information and making bad environmental decisions based on it.[33]

Upon obtaining such information, the citizen can do little about the agency's behavior without challenging the process in court, and victory is increasingly unlikely due to the administrative and procedural focus of American jurisprudence. Here, policymakers could learn from environmental science and assume that the best way to avoid damage to the natural world is to use the "learn as you go" approach, based on continuous and systematic monitoring with periodic reassessments or adjustments of policy decisions. In effect, government environmental performance would become a holistic process of learning and adapting.[34] But for now, American environmental law front-loads investigation before agency decisions are made – certainly making government-held information voluminous, but also making it decreasingly useful to citizens who would like to utilize that information to fight pollution and other types of damage to the natural world.

The true long-term and fundamental impacts of transparency and disclosure on American public policy are still to be discovered. Environmental law employs a number of specific transparency provisions that have been tailored to address specific problems. At the higher level, American transparency as embodied in the Freedom of Information Act is still a work in progress.[35] Greater enforcement of existing regulations, and a cultural and administrative shift away from secrecy and toward disclosure, are necessary before citizens can truly participate in policymaking in a way that levels the playing field and gives citizens the ability to truly protect their interests against power players in government and industry.[36]

Citizen activists would be wise to avoid the assumption that the wide-ranging substantive policy goals of statutes like the National

Environmental Policy Act, Clean Air Act, or Endangered Species Act can lead to truly enlightened environmental decision-making. Administrative realities have steered American environmental law away from natural protection for its own sake and toward the observance of proper procedures, via a yet-to-be-proven belief by lawmakers that procedural minutiae will automatically lead to wise decisions. Modern American policy has made true freedom of environmental information imaginable, but that freedom has not yet been achieved because of the realities of our political and judicial system.

Chapter 8 Notes

[1] Herbert N. Foerstel, *Freedom of Information and the Right to Know: The Origins and Applications of the Freedom of Information Act* (Westport, Conn.: Greenwood Press, 1999), 71.

[2] Ibid., 71-72.

[3] Daniel Hoffman, *Government Secrecy and the Founding Fathers: A Study in Constitutional Controls* (Westport, Conn.: Greenwood Press, 1981), 261.

[4] Ibid.

[5] Ibid., 261-262.

[6] James Salzman and Barton H. Thompson, Jr., *Environmental Law and Policy* (New York: Foundation Press, 2003), 45-46.

[7] Richard J. Lazarus, *The Making of Environmental Law* (Chicago: University of Chicago Press, 2004), 19-28. A pertinent example of inter-agency conflict, discussed previously, is the reluctance of many federal regulatory agencies to coordinate with the U.S. Fish & Wildlife Service for research into endangered species protection and proposed mitigation measures.

[8] Louis D. Brandeis, *Other People's Money: and How the Bankers Use It* (New York: F.A. Stokes, 1914), 92, 98. Here Brandeis was discussing political efforts during the age of large trusts (controlled by financiers like J.P. Morgan) to increase the transparency of the financial sector.

[9] Bradley C. Karkkainen, "Whither NEPA?," *New York University Environmental Law Journal* 12 (2004): 362.

[10] Mary Graham, *Democracy by Disclosure: The Rise of Technopopulism* (Washington, D.C.: Brookings Institution Press, 2002), 2.

[11] Ibid., 4.

[12] Ibid., 5.

[13] Vivek Ramkumar and Elena Petkova, "Transparency and Environmental Governance," in *The Right to Know: Transparency in an Open World*, ed. Ann Florini (New York: Columbia University Press, 2007), 305.

[14] Hoffman, 261-262.

[15] Ramkumar and Petkova, 300.

[16] Nicholas C. Yost, "NEPA's Promise – Partially Fulfilled," *Environmental Law* 20 (1990): 547-549.

[17] Lynton K. Caldwell, "A Constitutional Law for the Environment: 20 Years with NEPA Indicates the Need," *Environment* 31 (Dec. 1989): 6, 25-26.

[18] Yost, 549.

[19] Susannah T. French, "Judicial Review of the Administrative Record in NEPA Litigation," *California Law Review* 81 (1993): 964.

[20] Mark Seidenfeld, "Cognitive Loafing, Social Conformity, and Judicial Review of Agency Rulemaking," *Cornell Law Review* 87 (2002): 517-522.

[21] This pattern of agency deference to agency expertise and decision-making processes is constrained by the *Chevron* doctrine (based on a 1984 Supreme Court ruling), which is cited in many, if not most, rulings in which a citizen has challenged a matter of agency procedure or the substantive results of an agency decision. The *Chevron* doctrine instructs courts to defer to agency discretion if the agency's governing statute is sufficiently open-ended to indicate that Congress intended the agency to regulate complex phenomena on a case-by-case basis and with its own best judgment. *Chevron* has since become one of the defining precedents for the entire realms of administrative law and judicial review, with a prevailing philosophy of discouraging excessive judicial branch second-guessing of the actions of executive branch agencies. Chevron USA, Inc. v. Natural Resources Defense Council, 467 U.S. 837 (1984).

[22] Vermont Yankee Nuclear Power Corp. v. Natural Resources Defense Council, 435 U.S. 519, 548-549 (1978).

[23] 42 U.S.C. § 4331.

[24] Colin S. Diver, "Policymaking Paradigms in Administrative Law," *Harvard Law Review* 95 (1981): 433-434.

[25] Colin S. Diver, "Policymaking Paradigms in Administrative Law," *Harvard Law Review* 95 (1981): 433-434.

[26] Joseph L. Sax, "The (Unhappy) Truth About NEPA," *Oklahoma Law Review* 26 (1973): 239-240.

[27] Ibid., 248.

[28] Ibid.

[29] Bradley C. Karkkainen, "Toward a Smarter NEPA: Monitoring and Managing Government's Environmental Performance," *Columbia Law Review* 102 (2002): 938.

[30] Ibid., 938-940.

[31] Wendy E. Wagner, "Commons Ignorance: The Failure of Environmental Law to Produce Needed Information on Health and the Environment," *Duke Law Journal* 53 (2004): 1718.

[32] Ibid., 1719, 1738-1745.

[33] Karkkainen, "Toward a Smarter NEPA," 970.

[34] Ibid., 970-972.
[35] Graham, 6.
[36] Ramkumar and Petkova, 300.

Bibliography

Books and Articles

Abramson, Rachael. "The Migratory Bird Treaty Act's Limited Wingspan and Alternatives to the Statute: Protecting the Ecosystem without Crippling Communication Tower Development." *Fordham Environmental Law Journal* 12 (2000): 253-292.

Ackerman, John M., and Irma E. Sandoval-Ballesteros. "The Global Explosion of Freedom of Information Laws." *Administrative Law Review* 58 (2006): 85-130.

Adams, Ansel, and Nancy Newhall. *This is the American Earth*. San Francisco: Sierra Club, 1960.

Adams, John [anonymous]. "A Dissertation on the Canon and Feudal Law." *Boston Gazette*, 30 September 1765, page number unknown.

Adams, Thomas L. Esq. "Enforcement and Liability." In *Environmental Law Handbook*. Vol. 14. Edited by Thomas F.P. Sullivan, 42-71. Rockville, Md.: Government Institutes, Inc., 1997.

Allison, Henry E. *Kant's Transcendental Idealism: An Interpretation and Defense*. New Haven, Conn.: Yale University Press, 2004.

Andreen, William L. "Motivating Enforcement: Institutional Culture and the Clean Water Act." *Pace Environmental Law Review*, 24 (2007): 67-98.

Arora, Seema, and Timothy N. Cason. "An Experiment in Voluntary Environmental Regulation: Perception in EPA's 33/50 Program." *Journal of Environmental Economics and Management* 28 (1995): 271-286.

Atapattu, Sumudu. "The Right to a Healthy Life or the Right to Die Polluted: The Emergence of a Human Right to a Healthy Environment Under International Law." *Tulane Environmental Law Journal* 16 (2002): 65-126.

Audubon, John James. *Birds of America*. Self-published, 1827-1838.

Banks, James T. "EPA's New Enforcement Policy: At Last, a Reliable Roadmap to Civil Penalty Mitigation for Self-Disclosed Violations." *Environmental Law Reporter* 26 (1996): 10227-10238.

Barth, Alan. "Freedom and the Press." *The Progressive*, June 1862, 29.

Bartlett, Harvey. "Is NEPA Substantive Review Extinct, or Merely Hibernating? Resurrecting NEPA Section 102(1)." *Tulane Environmental Law Journal* 13 (2000): 411-449.

Bennett, Mark, and Kurt Zimmerman. "Politics and Preservation: The Endangered Species Act and the Northern Spotted Owl." *Ecology Law Quarterly* 18 (1991): 105-171.

Benson, W. Todd. *President Theodore Roosevelt's Conservation Legacy*. West Conshohocken, Pa.: Infinity Publishing, 2003.

Berland, Ava Holly. "Licensing Concerns, NEPA Sitings, Telecommunications Act Mandates: The FCC Perspective," *Proceedings of the Avian Mortality at Communications Towers Workshop*, 11 August 1999, http://www.towerkill.com/activism/workshop/html/pan10.html, accessed 23 June 2010.

Borchers, Doyle J. "The Practice of Regional Regulation Under the Clean Air Act." *Natural Resources Lawyer* 3 (1970): 59-65.

Bradley, Kathy. "Do You Feel the Sunshine? Government in the Sunshine Act: Its Objectives, Goals, and Effect on the FCC and You." *Federal Communications Law Journal* 49 (1997): 474-489.

Brandeis, Louis D. *Other People's Money: and How the Bankers Use It*. New York: F.A. Stokes, 1914.

Bregman, Jacob I. *Environmental Impact Statements*, 2nd ed. Boca Raton, Fla.: Lewis Publishers: 1999.

Brown, Richard D. *The Strength of a People: The Idea of an Informed Citizenry in America, 1650-1870*. Chapel Hill, NC: University of North Carolina Press, 1996.

Brucker, Herbert. *Freedom of Information*. New York: Macmillan Co., 1949.

Bruggers, James. "Toxic Legacy Revisited: Valley of the Drums, 30 Years Later." *Louisville Courier-Journal*, 14 December 2008, http://www.courier-journal.com/article/20081214/NEWS01/81214001, accessed 23 June 2010.

Caldwell, Lynton K. "A Constitutional Law for the Environment: 20 Years with NEPA Indicates the Need." *Environment* 31 (Dec. 1989): 6-11+.

Calland, Richard, and Allison Tilley, eds. *The Right to Know, the Right to Live: Access to Information and Socio-Economic Justice*. Cape Town, South Africa: Open Democracy Advice Center, 2002.

Cameron, Jenks. *The National Park Service: Its History, Activities, and Organization*. New York: D. Appleton & Co., 1922.

Carson, Rachel. *Silent Spring*, 40th Anniversary ed. Boston: Houghton Mifflin, 2002.

"Censorship at the Pentagon." *Time*, 4 July 1955, 62.

Center for Public integrity, The. *Wasting Away: Superfund's Toxic Legacy*. http://projects.publicintegrity.org/superfund/?gclid=COyGraCF3ZgCFQu-GgoduVWOeA, accessed 23 June 2010.

Chafee, Zechariah Jr. *Government and Mass Communications: A Report from the Commission on Freedom of the Press*. Vol. 1. Chicago: University of Chicago Press, 1947.

Coggins, George Cameron. "Conserving Wildlife Resources: An Overview of the Endangered Species Act of 1973." *North Dakota Law Review* 51 (1974): 315-340.

Coggins, George C. & Robert L. Glicksman. *Public Natural Resources Law*, 2nd ed. Vol. 1. Eagan, Minn.: Thomson/West, 2007.

Cone, Marla. "EPA is Faulted as Failing to Shield Public from Toxins." *Los Angeles Times*, 13 July 2005, A18.

"Contaminated Town is Relegated to History." *New York Times*, 14 April 1985, A26.

Cooley. Thomas. *A Treatise on Constitutional Limitations*. 8th ed. Vol. 2. Boston: Little, Brown, 1927.

Cooper, Kent. *The Right to Know: An Exposition of the Evils of News Suppression and Propaganda*. New York: Farrar, Strauss and Cudahy, 1956.

Cramer, Benjamin W. "The Human Right to Information, the Environment, and Information About the Environment: From the Universal Declaration to the Aarhus Convention." *Communication Law & Policy* 14 (2009): 73-103.

Cross, Frank B. "The Judiciary and Public Choice." *Hastings Law Journal* 50 (1999): 355-382.

Cross, Harold L. *The Right to Know: Legal Access to Public Records and Proceedings*. New York: Columbia University Press, 1953.

Cushman, John H. Jr. "Gore Asks Chemical Industry to Test for Any Toxic Effects." *New York Times*, 22 April 1998, A24.

de Quincey, Thomas. *Recollections of the Lakes and the Lake Poets: Coleridge, Wordsworth, and Southey.* Edinburgh: Adam and Charles Black, 1862.

de Tocqueville, Alexis. *Democracy in America.* New York: The Library of America, 2004.

Dienes, C. Thomas, Lee Levine, and Robert C. Lind. *Newsgathering and the Law.* Vol. 2. Charlottesville, Va.: Lexis Law Publishing, 1999.

Diver, Colin S. "Policymaking Paradigms in Administrative Law." *Harvard Law Review* 95 (1981): 393-434.

Dreyfus, Daniel A., and Helen M. Ingram. "The National Environmental Policy Act: A View of Intent and Practice." *Natural Resources Journal* 16 (1976): 243-262.

Dunford, Bruce. "Danny's Highway to Finally Open in Oahu, Hawaii." *Los Angeles Times,* 14 December 1997, 34.

Editorial, *Wall Street Journal,* 27 September 1951, 6.

Elliott, E. Donald, Bruce A. Ackerman, and John C. Millian. "Toward a Theory of Statutory Evolution: The Federalization of Environmental Law." Journal of Law, Economics, & Organization 1 (1985): 313-340.

Emerson, Ralph Waldo. *Nature.* New York: Duffield & Co., 1909.

———. *Selected Writings of Ralph Waldo Emerson.* Edited by William H. Gilman. New York: Signet Classic, 2003.

Emerson, Thomas I. "Toward a General Theory of the First Amendment." *Yale Law Journal* 72 (1963): 877-956.

Endangered Species Coalition. "President Obama Restores Endangered Species Protections." Press release, 3 March 2009, http://stopextinction.org/species/profiles/89-release-president-obama-restores-endangered-species-protections.html, accessed 23 June 2010.

Farrand, Max, ed. *The Records of the Federal Convention of 1787.* Vol. 3. New Haven, Conn.: Yale University Press, 1911.

"The Federal Administrative Procedure Act: Codification or Reform?" *Yale Law Journal* 56 (1947): 670-705.

Fischman, Robert L. "The EPA's Duties and Ecosystem Services." *Stanford Environmental Law Journal* 20 (2001): 497-536.

Flippen, J. Brooks. *Conservative Conservationist: Russell E. Train and the Emergence of American Environmentalism.* Baton Rouge, La.: Louisiana State University Press, 2006.

———. *Nixon and the Environment.* Albuquerque, N.M.: University of New Mexico Press, 2000.

Florini, Ann. "The Battle Over Transparency." In *The Right to Know: Transparency in an Open World.* Edited by Ann Florini, 1-16. New York: Columbia University Press, 2007.

———. "The End of Secrecy," *Foreign Policy* 111 (1998): 50-63.

———. "Whither Transparency?" In *The Right to Know: Transparency in an Open World.* Edited by Ann Florini, 337-348. New York: Columbia University Press, 2007.

Foerstel, Herbert N. *Freedom of Information and the Right to Know: The Origins and Applications of the Freedom of Information Act.* Westport, Conn.: Greenwood Press, 1999.

Foster, Sheila. "Environmental Justice in an Era of Devolved Collaboration." *Harvard Environmental Law Review* 26 (2002): 459-498.

Fox, Steven. *The American Conservation Movement: John Muir and His Legacy.* Madison, Wis.: University of Wisconsin Press, 1985.

Franklin, Benjamin. *Poor Richard's Almanack.* Waterloo, Ia.: U.S.C. Publishing, 1914.

Franz, David P., and William H. Hefter. "Providing Reliable Information to Clients: The Case of Environmental Remediation. " *International Journal of Applied Quality Management* 2 (1999), 211-220.

"Freedom of Information," *U.S. News and World Report*, 24 August 1956, 114.

French, Susannah T. "Judicial Review of the Administrative Record in NEPA Litigation." *California Law Review* 81 (1993): 929-990.

Frost, Don J. Jr. "*Amoco Production Co. v. Village of Gambel* and *Motor Vehicle Manufacturers Association v. State Farm Mutual Automobile Insurance Co.*: Authority Warranting Reconsideration of the Substantive Goals of the National Environmental Policy Act." *Alaska Law Review* 5 (1988): 15-67.

Gates, Paul H. Jr., and Bill F. Chamberlin. "Madison Misinterpreted: Historical Presentism Skews Scholarship." *American Journalism* 13 (1996): 38-47.

Gaynor, Kevin. "The Toxic Substances Control Act: A Regulatory Morass." *Vanderbilt Law Review* 30 (1977): 1149-1195.

Gerrard Michael B., and Michael Herz. "Harnessing Information Technology to Improve the Environmental Impact Review Process." *New York University Environmental Law Journal* 12 (2003): 18-49.

Glitzenstein, Eric. "Project Modification: Illegitimate Circumvention of the EIS Requirement or Desirable Means to Reduce Environment Impacts?" *Ecology Law Quarterly* 10 (1982): 253-280.

Gould, Lewis L. *America in the Progressive Era*, 1890-1914. New York:
   Longman, 2001.
Graham, Mary. *Democracy by Disclosure: The Rise of Technopopulism*.
   Washington, D.C.: Brookings Institution Press, 2002.
Grinnell, George Bird. "American Game Protection: A Sketch." In
   Conservation in the Progressive Era: Classic Texts. Edited by David
   Stradling, 45-49. Seattle: University of Washington Press, 2004.
Hall, Ridgway M. Jr. "The Clean Water Act of 1977." *Natural Resources
   Lawyer* 11 (1978): 343-372.
Halstuk, Martin E. "Policy of Secrecy – Pattern of Deception: What Federalist
   Leaders Thought About a Public Right to Know, 1794-1798."
   Communication Law & Policy 7 (2002): 51-76.
———. "When Secrecy Trumps Transparency: Why the OPEN Government
   Act of 2007 Falls Short." *CommLaw Conspectus* 16 (2008): 427-469.
Halstuk, Martin E., and Bill F. Chamberlin. "The Freedom of Information Act
   1966-2006: A Retrospective on the Rise of Privacy Protection Over the
   Public Interest in Knowing What the Government's Up To."
   Communication Law & Policy 11 (2006): 511-564.
Hays, Samuel P. *Beauty, Health, and Permanence: Environmental Politics in
   the United States, 1955-1985*. New York: Cambridge University Press,
   1987.
———. *Wars in the Woods: The Rise of Ecological Forestry in America*.
   Pittsburgh, Pa.: University of Pittsburgh Press, 2007.
Healy, Michael P. "Direct Liability for Hazardous Substance Cleanups Under
   CERCLA: A Comprehensive Approach." *Case Western Reserve Law
   Review* 65 (1992): 65-146.
Herson, Albert I. "Project Mitigation Revisited: Most Courts Approve Findings
   of No Significant Impact Justified by Mitigation." *Ecology Law Quarterly*
   13 (1986): 51-72.
Herz, Michael. "Parallel Universes: NEPA Lessons for the New Property."
   Columbia Law Review 93 (1993): 1668-1737.
Hirsch, Jeff. "Superfund May Not Be So Super." Massachusetts Institute of
   Technology News, 5 August 2008,
   http://web.mit.edu/newsoffice/2008/superfund-0805.html, accessed 23
   June 2010
Hoffman. Daniel. *Government Secrecy and the Founding Fathers: A Study in
   Constitutional Controls*. Westport, Conn.: Greenwood Press, 1981.

Hornstein, Donald T. "Reclaiming Environmental Law: A Normative Critique of Comparative Risk Analysis." *Columbia Law Review* 92 (1992): 562-633.

Houck, Oliver. "The Endangered Species Act and Its Implementation by the U.S. Departments of Interior and Commerce." *University of Colorado Law Review* 64 (1993): 278-370.

Huffman, James L. "A History of Forest Policy in the United States." *Environmental Law* 8 (1978): 239-280.

Hughes, J. Donald. *Ecology in Ancient Civilizations.* Albuquerque, N.M.: University of New Mexico Press, 1975.

———. *Pan's Travail: Environmental Problems of the Ancient Greeks and Romans.* Baltimore: Johns Hopkins University Press, 1994.

Hunt, Gaillard, ed. *The Writings of James Madison.* Vols. 6 and 9. New York: Putnam, 1900-1910.

Hutton, Gerald L. "Public Information and Rule Making Provisions of the Administrative Procedure Act of 1946." *Temple Law Quarterly* 33 (1959): 58-76.

Ingelhart, Louis Edward, ed. *Press and Speech Freedoms in America, 1619-1995: A Chronology.* Westport, Conn.: Greenwood Press, 1999.

International Monetary Fund. *Report of the Working Group on Transparency and Accountability.* Washington: International Monetary Fund. 1998.

Jackson, Henry. "Environmental Policy and the Congress." *Natural Resources Journal* 11 (1971): 403-415.

Jaffe, Natasha Rossell, and Jordan D. Weiss. "The Self-Regulating Corporation: How Corporate Codes Can Save Our Children." *Fordham Journal of Corporate and Financial Law* 11 (2006): 893-922.

Jones, Elise S., and Cameron P. Taylor. "Litigating Agency Change: The Impact of the Courts and Administrative Appeals on the Forest Service." *Policy Studies Journal* 23 (1995): 310-336.

Kant, Immanuel. *Critique of Pure Reason.* Translated by J.M.D. Meiklejohn. New York: P.F. Collier & Son, 1901.

Karkkainen, Bradley C. "Information-Forcing Environmental Regulation." *Florida State University Law Review* 33 (2006): 861-902.

———. "Toward a Smarter NEPA: Monitoring and Managing Government's Environmental Performance." *Columbia Law Review* 102 (2002): 903-972.

———. "Whither NEPA?" *New York University Environmental Law Journal* 12 (2004): 333-363.

Knickerbocker, Brad. "Northern Spotted Owl's Decline Revives Old
Concerns." *Christian Science Monitor*, 27 June 2007,
http://www.csmonitor.com/2007/0627/p02s01-sten.html, accessed 23 June
2010.

Lachenmeier, Rudy R. "The Endangered Species Act of 1973: Preservation or
Pandemonium?" *Environmental Law* 5 (1974): 29-83.

Landfair, Stanley W. "Toxic Substances Control Act." In *Environmental Law
Handbook*. Vol. 14. Edited by Thomas F.P. Sullivan, 226-283. Rockville,
Md.: Government Institutes, Inc., 1997.

Large, Kimberly M. "The Mischaracterization of Justice Scalia as
Environmental Foe: What Harm to Standing Following the Court's Stance
in *Laidlaw Environmental v. Friends of the Earth*?" *Widener Law Review*
10 (2004): 561-584.

Lavelle, Marianne. "Environmental Vise: Law, Compliance." *National Law
Journal* 15 (30 August 1993): S1-S9.

Lazarus, Richard J. *The Making of Environmental Law*. Chicago: University of
Chicago Press, 2004.

Lee, Hye-Jong Linda. "The Pragmatic Migratory Bird Treaty Act: Protecting
'Property'." *Boston College Environmental Affairs Law Journal* 31
(2004): 649-681.

Leopold, Aldo. *A Sand County Almanac*. New York: Oxford University Press,
2001.

Lieben, Ivan. "Catch Me if You Can – The Misapplication of the Federal
Statute of Limitations to Clean Air Act PSD Permit Program Violations."
Environmental Law 38 (2008): 667-709.

Lindstrom, Matthew J. "Procedures Without Purpose: The Withering Away of
the National Environmental Policy Act's Substantive Law." *Journal of
Land Resources & Environmental Law* 20 (2000): 245-267.

Liroff, Richard A. *A National Policy for the Environment: NEPA and its
Aftermath*. Bloomington, Ind: Indiana University Press, 1976.

Lynch, John A. "Justice Douglas, the Chesapeake & Ohio Canal, and Maryland
Legal History." *University of Baltimore Law Forum* 35 (2005): 104-125.

Maher, Neil M. *Nature's New Deal: The Civilian Conservation Corps and the
Roots of the American Environmental Movement*. New York: Oxford
University Press, 2008.

Manville, Albert M. "The ABCs of Avoiding Bird Collisions at
Communication Towers: The Next Steps." *Proceedings of the Avian*

Interactions Workshop, December 2, 1999, reprinted at http://library.fws.gov/bird_publications/tower_collisions00.htm, accessed 23 June 2010.

Marcuse, Peter. "Conservation for Whom?" *In Environmental Quality and Social Justice in Urban America: An Exploration of Conflict and Concord Among Those Who Seek Environmental Quality and Those Who Seek Social Justice*. Edited by James N. Smith, 17-36. Washington: Conservation Foundation, 1974.

Marsh, George Perkins. *Man and Nature: On Physical Geography as Modified by Human Action*. New York: Charles Scribner, 1864.

Martin, Anne. "Tell the Forest Service: Strong Oil and Gas Regulations Needed on National Forests." American Lands Alliance, 18 February 2009, reprinted at http://www.alleghenydefense.org/hchronicles/?p=68, accessed 23 June 2010.

Mattix, Carla, and Kathleen Becker. "Scientific Uncertainty Under the National Environmental Policy Act." *Administrative Law Review* 54 (2002): 1125-1165.

May, Randolph. "Reforming the Sunshine Act." *Administrative Law Review* 49 (1997): 415-419.

McEvoy, James. "The American Concern with the Environment." In *Social Behavior, Natural Resources, and the Environment*. Edited by William Burch, Neil H. Cheek, Jr., and Lee Taylor, 214-236. New York: Harper & Row, 1972.

McKibben, Bill, ed. *American Earth: Environmental Writing Since Thoreau*. New York: The Library of America, 2008.

Meiklejohn, Alexander. "The First Amendment is an Absolute." *Supreme Court Review* 1961 (1961): 245-266.

Melious, Jean O. "Enforcing the Endangered Species Act Against the States." *William & Mary Environmental Law & Policy Journal* 25 (2001): 605-674.

Meltzer, Milton. *Henry David Thoreau: A Biography*. Minneapolis, Minn.: Twenty-First Century Books, 2007.

Mill, John Stuart. *On Liberty*, Penguin Classics ed. Baltimore: Penguin, 1974.

Millet, Saralaine. "Birds Make Comeback." *Atlanta Journal-Constitution*, 2 August 2007, A19.

Morreale, Eva H. "Federal Power in Western Waters: The Navigation Power and the Rule of No Compensation." *Natural Resources Journal* 3 (1963): 1-77.

Mortimer, Michael J. "The Delegation of Law-Making Authority to the United States Forest Service: Implications in the Struggle for National Forest Management." *Administrative Law Review* 54 (2002): 907-982.

National Research Council, Committee on Risk Characterization & Commission on Behavioral and Social Sciences and Education. *Understanding Risk: Informing Decisions in a Democratic Society.* Edited by P.C. Stern and H.V. Fineberg. Washington, D.C.: National Academy Press, 1996.

National Research Council of the National Academies. *Public Participation in Environmental Assessment and Decision Making.* Washington, D.C.: The National Academies Press, 2008.

Neuman, Laura, and Richard Calland. "Making the Law Work: The Challenges of Implementation." In *The Right to Know: Transparency in an Open World.* Edited by Ann Florini, 179-213. New York: Columbia University Press, 2007.

Niro, William L. "Standing to Sue in Environmental Litigation: *Sierra Club v. Morton.*" *DePaul Law Review* 22 (1973): 451-460.

O'Reilly, James T. *Federal Information Disclosure.* Vol. 1. St. Paul, Minn.: West Group, 2000.

Organization for Economic Co-Operation and Development. *Open Government: Fostering Dialogue with Civil Society.* Paris: Organization for Economic Co-Operation and Development, 2003.

Otenyo, Eric E., and Nancy S. Lind. "Faces and Phases of Transparency Reform in Local Government." *International Journal of Public Administration* 27 (2004): 287-307.

Outka, Uma. "NEPA and Environmental Justice: Integration, Implementation, and Judicial Review." *Boston College Environmental Affairs Law Review* 33 (2006) 601-625.

Paine, Thomas. Common Sense (1776), http://www.earlyamerica.com/earlyamerica/milestones/commonsense/text.html, accessed 23 June 2010.

Panizza, Francisco. "Introduction." In *Populism and the Mirror of Democracy.* Edited by Francisco Panizza, 1-31. New York: Verso, 2005.

Parks, Wallace. "The Open Government Principle: Applying the Right to Know Under the Constitution." *George Washington Law Review* 26 (1957): 1-22.

Penn, William. "Concessions to the Province of Pennsylvania," 11 July 1681, http://www.teachingamericanhistory.org/library/index.asp?document=227 1, accessed 23 June 2010.

Pierce, Richard J. "Two Problems in Administrative Law: Political Polarity on the District of Columbia Circuit and Judicial Deference to Agency Rulemaking." *Duke Law Journal* 1988 (1988): 300-328.

Pinchot, Gifford. *Breaking New Ground.* New York: Harcourt, Brace: 1947.

Powell, John Wesley. *The Exploration of the Colorado River and Its Tributaries.* New York: Penguin Books, 2003.

————. *Report on the Lands of the Arid Region of the United States,* 2nd ed. Washington: Government Printing Office, 1879.

"President Urges Limits by Press," *New York Times,* 28 April 1961, 14.

"Press is Divided on Kennedy Talk," *New York Times,* 30 April 1961, 68.

Rachliniski, Jeffrey J. "Noah by the Numbers: An Empirical Evaluation of the Endangered Species Act." *Cornell Law Review* 82 (1997): 356-389.

Ramkumar, Vivek, and Elena Petkova. "Transparency and Environmental Governance." *The Right to Know: Transparency in an Open World.* Edited by Ann Florini, 279-308. New York: Columbia University Press, 2007.

Ressmeyer, Kellen. "The Information Quality Act: The Little Statute That Could (or Couldn't)? Applying the Safe Drinking Water Act Amendments of 1996 to the Federal Communications Commission." *Federal Communications Law Journal* 59 (2006): 215-235.

Revesz, Richard. "Environmental Regulation, Ideology, and the D.C. Circuit." *Virginia Law Review* 83 (1997): 1717-1772.

Roberts, Alasdair. *Blacked Out: Government Secrecy in the Information Age.* New York: Cambridge University Press, 2006.

Robinson, Glen O. "Access to Government Information: The American Experience." *Federal Law Review* 14 (1983): 35-61.

Roosevelt, Theodore. Speech at Grand Canyon, Ariz., 6 May 1903. *A Compilation of the Messages and Speeches of Theodore Roosevelt, 1901-1905.* Edited by Alfred Henry Lewis, 327-328. Washington: Bureau of National Literature and Art, 1905.

Rosen, Frederick. *Classical Utilitarianism from Hume to Mill.* New York: Routledge, 2003.

Salzman, James, and Barton H. Thompson, Jr. *Environmental Law and Policy.* New York: Foundation Press, 2003.

Sartori, Giovanni. *The Theory of Democracy Revisited.* Chatham, N.J.: Chatham House, 1987.

Sax, Joseph L. "Property Rights and the Economy of Nature: Understanding *Lucas v. South Carolina Coastal Council.*" *Stanford Law Review* 45 (1993): 1433-1455.
———. "The (Unhappy) Truth About NEPA." *Oklahoma Law Review* 26 (1973): 239-248.
Scalia, Antonin. "The Freedom of Information Act Has No Clothes." *Regulation* 6 (1982): 14-19.
Schement, Jorge Reina. "Broadband, Internet, and Universal Service: Challenges to the Social Contract of the Twenty-First Century." In ...*And Communications for All: A Policy Agenda for the New Administration.* Edited by Amit M. Schejter, 3-27. Lanham, Md.: Lexington Books, 2009.
Schneider, Paul. *The Adirondacks: A History of America's First Wilderness.* New York: H.H. Holt & Co., 1997.
Scott, Doug. *The Enduring Wilderness: Protecting Out Natural Heritage Through the Wilderness Act.* Golden, Colo.: Fulcrum, 2004.
Seidenfeld, Mark. "Cognitive Loafing, Social Conformity, and Judicial Review of Agency Rulemaking." *Cornell Law Review* 87 (2002): 486-548.
Shabecoff, Philip. *A Fierce Green Fire: The American Environmental Movement.* Washington: Island Press, 2003.
Smith, Adrienne. "Standing and the National Environmental Policy Act: Where Substance, Procedure, and Information Collide." *Boston University Law Review* 85 (2005): 633-662.
Smith, James N. "The Coming of Age of Environmentalism in American Society." In *Environmental Quality and Social Justice in Urban America: An Exploration of Conflict and Concord Among Those Who Seek Environmental Quality and Those Who Seek Social Justice.* Edited by James N. Smith, 1-16. Washington: Conservation Foundation, 1974.
Smith, Jeffrey A. *War and Press Freedom: The Problem of Prerogative Power.* New York: Oxford University Press, 1999.
Speakman, Joseph M. *At Work in Penn's Woods: The Civilian Conservation Corps in Pennsylvania.* State College, Pa.: Pennsylvania State University Press, 2006.
Spensley, James W. Esq. "National Environmental Policy Act." In *Environmental Law Handbook.* Vol. 14. Edited by Thomas F.P. Sullivan, 404-429. Rockville, Md.: Government Institutes, Inc., 1997.
Sperber, A.M. *Murrow: His Life and Times.* New York: Freundlich Books, 1986.

Steen, Harold K. *The U.S. Forest Service: A History.* Durham, N.C.: Forest History Society, 2004.

Stevenson, Robert Louis. "Henry David Thoreau: His Character and Opinions." *Cornhill Magazine*, June 1860, page number unknown.

Stewart, Richard B. "The Reformation of American Administrative Law." *Harvard Law Review* 88 (1975): 1667-1813.

Stiglitz, Joseph E. "Foreword." *In The Right to Know: Transparency in an Open World.* Edited by Ann Florini, vii-viii. New York: Columbia University Press, 2007.

Stokey, Edith, and Richard Zeckhauser. *A Primer for Policy Analysis.* New York: W.W. Norton, 1978.

Stratton-Lake, Philip. "Classical Idealism: An Introduction." In *The Edinburgh Encyclopedia of Continental Philosophy.* Edited by Simon Glendenning, 23-31. Edinburgh: Edinburgh University Press, 1999.

Thoreau, Henry David. *Walden, or: Life in the Woods.* New York: Thomas V. Crowell & Co., 1910.

Train, Russell E. *Politics, Pollution, and Pandas: An Environmental Memoir.* Washington: Shearwater, 2003.

Tuchman, Barbara. *A Distant Mirror: The Calamitous 14th Century.* New York: Knopf, 1978.

Turner, Frederick. *John Muir: Rediscovering America.* Cambridge, Mass.: Perseus Publishing, 2000.

United Nations. *Draft Declaration of Principles on Human Rights and the Environment.* 16 May 1994, United Nations, Annex I., E/CN.4/Sub.2/1994/9, reprinted at http://www.sojust.net/documents/declaration_of_principles.html, accessed 23 June 2010.

U.S. Environmental Protection Agency. "DDT Ban Takes Effect." Press release, 31 December 1972.

———. *Summary of the National Environmental Policy Act,* http://www.epa.gov/lawsregs/laws/nepa.html, accessed 23 June 2010.

———. *Summary of the Resource Conservation and Recovery Act,* http://www.epa.gov/lawsregs/laws/rcra.html, accessed 23 June 2010.

———. New Chemical Program. *What is the TSCA Chemical Substance Inventory?*, http://www.epa.gov/opptintr/newchems/pubs/invntory.htm, accessed 23 June 2010.

U.S. Federal Communications Commission, Wireless Telecommunications Bureau, *Compliance with Commission's Rules Implementing the National*

Environmental Policy Act of 1969,
http://wireless.fcc.gov/siting/npaguid.html, accessed 23 June 2010.

U.S. Government, NEPA Task Force. *Report to the Council on Environmental Quality: Modernizing NEPA Implementation*, September 2003, http://ceq.hss.doe.gov/ntf/report/finalreport.pdf, accessed 23 June 2010.

U.S. White House, *Office of the Press Secretary. Memorandum for the Heads of Executive Departments and Agencies, Subject: The Endangered Species Act*, 3 March 2009, http://www.whitehouse.gov/the_press_office/Memorandum-for-the-Heads-of-Executive-Departments-and-Agencies/, accessed 23 June 2010.

Verhovek, Sam Howe. "After 10 Years, the Trauma of Love Canal Continues." *New York Times*, 5 August 1988, B1.

Wagner, Wendy E. "Commons Ignorance: The Failure of Environmental Law to Produce Needed Information on Health and the Environment." *Duke Law Journal* 53 (2004): 1619-1745.

Weidel, Ruth Ann, John R. Mayo, and F. Michael Zachara. "The Erosion of *Mens Rea* in Environmental Criminal Prosecutions." *Seton Hall Law Review* 21 (1991): 1100-1124.

Weil, David, Archon Fung, Mary Graham, and Elena Fagotto. "The Effectiveness of Regulatory Disclosure Policies." *Journal of Policy Analysis and Management* 25 (2006): 155-181.

Weinberg, Philip. "Endangered Statute? The Current Assault on the Endangered Species Act." *Villanova Environmental Law Journal* 17 (2006): 389-410.

Wells, Christina E. "'National Security' Information and the Freedom of Information Act." *Administrative Law Review* 56 (2004): 1195-1221.

Wilcove, Davis S., and Lawrence L. Master. "How Many Endangered Species are There in the United States?" *Frontiers in Ecology and the Environment* 3 (October 2005): 414-420.

Williams, Cynthia A. "The Securities and Exchange Commission and Corporate Transparency." *Harvard Law Review* 112 (1999): 1197-1311.

Wilson, Ernest J. III. "Digital Media, Modern Democracy, and Our Truncated National Debate." In *...And Communications for All: A Policy Agenda for the New Administration*. Edited by Amit M. Schejter, 29-39. Lanham, Md.: Lexington Books, 2009.

Wisman, Phil. "EPA History." U.S. Environmental Protection Agency, http://www.epa.gov/history/topics/epa/15b.htm, accessed 23 June 2010.

World Resources Institute. *Decisions for the Earth: Balance, Voice, and Power 2002-2004.* Washington: World Resources Institute, 2003.

Worster, Donald. *A Passion for Nature: The Life of John Muir.* New York: Oxford University Press, 2008.

Yang, Julie. "Confidential Business Information Reform Under the Toxic Substances Control Act." *The Environmental Lawyer* 2 (1995): 219-238.

Yost, Nicholas C. "NEPA's Promise – Partially Fulfilled." *Environmental Law* 20 (1990): 533-549.

Websites and Databases

Privacy International. *National Freedom of Information Laws 2007.* http://www.privacyinternational.org/issues/foia/foia-laws.jpg, accessed 23 June 2010.

RTK Net: The Right-to-Know Network. http://www.rtknet.org, accessed 23 June 2010.

Scorecard: The Pollution Information Site. http://www.scorecard.org, accessed 23 June 2010.

Transparency International. *About Us.* http://www.transparency.org/about_us, accessed 23 June 2010.

U.S. Environmental Protection Agency. *About EPA.* http://www.epa.gov/epahome/aboutepa.htm, accessed 23 June 2010.

———. EPA Office of Federal Activities. *EISs Filed by Year, 1973-2006,* http://epa.gov/enforcement/resources/publications/nepa/number_eis_1973 _2006.pdf, accessed 23 June 2010.

———. *How Sites are Deleted from the NPL.* http://www.epa.gov/superfund/programs/npl_hrs/nploff.htm, accessed 23 June 2010.

———. *National Environmental Policy Act: EIS Filing System Guidance,* 1989. http://www.epa.gov/compliance/resources/policies/nepa/fileguide.html, accessed 23 June 2010.

———. *National Priorities List.* http://www.epa.gov/superfund/sites/query/queryhtm/npltotal.htm, accessed 23 June 2010.

———. *RCRA Online.* http://www.epa.gov/epawaste/inforesources/online/index.htm, accessed 23 June 2010.

———. *Superfund Information Systems.*
http://www.epa.gov/superfund/sites/cursites/, accessed 23 June 2010.
———. *Title V Petition Database.*
http://www.epa.gov/region07/air/title5/petitiondb/petitiondb.htm, accessed
23 June 2010.
U.S. Fish & Wildlife Service. *Conserving the Nature of America.*
http://www.fws.gov/index.html, accessed 23 June 2010.

Court Cases

Abrams v. United States, 250 U.S. 616 (1919)
Alaska v. Andrus, 580 F.2d 465 (D.C. Cir. 1978)
American Bird Conservancy v. Federal Communications Commission, 408
    F.Supp.2d 987 (D.Hawai'i, 2006)
American Federation of Government Employees v. Department of Commerce,
    907 F.2d 203 (D.C. Cir. 1990)
American Mining Congress v. Environmental Protection Agency, 907 F.2d
    1179 (D.C. Cir. 1990).
Arlington Coalition on Transportation v. Volpe, 458 F.2d 1323 (4th Cir. 1972)
Association of Data Processing Service Organizations Inc. v. Camp, 397 U.S.
    150 (1970)
Atlantic States Legal Foundation v. Buffalo Envelope, 823 F. Supp. 1065
    (W.D.N.Y. 1993)
Atlantic States Legal Foundation v. Whiting Roll-Up Door Manufacturing
    Corp., 772 F. Supp. 745 (W.D.N.Y. 1991)
Baker v. Carr, 389 U.S. 186 (1962)
Baltimore Gas & Electric Company v. Natural Resources Defense Council, 462
    U.S. 87 (1987)
Barlow v. Collins, 397 U.S. 159 (1970)
Burford v. Sun Oil Co., 319 U.S. 315 (1943)
Burka v. Department of Health and Human Services, 87 F.3d 508 (D.C. Cir.
    1996)
Cabinet Mountains Wilderness v. Peterson, 685 F.2d 678 (D.C. Cir. 1982)
California v. Block, 690 F.2d 753 (9th Cir. 1982)
Calvert Cliffs Coordinating Committee v. Atomic Energy Commission, 449
    F.2d 1109 (D.C. Cir. 1971)
Campbell v. Department of Justice, 164 F.3d 20 (D.C. Cir. 1998)

Chevron USA, Inc. v. Natural Resources Defense Council, 467 U.S. 837 (1984)

Chevron USA, Inc. v. Yost, 919 F.2d 27 (5th Cir. 1990)

Citizens Commission on Human Rights v. Food & Drug Administration, 45 F.3d 1325 (9th Cir. 1995)

Citizens to Preserve Overton Park, Inc. v. Volpe, 401 U.S. 402 (1971)

City of Davis v. Coleman, 521 F.2d 661, 678 (9th Cir. 1975)

City of West Chicago v. Nuclear Regulatory Commission, 701 F.2d 632 (7th Cir. 1983)

CleanCOALition v. TXU Power, 536 F.3d 469 (5th Cir. 2008); cert. denied, 129 S. Ct. 648 (2008)

Commission for Nuclear Responsibility, Inc. v. Seaborg, 463 F.2d 796 (D.C. Cir. 1971)

Corrosion Proof Fittings v. Environmental Protection Agency, 947 F.2d 1201 (5th Cir. 1991)

Defenders of Wildlife v. Administrator, Environmental Protection Agency, 882 F.2d 1294 (8th Cir. 1989)

Department of the Air Force v. Rose, 425 U.S. 352, 361 (1976)

Department of Defense v. Federal Labor Relations Authority, 510 U.S. 487 (1994)

Department of Justice v. Reporters Committee for the Freedom of the Press, 489 U.S. 749 (1989)

Department of Justice v. Tax Analysts, 492 U.S. 136 (1989)

Department of Transportation v. Public Citizen, 541 U.S. 752 (2004)

Dobronski v. Federal Communications Commission, 17 F.3d 275 (9th Cir. 1994)

Don't Waste Arizona v. McLane Foods Inc., 950 F. Supp. 972 (D.Ariz. 1996)

Dow Chemical Company v. Environmental Protection Agency, 605 F.2d 673 (3rd Cir. 1979)

Edwards Woodruff v. North Bloomfield Gravel Mining Company, 18 F9 753 (9th Cir. 1884)

Engine Manufacturers Association v. South Coast Air Quality Management District, 541 U.S. 246 (2004)

Environmental Defense Fund v. Army Corps of Engineers, 325 F.Supp. 749 (E.D. Ark. 1971)

Environmental Defense Fund v. Army Corps of Engineers, 348 F.Supp. 916, 933 (N.D. Miss. 1972)

Environmental Defense Fund v. Costle, 439 F.Supp. 980 (E.D.N.Y. 1977)

Environmental Defense Fund v. Environmental Protection Agency, 852 F.2d
    1309 (D.C. Cir. 1988)
Environmental Defense Fund v. Ruckelshaus, 439 F.2d 584 (D.C. Cir. 1974)
Environmental Protection Agency v. Mink, 410 U.S. 73 (1973).
Farmland Preservation Association v. Adams, 491 F.Supp. 601 (N.D. Iowa,
    1979)
Forsham v. Harris, 445 U.S. 169 (1980)
Gitlow v. New York, 268 U.S. 652 (1925)
Griswold v. Connecticut, 381 U.S. 479 (1965)
Grosjean v. American Press Company, 297 U.S. 233 (1936)
Honeywell International, Inc. v. Environmental Protection Agency, 372 F.3d
    441 (D.C. Cir. 2004)
Houchins v. KQED, 438 U.S. 1 (1978)
I-291 WHY? Association v. Burns, 517 F.2d 1077 (2nd Cir. 1975)
Izaak Walton League v. Butz, 522 F.2d 945 (4th Cir. 1975)
Kissinger v. Reporters Committee for Freedom of the Press, 445 U.S. 136, 157
    (1980)
Kleppe v. Sierra Club, 427 U.S. 390, 410 (1976)
LaFlamme v. Federal Energy Regulatory Commission, 852 F.2d 389 (9th Cir.
    1988)
Lamont v. Postmaster General, 381 U.S. 301 (1965)
Life of the Land v. Brinegar, 485 F.2d 460 (9th Cir. 1973)
Linemaster Switch Corporation v. Environmental Protection Agency, 938 F.2d
    1299 (D.C. Cir. 1991)
Logan v. Commercial Union Insurance Company, 96 F.3d 971 (7th Cir. 1996)
Long v. Internal Revenue Service, 596 F. 2d 363 (9th Cir. 1979)
Lucas v. South Carolina Coastal Council, 505 U.S. 1003 (1992)
Lujan v. Defenders of Wildlife, 504 U.S. 555 (1992)
Lujan v. National Wildlife Federation, 497 U.S. 871 (1990)
Marsh v. Oregon Natural Resources Council, 490 U.S. 360 (1989)
Martin v. City of Struthers, 319 U.S. 141 (1943)
Metropolitan Edison Co. v. People Against Nuclear Energy, 460, U.S. 766
    (1983)
Nation Magazine v. United States Customs Service, 71 F.3d 885 (D.C. Cir.
    1995)
National Labor Relations Board v. Sears, Roebuck & Company, 421 U.S. 132
    (1975)

National Mining Association v. Environmental Protection Agency, 59 F.3d
1351 (D.C. Cir. 1995)

National Parks & Conservation Association v. Babbitt, 241 F.3d 722 (9th Cir.
2001)

Natural Resources Defense Council v. Environmental Protection Agency, 25
F.3d 1063 (D.C. Cir. 1994)

Natural Resources Defense Council v. Hodel, 865 F.2d 288 (D.C. Cir. 1988)

Natural Resources Defense Council v. Morton, 458 F.2d 827 (1972)

Natural Resources Defense Council v. Nuclear Regulatory Commission, 547
F.2d 633 (D.C. Cir. 1976)

Natural Resources Defense Council v. Train, 1976 U.S. Dist. LEXIS 14700
(D.D.C. 1976)

Neighbors for a Toxic Free Community v. Vulcan Materials Company, 964 F.
Supp. 1448 (D.Colo. 1997).

Nelson Acschliman v. Nuclear Regulatory Commission, 547 F.2d 622 (D.C.
Cir. 1976)

Northern Spotted Owl v. Hodel, 716 F. Supp. 479 (W.D. Wash. 1988)

Norton v. Southern Utah Wilderness Alliance, 542 U.S. 55 (2004)

Open America v. Watergate Special Prosecution Force, 547 F.2d 605 (D.C. Cir.
1976)

Pell v. Procunier, 417 U.S. 817 (1974)

Portland Audubon Society v. Endangered Species Committee, 984 F.2d 1534
(9th Cir. 1993)

Postal Service v. Phelps Dodge Refining Corp., 852 F.Supp. 156 (E.D.N.Y.
1994)

Reno v. Condon, 528 U.S. 141 (2000)

Resources Limited, Inc. v. Robertson, 789 F.Supp 1529 (D. Mont. 1991)

Robertson v. Methow Valley Citizens Council, 490 U.S. 332 (1989)

Rocap v. Indiek, 539 F.2d 174 (D.C. Cir. 1976)

Saxbe v. Washington Post, 417 U.S. 843 (1974)

Scenic Hudson Preservation Conference v. Federal Power Commission, 354
F.2d 608 (2nd Cir. 1965)

Schenck v. United States, 249 U.S. 47, 52 (1919)

Sierra Club v. Army Corps of Engineers, 701 F.2d 1011 (2nd Cir. 1982)

Sierra Club v. Bosworth, 510 F.3d 1016 (9th Cir. 2007)

Sierra Club v. Georgia Power Company, 443 F.3d 1346 (11th Cir. 2006)

Sierra Club v. Johnson, 541 F.3d 1257 (11th Cir. 2008)

Sierra Club v. Leavitt, 368 F.3d 1300 (11th Cir. 2004)

Sierra Club v. Morton, 405 U.S. 727 (1972)
Sierra Club v. Sigler, 695 F.2d 957 (5th Cir. 1983)
Society Hill Towers Owners' Association v. Rendell, 210 F.3d 168 (3rd Cir.
    2000)
South Florida Water Management District v. Miccosukee Tribe of Indians, 543
    U.S. 805 (2004)
State of Missouri v. Holland, 252 U.S. 416 (1920)
Stop H-3 Association v. Dole, 870 F.2d 1419 (9th Cir. 1989)
Strout v. United States Parole Commission, 40 F.3d 136 (6th Cir. 1994)
Strycker's Bay Neighborhood Council, Inc. v. Karlen, 444 U.S. 223 (1980)
Tennessee Valley Authority v. Hill, 437 U.S. 153 (1978)
Trout Unlimited v. Morton, 509 F.2d 1276 (9th Cir. 1974)
United States v. Ashland Oil and Transportation Company, 504 F.2d 1317 (6th
    Cir. 1974)
United States v. Carr, 880 F.2d 1550 (2nd Cir. 1989)
United States v. Goldsmith, 978 F.2d 643 (11th Cir. 1992)
United States v. Kennecott Copper Corporation, 523 F.2d 821 (9th Cir. 1975)
United States v. Laughlin, 10 F.3d 961 (2nd Cir. 1993)
United States v. Protex Industries, Inc., 874 F.2d 740 (10th Cir. 1989)
United States v. Self, 2 F.3d 1071 (10th Cir. 1993)
United States v. Sellers, 926 F.2d 410 (5th Cir. 1991)
United States v. Students Challenging Regulatory Agency Procedures, 412 U.S.
    669 (1973)
United States v. Ward, 448 U.S. 242 (1980)
Vermont Yankee Nuclear Power Corp. v. Natural Resources Defense Council,
    435 U.S. 519 (1978)
Warm Springs Dam Task Force v. Gribble, 621 F.2d 1017 (9th Cir. 1980)
Weinberger v. Catholic Action of Hawai'i/Peace Education Project, 454 U.S.
    139 (1981)
Weisberg v. Department of Justice, 631 F.2d 824 (D.C. Cir. 1980)
Weyerhauser v. Costle, 590 F.2d 1011 (D.C. Cir. 1978)
Whitney v. California, 274 U.S. 357 (1927)

Index